THE
NEW MISSION
OF
Pope John XXIII

THE
NEW MISSION
OF
Pope John XXIII

BY

VITTORIO GORRESIO

TRANSLATED BY CHARLES LAM MARKMANN

FUNK & WAGNALLS

NEW YORK

Contents

I

Habemus Papam!

White smoke on October 28, 1958.
Pius XII in his declining years.
Pacelli's last illness and death.
Cardinal Tardini's harsh judgments.
The Curia in crisis.

PREMIER Amintore Fanfani was scheduled to discuss Italy's foreign-trade balance in Montecitorio * on the afternoon of October 28, 1958. But the Chamber was almost empty, and it was in vain that the summons bells shrilled in all the corridors to call the deputies back to their seats; instead they thronged into the bar of the Transatlantico, † clustering round an old-fashioned radio that was broadcasting a Vatican news program. The smoke of the conclave's sixth ballot had begun to rise at four forty-five, first almost dark gray, and then lightening steadily until it was white beyond any doubt.

In the bar, Mariano Rumor, at that time vice-secretary of the Christian Democratic Party, was the first to hear the new pope's name on the radio and to shout it out almost with a note of victory: "Roncalli! Roncalli! I could call him my friend if he weren't the pope now. I know him extremely well. Only recently I was with him at the dedication of a new school. He is an enlightened man and he will be a great pope." Then he ran out to give the news to Fanfani, who had not left the government bench in the empty Chamber. "Personally," Fanfani said, "I don't know him; but I know enough about him—more than enough, in fact—to have the highest hopes."

* The meeting place of the Chamber of Deputies.—TRANSLATOR.
† A restaurant.—TRANSLATOR.

3

Fanfani then asked for the floor, and he addressed the returned deputies: "I have the honor to inform the Chamber that I have been notified that the troop of the Papal Guards has entered the conclave's premises in order to pay tribute to the new pope as soon as he has been proclaimed. I therefore suggest to the Speaker of the Chamber that it would be fitting to adjourn the session." The Speaker was Giovanni Leone, who could not reply immediately because of the cheering of many deputies. Finally Leone was able to make himself heard: "I am certain that I am expressing the feelings of the Italian people in stating the hope that the new pontiff will be able to continue the radiant tradition of the rule of justice, truth, and peace." As if it were a kind of competition, Fanfani had another turn; as soon as the applause for Leone and the Christian Democrats' shouts of *Viva il papa!* had died away, he said: "On behalf of the government I share that hope, invoking God's lavish blessings on the new pope, on our nation, and on the whole world for peace with justice. May the accession of John XXIII be joined with divine protection for the peace and prosperity of all mankind."

The session was adjourned. Many of the ministers and deputies went to St. Peter's Square to receive the new pope's first blessing. Giuseppe Saragat stayed in front of the television in Montecitorio, commenting: "Did you hear that beautiful voice? Sonorous! I know Roncalli well, and until yesterday I could have regarded him as a colleague of mine, because we were in Paris together in forty-four— he as papal nuncio, I as ambassador of Italy. He was immeasurably helpful to me in aid for Italians who were at that time prisoners of war in France, and in fact, when I came back to Rome, I asked Pius XII for an audience in order to thank him for what his nuncio had done. And personal relations between us have always been of the best; my family has the fondest recollections of him. He is really a man full of common sense, as well as a holy man."

The conviction that the new pope was an excellent choice even in terms of Italian public affairs, given the importance of the pope for Italy and her policies, spread with amazing rapidity. It was as if everyone knew Roncalli well and was in a position to predict his behavior. Perhaps it was only relief that a change had finally come—the pontificate of Pius XII had lasted almost twenty years— in combination with the conviction that a breath of fresh air in the Vatican would be beneficial. It was conceded that the legacy of Pius XII would be onerous to assume, but the very fact enhanced the affectionate sympathy in which John XXIII was held. It was possible that he was destined to be only a transition pope, inasmuch as he was ascending the throne when he was already old—seventy-seven—but even a mere transition was welcome after the rigor of the reign of Pius XII.

"Like a lighthouse contemptuous of the changes in the sea beneath," Henri Fesquet said in his book *Rome s'est- elle convertie (Has Rome Been Converted)?* when he was describing the atmosphere of Rome during the Pacelli years. "The Church sat enthroned, inaccessible and pharisaical, confounding the absolute with absolutism, firmness with sclerosis, intransigence with incomprehension, culture with imitation, certainty with prejudices, transcendency with unreality, reform with treason. . . ." This was in fact the face that Pacelli's Curia showed, and the fear of falling

5

into disgrace was the more conducive to hypocrisy and to the avoidance of responsibility, while a new form of heresy, papolatry, began to spread its infection through Catholic doctrine.

Ecclesia, a religious encyclopedia that was published in 1948, at the full flowering of *pacellismo,* contained a chapter devoted to the conclave, and this was its disconcerting introduction: "The pope is not immortal. He is subject to the destiny common to all, and he dies." A book of meditations on Don Bosco,* published in Turin in 1957, offered a definition of the pope that was so remarkable as to insinuate into simple minds the notion that his fate might even be different from that of humanity:

> The pope is God on earth. Jesus has placed him above the prophets, above John the Baptist, above the angels. Jesus has placed the pope on the same level as God. In fact, he said to Peter and his successors: "He that heareth you, heareth me: and he that despiseth you, despiseth me: and he that despiseth me, despiseth him that sent me" (Luke X:16).

There had been veritable aberrations. A rumor was circulated, with the help of various popular magazines and without any official denial by the Vatican at any time, that in 1955 Pius XII had bestowed sight on a little girl born blind, merely by placing his hands on her eyes, just as easily as Jesus Christ had given sight to the blind at Jericho, Bethesda, and the pool of Shiloh: "So Jesus had compassion on them, and touched their eyes: and immediately their eyes received sight, and they followed him" (Matthew XX:34; Mark VIII:25; John IX:6–7). Then there was the long-distance cure of Brother Simon Blasco Traver of

---

* San Giovanni Bosco, a Piedmontese priest, who founded the Salesian Order.—TRANSLATOR.

6

Granollers, who was afflicted with a cancer of the throat and was already dying. He had refused medication and even rejected sedatives, requesting instead an image of Pius XII. It was given to him, and fifteen minutes later he was cured.

On another occasion it was announced that Pius XII had seen the Madonna two or three times. On October 13, 1951, in fact, the Associated Press informed the editors of the world's newspapers: "Cardinal says Pope Pius XII saw Virgin twice." Seeing the item on the AP's teletype machines, many newspapermen assumed that it was an irreverent joke by anti-papists, but instead it soon became clear that it was based on a speech that Federico Cardinal Tedeschini, the papal legate, had made in Portugal before a crowd "estimated to number one million" (*Civiltà cattolica*, No. 2433, October 27, 1951, p. 325) at the Cova da Iria, the famous grotto of Fatima where the Madonna is supposed to have appeared to three shepherd children (two girls and a boy) on May 15 and October 13, 1917.

These million faithful had been told by the cardinal: "It was four o'clock on the afternoons of October 30 and 31 and November 1 last year, 1950; it was the same time in the octave of November 1—in other words, of the day of the definition of the Assumption of Mary into heaven. Walking in the Vatican gardens, the Holy Father looked up at the sun; and then before his eyes he saw repeated the miracle of this valley and this date. The sun's disc is surrounded by a halo: who would be able to look at it? But the pope could: All through those four days he was enabled, by Mary's hand, to endure the sight of the sun. The sun was shaken, all convulsed, transformed into an image of life, a spectacle of celestial movements, a transmission of silent but eloquent messages to the Vicar of Christ. Was not this Fatima transported to the Vatican? Was not this the Vatican transformed into Fatima?"

The cardinal said again that he was speaking only for himself, but precisely because he was personally worthy of the utmost credit (he was a highly respectable veteran of the purple, bishop of Frascati, archpriest of the Patriarchal Basilica of the Vatican, and datary to His Holiness), it is impossible to imagine that he would have made his statement without the knowledge of Pius XII. Indeed, the Italian newspapers took the cardinal's disclosure at face value, except that they prefaced it with interrogative headlines open to any interpretation: "DID THE VIRGIN MARY APPEAR TO PIUS XII IN THE VATICAN?" and: "WAS PONTIFF'S VISION ACCOMPANIED BY REVELATIONS?" The Holy See's own organ, *l'Osservatore romano*, as authoritative on the religious as on the political plane, manifested no doubt. Quoting Cardinal Tedeschini, it spoke of a "memorable communication" and described the miracle in the Vatican gardens as a "formidable sign of the omnipotent repeated in the sight of Pius XII." By way of clarification, the newspaper explained: "Since God has decided on unaccustomed movement in the sun, he has done so specifically in order to show that the forces of nature will have to yield to the power of regenerated souls."

So it was a matter of repetition—that is, repetition of the miracle of Fatima and therefore the Virgin's second "dogmatic" appearance during our century, which in fact the theologians of Pacelli's Curia had named "the age of Fatima." As in the case of the Portuguese shepherd children in 1917, the sun, in the pontiff's eyes, had assumed the appearance of a perfect disc of silver dizzily whirling in the pale sky of twilight. Clusters of fire formed its halo: "In what manner the hand of Mary governed the miracle," it was later written, after the announcement by the cardinal, "and in what manner admonitions and prophecies stood forth from the miracle—these are matters beyond theology, in a field barred to investigation. Admonitions and prophecies, in any event, accompanied the miracle, and Catholics are wondering whether Pius XII is now the depository of new predestinations and new hopes." Only he could have resolved the question, but he abstained. In fact, just when expectations were at their peak, on October 29, 1951, he chose as his subject for a major speech a different theme: the mission of the midwife.

It was not until three years later, toward the end of 1954, that he returned to the subject of miracles: then he told of one that had occurred to him during an illness. He was suffering from an abdominal hernia that caused him to have acute attacks of hiccoughs, and there was fear for his life. But at dawn of December 2, Jesus Christ walked into his bedroom. By sheer chance, as *l'Osservatore romano* was to say a year later (December 11, 1955, under the headline: "IT IS THE LORD"), "in that solemn moment there was no one in the bedchamber of His Holiness; in spite of the solicitous and constant attention lavished on the invalid, there were merely a few persons in the next room." Thus the supernatural meeting was held in private, and, for lack of other testimony, one must rely on the account given by Pius XII himself to the first human being who called on him on that morning. The visitor's name is not given in the account in *l'Osservatore*, although it is otherwise most detailed; but in all probability the first

9

visitor was a physician, most likely the chief physician, Doctor Riccardo Galeazzi-Lisi:

Having entered the Holy Father's bedchamber at about nine o'clock on the morning of December 2, the visitor had barely knelt and presented his morning greetings and good wishes when he heard the Holy Father say, as if in reply: "This morning I saw Our Lord!" Then the pope added that, the day before, he had heard a very clear voice announce quite distinctly that he would have a vision; and now this morning, while he was repeating the prayer of the *Anima Christi—In hora mortis meae voca me—* the Lord had come and remained a little time with him. At that moment His Holiness had suddenly thought of the well-known passage in the Gospel according to Saint John: *"Magister adest et vocat te"* (John XI:28, when Martha went to call Mary), and immediately he had therefore added the next verse of the same prayer, *Anima Christi: Et jube me venire ad te.* The entire story was told by the Holy Father with remarkable presence and clarity of mind. It should also be pointed out that . . . precisely on that same morning of December 2 the Holy Father, having briefly described what had happened, turned to current business and, among other things, made his final revision of his speech to the Catholic lawyers, the text of which was read to their convention on the following day.

Even though he had to expedite current business during that remarkable morning, Pius XII came back to the subject of his divine visitor, according to the evidence of autograph memoranda left by Monsignor Domenico Tardini, at that time deputy secretary of state for extraordinary ecclesiastical matters. On that December 2, a Thursday, Tardini had gone to have his customary audience with the pope at twelve forty-five in the afternoon:

He was on a couch. He seemed much worse to me. Every five minutes he had an attack of nausea and brought up something coffee-colored (waste matter, not blood). His mind was still serene. He said to me: "I will tell you something: the others might think it was a sick man's hallucination. Yesterday morning I clearly heard a voice, a clear voice! (and as he said this the pope touched his right ear) that said: 'Now a vision is coming.' But nothing happened. This morning, while I was hearing mass, I saw the Lord for a second. It was only a second, but I saw him clearly."

Monsignor Tardini's notes contain no comments, not even his own reply when the pope made the great disclosure to him; he notes merely a conclusion: "At one thirty I left." Two days later, on Saturday, November 4, he went back, and again he recorded his recollections:

Twelve-forty. The pope was in bed. He was pleased with the medical visit. He spoke highly of the physicians and said that they were very optimistic, especially Professor Paolucci. He opened his arms, spreading them as if he were offering a benediction, looked up toward heaven, and said: *"Voca me!"* Then he added: "I thought that Our Lord was calling me. But no!"

More than once during that ominous December of 1954 Pius XII told Monsignor Tardini that, if he had been condemned to remain bedridden, he would have renounced the papacy: "I remain at my post," he told Tardini, "only because the doctors have assured me that I shall be as strong as I was before." Indeed he did recover and live four years more, constantly working hard, until October of 1958. He was still in his summer residence in Castel Gandolfo when suddenly his health declined. He had been extremely active just before: on September 28 he had addressed the delegates to the Seventh International Congress of the Gas Industry; on October 2 he had made a speech to the delegates to the Convention of Railway-station Booksellers; on October 4 he had addressed the participants in the Tenth National Congress of the Italian Plastic Surgeons' Society; and on Sunday, October 5, he had spoken to the delegates to the Fifth International Congress of Latin Notaries.

It was this last group that saw how very weak and pale he seemed. He was holding a watch in his hands and at one point it fell to the floor; he took leave of his listeners with a significant *adieu!* Then, in private audience, he received Monsignor Angelo Dell'Acqua of the Secretariat of State, who asked him anxiously how he was feeling; Pius XII replied deliberately: "We have come to the end." By next morning alarm over the seriousness of his condition had spread beyond the papal palace because a newly married couple—Alessandro Ceccarel and Maria Bianchini—had arrived at the gates immediately after their wedding for a scheduled private audience, but a policeman had told them to leave because the pope's health was "extremely precarious."

At eight thirty that morning, in fact, Pius XII had suffered a thrombosis or spasm causing a collapse in the cerebral arteries. It was reported that just before he lost consciousness, he had cried out: "I can't see—Immaculate Madonna, help me!" Later in the day he regained consciousness and spoke for some time with his physicians about the details of the treatment that they were planning for him; he insisted on seeing the medicine bottles, as if he feared that they might deceive him by concealing his true state. A prelate of his antechamber, Monsignor L, however, when talking with reporters, shook his head skeptically and even let slip a Roman idiom: "He's got away from us." Subsequently, an optimisic bulletin was read out by Professor Antonio Gasbarrini; it began: "On the whole, the Holy Father continues to improve." His breathing was described as normal and it was stated definitely that he had been able to take nourishment.

A day later, on October 7, his temperature had risen. "You are keeping the truth from me," Pius XII said once more, and in reply he was handed a copy of *l'Osservatore* with a headline that filled the front page: "THE HOLY FATHER IS IMPROVING." The sight of the words printed in the newspaper seemed to reassure him, but still he said to Monsignor Tardini: "This is my last day." He asked for communion and then plunged himself into prayer. Tardini recalled in his notes:

His nurses gave him some hot broth. Brought back to the reality of everyday life, the pope gestured that they should wait. A further interval passed and there was no sign that his prayer was coming to an end. A second bowl of broth was brought, the first having grown cold. Again the broth was shown to the pope, again he motioned that it must wait. Much more insistence, affectionate but firm, was required to make him drink any of the broth. By then a third bowl had been brought because the second too had grown cold.

This was the pope's last day of conscious life. On the previous evening, in response to an emergency appeal, Paul Niehans, the Swiss biologist, had arrived in Rome by plane; four years earlier he had given the pope a treatment consisting of a series of injections with live meat cells. Bitter controversy had followed in medical circles, and the Vatican had split into two parties, one backing Niehans and the other attacking him. At the time of Jesus Christ's visit to Pius XII on December 2, 1954, too, the chief physician, Galeazzi-Lisi, had issued a long medical bulletin repudiating the Swiss scientist's treatment. "Un-

13

der present conditions," it concluded, "all other treatments have been suspended."

Now that Niehans had unexpectedly returned to Rome, some of his enemies hastened to make it known at noon of October 7, by means of the Christian Democratic Party's press agency, Italia, that it had been learned from an unimpeachable source that Doctor Niehans had not been summoned to the pontiff's bedside. On the other hand, the Swiss biologist was seen arriving at Castel Gandolfo at four o'clock that afternoon. He seemed to be panting, and in his haste to escape the reporters he slipped and fell full length at the entrance to the palace.

He spent almost an hour with the pope and, when he emerged, the reporters followed him again, even going into the church of Saint Thomas. "I can say nothing," Niehans said over and over, defensively; "I am a physician, not a microphone. What do you want me to tell you? Certainly the pope is better, but his condition is still critical." Meanwhile the other physicians in the castle had relieved Niehans at Pius' bedside, and then they issued a bulletin: "The therapeutic procedures that have previously been decided on are now being carried out." In other words, Niehans' visit had brought about no change in the treatment, as previously at the time of the 1954 miracle. The bulletin added that the improvement was steady, the pope's sense organs were functioning normally, and his motor responses were unimpaired. In short, in a few hours the pope had miraculously come through the acute phases of a cerebral thrombosis, a kidney blockage, and the hiccoughs caused by the diaphragm hernia; in addition, he had completely recovered his intellectual and mnemonic faculties. "Do you know when I began to hope again?"

Galeazzi-Lisi said to the press. "When the hiccoughs disappeared. And doesn't it signify anything to you that we doctors are now going to leave Castel Gandolfo for a few hours?"

Unfortunately, however, the last hopes were destroyed at nine thirty the next morning. There was a report that the pope had suffered a new attack and lost consciousness, and the square in Castel Gandolfo became a camping ground for newspapermen, radio correspondents from everywhere in the world, and film and television cameramen. It was like a siege. What was even more intense than anticipation or anxiety, however, was impatience—a cruel, irreverent impatience born of the conviction that now Pacelli's doom had been sealed. So great, in fact, was the haste to turn the last page that the biggest newspapers in Rome printed the news of the pope's death almost twenty-four hours before it came—on that same morning of October 8 —and every edition sold out instantly.

A group of reporters holding their death watch outside the castle apparently had made a joint agreement with a monsignor whose duties required him to work near the pope's chamber. This monsignor was supposed, as soon as the pope died, to open a specific window; but by chance it was opened by a servant who had gone off duty, and so it was that at eleven o'clock that morning Italia broke into its normal transmissions with a flash: "The pope is dead. The actual time of death came a few minutes before eleven o'clock." In Rome *Il Tempo* was specific in its headline: "POPE DIES AT 10:40." *Momento-Sera* was ostensibly even better informed: "The last words that Pope Pacelli left for the world were these: 'I bless all mankind, I pray for peace, peace, peace, I bless Rome. Pray for me.' " *Il Messaggero* and *Il Giornale d'Italia* were rich in detailed, reasonably plausible reports on the death and the official confirmation of it, as well as all the procedures ritually connected with such an event, none of which had altered in centuries. Thus these newspapers described how the senior cardinal knelt at the pope's ear and called him three times by his baptismal name, Eugenio, before turning to the other persons present and announcing: *"Vere, papa Pius mortuus est*—Pope Pius is truly dead."

When copies of these newspapers reached Castel Gandolfo they were burned in the public square for blasphemy. Three hundred fifty Bavarian pilgrims were reciting their rosaries outdoors and a priest, Don Lorenzo B, had spent twelve hours kneeling in prayer. An old woman was howling invocations to the Madonna, demanding that this time she perform a true miracle and save the pope's life: "He is a saint, he is a saint!" the old woman shrieked. "For me it's as if he were someone in my family." Her emotion seemed genuine, on the whole, even if tainted with a certain exhibitionism; but, aside from the minor burning at the stake of the blasphemous newspapers, there were no unseemly incidents. There was only the flourishing little traffic in relics, among which the special items were scraps of the pope's handkerchief. *L'Osservatore romano* protested formally against the frivolity of the Italian newspapers that had exploited the "fearful, anxious" vigil of Catholics "in these hours of anguish," and meanwhile Pius XII still lingered almost until dawn of the next day, Thursday, October 9, when finally the *Gazzetta Ufficiale della Repubblica Italiana*—*Official Gazzette of the Italian Republic* (Vol. XCIX, No. 244)—published the universally expected announcement in proper and historically accurate form between two heavy mourning leads across the lower half of its front page: "At three fifty-two this morning, October 9, the Supreme Pontiff Pius XII (Eugenio Pacelli) reached the end of his life." In smaller type at the foot of the page the newspaper added:

The government has given specific instructions in order to assure the strict observance of Article XXI of the Lateran Treaty of 11 February 1929, which was given legal effect by the law of 29 May 1929, No. 810, and in particular to guarantee the complete freedom of the cardinals and to prohibit the performance of any acts on Italian territory that might trouble the convocation of the conclave.

The real trouble was inside Castel Gandolfo, where for the first time it was necessary to face the extremely great, even if only formal, problems posed by a pope's death when it occurs outside the Holy See. Igor Man, who was a reporter officially assigned to the occasion, noted in his diary that he had seen *monsignori* dashing in circles like maddened moths while the physicians were arranging the corpse on a bier. The head of the bearers of the gestatorial chair, using a white silk neck scarf, was measuring the very narrow doors, which made it difficult to transport the heavy walnut litter draped in purple velvet. Beneath the pope's head, which was covered by his ermine-edged *camauro* (the papal cap), someone thrust two red cushions; the whole was then enclosed in an envelope of cellophane.

In the doorways it was still necessary to tilt the litter somewhat. Igor Man wrote:

The pope's body rolled a quarter-turn, first to the right, then to the left, depending how the bier was tilted. The bearers were sweating with fear. Broken only by warnings to "be very careful," the mixed, disordered procession's passage took an extremely

long time. In the drawing room that precedes the hall of the
Swiss Guards, Princess Pacelli, the wife of the pope's nephew,
Marcantonio, seemed to be at the very limit of her resistance.
Don Marcantonio turned to an officer and asked him to open a
door so that the princess could go outside for some fresh air.
Rather discourteously and in fact churlishly, the officer retorted
that no one could leave. No one, not even Princess Pacelli, the
wife of the pope's favorite nephew. Now that "the master is
dead," the pettiness begins at once.

It required a half-hour to progress through a few rooms.
When the bier had been placed in the center of the hall of
the Swiss Guards, someone noticed that the pope's head
was not sufficiently elevated. A cushion was taken from an
armchair and swiftly placed beneath the pope's neck—the
movements were not irreverent but quick, in order that
each of the four tassels fall properly on its own side.
Father P, who was attached to the papal family, had considerable work in assembling rosaries, images, and medals
to be placed in contact with the remains so that they could
become relics for devotional use. Igor Man, who knew the
priest, saw how extremely weary and nervous he was, and
asked him solicitously: "Are you all right, Father?" "*Dot-
tore mio*, my feet are on fire," Father P replied. The
"headlights" were turned on in order to enable the news-
reel and television cameramen to photograph the remains.
The lights created reflections in the cellophane envelope
that made the pope seem bathed in an evanescent cloud of
all the colors of the rainbow. An assistant to the chief
physician who had embalmed Pius XII, employing special
methods of his own invention based on aromatics, ordered
the lighting crews: "Easy with those projectors or you'll
melt him right under my hands!" He could not be silenced

until at last a black and tragic monk began to intone the *Miserere.*

The next day, when the coffin was placed inside a hearse belonging to the Roman city government, it was not properly covered with the ritual flag. "Use a sword!" an officer of the Palatine Guard shouted; and in fact the point of a regulation sword was used to fix the folds of the pall on either side of the coffin. The hearse started off, but within a few yards one of its tires was punctured. A jack was placed under the hearse, but badly: beneath the mudguard instead of in the socket built into the chassis for the purpose. Amid terror and horror, the hearse canted over to one side. This was soon remedied, but what was really irremediable was discovered in Rome: the method used for embalming the corpse was technically flawed. Putrefaction, indeed, had set in regardless, and, worse, it was extremely speedy; the stench caused more than one of the nobleman's guard on duty at the catafalque to swoon. Igor Man, who was there, described it:

There was not a man who did not whisper something into the next man's ear. I heard one exchange of remarks that made me jump. A monsignor sniffed and said: "What a strange smell; it must be the aromatics." Another, holding his nose, retorted: "What are you talking about, aromatics? That's stench!" And a third monsignor added: "*Iam foetet*—By this time he stinketh" (John XI:39).

Whenever a pope dies it is an occasion for changes at court, with the more or less rapid dispersal of familiars and favorites, but the period of Pacelli's death was full of presages that something more than the usual replacement episodes was in store. Indications of widespread disquiet were evident, and even the most cautious and conformist of the newspapers expressed themselves in critical terms, in sharp contrast to the excesses of conventional obsequiousness previously lavished on Pius XII.

Even while the pope was still alive, a paper as conservative as *Il Tempo* of Rome, in the special edition that it mistakenly published on October 8, had rhetorically reversed the position that it had held for so many years, going over openly to the attack against Pius XII:

> It was unquestionably Pope Pacelli's continually centralist attitude that multiplied and aggravated the problems inevitably created by any absolute government. . . . Centralization finished in the end by actually becoming its opposite: a certain diffuseness, a certain variety of judgments and opinions, a multiplicity of tendencies that are among the most ruinous dangers to the Church.

This denunciation was no mere eruption of freedom after prolonged and enforced reverence; it was, rather, revelatory of the serious apprehensions that were widespread in many quarters—clerical as well as lay, reactionary or not reactionary—over the state of crisis in which Pius XII was leaving the Church, and in particular ecclesiastic headquarters in the Vatican, at the end of his twenty-year pontificate.

More than for his visions, which were probably no more than a symptom of his illness, he was in fact to be reproached for the manner that he had adopted in the conduct of Chur h affairs; the arrogant isolation in which he had kept himself; the lack of trust in others, and his incapability of working with them, hence of gaining their collaboration. Lacking the capacity to open his spirit and to confide, Pius XII was ill at ease among people; he was a solitary to whom personal contacts were a burden, and it gave him no pleasure to see new faces round him. He had offered his confidence only to a very few intimates, and of necessity this confidence had been extremely broad and not always deserved. Otherwise he stood alone, avoiding even the presence of a secretary during the day or of a servant in the evening.

L'Osservatore romano was under orders to pay homage to Pius' manner of living and working. One day in 1957, *Il Mondo* reported that Father Giacomo Martegani, assistant for Italy to the provost general of the Society of Jesus, was among the most respected counselors of Pius XII. *L'Osservatore* published a denial that was out of all proportion to the original report; it said that, while Father Martegani did occasionally visit the Vatican, he spent his time there "listening, if anything, to some reflections by the Holy Father and certainly offering none of his own," inasmuch as Pius XII, "because of his strong-willed energy, his indefatigable toil, his unshakable tenacity, . . . his most punctilious supervision of every act that emanates from his authority, was likened to Innocent XI, that great pope whose custom it was to say: 'I will do it myself.' "

Perhaps, if what was desired was to pay homage to the energy of Pius XII, it would have been better to have chosen other criteria, for historians of the Church have inclined to be negative in their assessments of Innocent XI. Ludwig von Pastor says that he was a conscientious pope, but von Pastor adds that "one result of his meticulousness was a certain pettiness, extreme circumspection in everything, and the utmost difficulty in making decisions." All these statements, for that matter, were true of Pius XII as well. Von Pastor added that Innocent XI "had only the most inadequate knowledge of European political condi-

21

tions"; that he was lacking in "understanding of men, and consequently it was easy to deceive him"; and, finally, that "there were measurable gaps in his theological education" (*Storia dei Papi—History of the Popes—*Vol. XIX, Part II. pp. 13–15).

Historical comparisons aside, there is no doubt that Pius XII did a great deal for himself and that he preferred to be isolated. "He loved solitude," Pope Paul VI, then a cardinal, wrote of him, "because the riches of his mind and his remarkable capacity for thought and work in fact concentrated on avoiding unnecessary distractions and useless diversions" (letter to *The Tablet,* June 29, 1963). Domenico Cardinal Tardini also remembers him as "*segregatus.* Pius XII was indeed like that: apart from everyone and everything. It was not that he was withdrawn or uninterested; but . . . he was by nature driven almost irresistibly to live within himself and to be remote from others." Having worked for Pacelli for a long time, Tardini epitomized in one quotation from him the only kind of relationship that it was possible to have with Pius XII: " 'I do not want collaborators, I want executors,' Pius XII said to me on November 5, 1944, when he told me that he was not going to appoint a successor to the late Cardinal Maglione."

It would appear that Pacelli was very timid. "He was not born with the fighter's temperament," Tardini said, recalling too that Pius XII had stammered.

Cardinal Pacelli suffered from a slight stammer, which became apparent in private conversations but disappeared when he spoke to a crowd. Therefore, whenever he had to address a small group of persons (for instance, the staff of his Secretariat of State), His Eminence instinctively raised his voice: in consequence whatever he said had a character of declamation and solemnity that at certain times was quite disproportionate. Once he had become pope, I no longer observed the slightest stammer in him, except in very rare instances (*Pio XII—Pius XII—* published by Tip. Poliglotta Vaticana, 1960, p. 137).

This too might have been a reason for his avoidance of human contacts, a characteristic that Tardini did not hesitate to describe in terms that might seem moved with pity.

The Holy Father Pius XII began to be afflicted with a certain shyness about receiving high Church dignitaries and priests. . . . During his reign, as a result, there was some diminution in direct personal contacts between the Supreme Pastor and the pastors of the various dioceses: contacts that not only would have been very valuable in themselves but also would have undoubtedly afforded the prelates the blessed opportunity of profiting by the pope's wisdom. . . .

The diction is euphemistic, but nonetheless its import is that of condemnation of the lack of relations between the pope and the bishops. Furthermore, Pius XII had even abolished the scheduled audiences that were the occasions for regular contact with the responsible figures in the Roman congregations—in other words, in the ministries of the Papal State.

In sum, Tardini regarded Pacelli as weak. Indeed, he explained that, being highly intelligent, Pius XII was able to comprehend in a flash all the positive and negative aspects of every question that was laid before him by his visitors: "Therefore he was sometimes unsure, vacillating, almost as if he had no self-confidence. He had to be allowed to contemplate and pray. But not everyone was willing to wait. There were those who pressed one choice on him and those who pressed another. . . . All this upset him." He did not like to make immediate decisions, and, when he was asked to do so, it embarrassed him. "Not only was he reluctant to seek a solution there and then; later, when he did find it, it seemed to be a great effort for him to put it into words." Precisely for this reason he preferred to concentrate in solitude, for he needed to prepare himself undisturbed, to the last detail, in a perfectionist concentration that fascinated and almost excited him.

It is well known, for example, that his speeches were the products of a specialized and, objectively, exaggerated preparation. When his schedule included an audience on September 28, 1958, for the delegates to the Seventh International Congress of the Gas Industry, he ordered a number of publications on the subject well in advance, some of them even coming from other countries.

I remember [Tardini said] that in the summer of 1958, as I arrived for an audience, I saw a huge, heavy package of books on a little table. The pope, who was not at all unaware of my curiosity, said: "See, all these books are about gas." In addition he was a pedant always in search of formal perfection, purity of phrase, appropriateness of language. Once the first draft of a speech had been written, . . . it was time for the dictionaries: the best known, the most exhaustive, the newest. He had a splendid collection of them. He was constantly consulting them in order to be sure whether a given word was correct, whether it was archaic, whether there were more appropriate synonyms. . . . Until the very last moment he made all his own corrections: he changed words and sentences, he recast paragraphs, he inserted and deleted, in such fashion that the text was final only at the very moment when he began to speak. In fact, there were times when he made even later changes on galley proofs of *l'Osservatore romano*, which he himself always insisted on checking.

If, then, his literary talent was brought under attack, the reaction was immediate. Reviewing a volume of essays and speeches by Pius XII in 1957, Carlo Falconi expressed some reservation with respect to their style, which he described as arid if not in fact lacking in incisiveness, originality, images, and movement. *L'Osservatore* characterized the pope's critic as "a street boy with the toga and the tone of a Cato," and *Il Quotidiano*, the spokesman for Catholic Action, assumed the pope's defense in lively language:

The cup of impiety and unbelief begins to run over! Not only is there concordance in the fullest recognition that all the *Scritti e Discorsi (Essays and Speeches)* of His Holiness Pius XII reveal the profound and individual personality of his style, which is remarkably rich in images and in spiritual and intellectual vibrations; but these qualities are all the more notable and, we might say, surprising when one reflects that the Holy Father— with all his respect, typical of a humanist, for language and for nicesness of expression—has never made any effort at or even given a thought to literary creation.

His virtuosity of style, therefore, was supposedly a supernatural endowment, and indeed it was said that Pius XII was imbued with the conviction that by the grace of the Holy Ghost he had been invested with the gift of tongues, or glossolalia, of which Saint Paul wrote (I Cor. 14) that the Apostles possessed it on Pentecost. As a matter of fact, Pius XII was always as harsh as any pedant in his criticisms of any fault in idiom or even of pronunciation in a foreign language. He made fun of Premier Alcide De Gasperi because one day De Gasperi had said to foreign reporters: "*Nous espérons supérer les difficultés* (We hope to overcome our difficulties)." He should have said *surmonter,* the pope commented. Tardini recalled having spoken to Pacelli about the Diocese of Rodez in Aveyron one day in December, 1954, just when the pope was very ill.

> I pronounced it *Rodés,* [Tardini wrote] that is, with the closed vowel. His Holiness interrupted me: "Now, Monsignor, the word is not pronounced *Rodés* but *Rodès,* with the vowel open." Partly because at the moment I was concentrating on getting through quickly, partly because I was concerned by the serious state of the pope's health, partly because I was merely distracted, I went on saying *Rodés.* Pius XII said nothing further. He dismissed me, as usual, very cordially. Two days later I had another audience, and I was rather surprised to see three or four large books on the Holy Father's bed. He greeted me with a smile and said at once: "Well, Monsignor, you have a fluent knowledge of French . . ." I interrupted him to say that unfortunately I did not deserve such praise, adding that I was rather like that Roman fellow who, when asked whether he spoke French, replied: "*Je m'arrange* (I manage)." The pope smiled again and said: "You know, the other day I told you that Rodez was pronounced *Rodès.* You, however, went right on saying *Rodés.* I assure you it is an exception. Here are the best French dictionaries, which remark on it." As he spoke he beckoned me closer to his bed so that I might see the dictionaries. There was nothing for me to do but apologize for my ignorance and my inattentiveness."

Purism and preciosity, moreover, were merely the outer evidences of his conviction that mastery of language was sufficient for all pastoral obligations and duties. He believed passionately in the high quality of his own oratory, certain that he was competent to answer everyone on every subject. Tardini said that Pius XII "often referred to the people's anticipation of his speeches and his own conviction that he—and he alone—was the infallible interpreter of the people's feelings and aspirations." Objectively Pius

XII scored successes with his speeches, and he loved success.

All these judgments were voiced by Tardini as the official speaker for the commemoration of Pius XII, a solemn ceremony that took place on October 20, 1959, in the hall of benedictions in the Vatican, in the presence of John XXIII, the Sacred College of Cardinals, the diplomatic corps, and a select gathering of clerics and laity. At one point, in fact, he felt obliged to point out to his audience:

> Let no one think that it has been my intention, in what I have considered it my duty to say, in any way to derogate the gigantic figure of Pius XII. I have sought only to be honest, certain as I am that the great pontiff would not have been pleased had I offered him adulation in death after having given him admiration, veneration, and love but never adultation in life. In any event, a man is what he is. Grace elevates nature: with divine aid good will gains great victories. To all human potentials, however, there is always a limit that cannot be overstepped.

It is common knowledge that Tardini's reservations with regard to Pius XII were an accurate reflection of the moods of the Roman Curia, which, paradoxically, felt that it had been betrayed by this very pope. For all that he personally was the most typical product of the Curia, it was Pacelli who had struck a staggering blow at his own origins. Himself of an aloof temperament, he had accepted intellectually certain ideas that were vaguely democratic. As a lone and authoritarian centralizer, however, he had come to the end of his pontificate under the banner of dangerous contradictions. Tardini said that, "confronted with conflicting proposals and recommendations, Pius XII no longer felt in control of a situation, divided as he was between his natural friendly compliance and the rigid dictates of his con-

27

science. Hence he did not like to make changes, and he preferred to procrastinate."

It would appear that his most grievous burden was the consistories—the selections of new cardinals. In fact, throughout the whole of his pontificate—almost twenty years—he convoked only two consistories, one in 1946 and the other in 1952. In 1946 he increased the number of non-Italian cardinals, who for the first time since the era of Pius II and Paul II, in the fifteenth century, became more numerous than the Italians. In order to make room for the outlanders, therefore, he reduced the number of cardinals in the Curia; but, while this gave point to the universality of the Church, its bureaucratic results were negative. When the old custom prevailed, under which the best spokesmen for the Curia were elevated to the purple, it was easier to re-staff the various Vatican offices when the highest posts periodically fell vacant. The effect of the innovation made by Pacelli, however, was to block advancement, cut off careers, and foment uneasiness and resentment in all offices. There was lamentation over the reduced prestige of the Curia cardinals, who constituted the real senate of the Church; but there was also a diminution in the efficiency of the central agencies because, for lack of cardinals, all their functions fell into the hands of the pope, who refused to have even a secretary of state collaborating with him after the death of Luigi Cardinal Maglione in 1944. Never in the history of the Church had there been a fourteen-year vacuum in the most important post in the ecclesiastical general staff.

One comes back to Tardini, this time for the disclosure of the underlying reasons for the resentments in the Curia:

Habemus Papam!

Thus the Roman Curia was afflicted with a certain stagnation, as when in the human body some irregularities in the circulation of the blood begin to be observed. We old men were still there blocking the passage and preventing the rise of forces that were fresher and stronger than ourselves.

In other words, Pius' own immediate collaborators (or, in more accurate terms, his closest subordinates) reproached him for having destroyed the old system of the ecclesiastical general staff without creating anything to take its place. Once he had taken the first step in the direction of a more modern conception of the life of the Church, Pius XII no longer had the courage or the ability to proceed farther.

II

Behind the Scenes
of the Conclave

The Curia would have preferred
Aloisi Cardinal Masella.
Tisserant, the head of the "French party."
Few eligible candidates.
The Church of France in Roncalli's debt.
At grips with de Gaulle.
"I shall be elected if they are looking
for a man with common sense."
"This morning I became pope."

ON the eve of the conclave, there was a rumor that Gregory Peter Cardinal Agagianian, the Armenian patriarch of Cilicia, pro-prefect of the Congregation for the Propagation of the Faith, and, as such, known as the "Red Pope," had an excellent chance of being elected. A Russian by birth, a Lebanese by passport, and a Vatican national by right in his capacity as a cardinal, in excellent physical condition and at an excellent age (he was sixty-three), with an excellent cultural background and broad international experience, learned, cautious, pious, a fluent orator in many languages, Agagianian seemed to be the incarnation of a pope who would have been at once a Roman and a foreigner, a man of the Curia and a missionary. In every list of eligible candidates put together for each of the succesive illnesses of Pius XII, his name had in fact always appeared, and he had to his credit in addition a prophecy made by Pius X, who had met Agagianian as a seminarist: "That young man will perform great services for the Church."

Agagianian's supporters, of course, made every effort to give this prophecy the widest circulation, but their man's chances were actually virtually nil. His candidacy, which on paper seemed perfect, was the outcome of rationalizations as rigid in form as they were lacking in contact with reality. Even the so-called "Orientals" who should have been Agagianian's natural backers were hostile to him—for instance, Ignace Gabriel Cardinal Tappuni of Iraq. What was worse, Agagianian was opposed by the dean of the Sacred College, Eugène Cardinal Tisserant, secretary of the Congregation of the Eastern Church, the traditional rival and competitor of the Congregation for the Propagation of the Faith. The latter, indeed, challenged the former's jurisdiction over whole regions that the Congregation for the Propagation of the Faith regarded as mission territories whereas its adversary claimed them as among the most ancient seats of Christendom. On the merits, moreover, Tisserant foresaw that Agagianian would have been another Pius XII, with his rigid temperament that was more Roman and Curial than open to the world. And Tisserant was right, as became apparent later, during Vatican Council II. Of all the moderators, Agagianian was the most reserved; he never once spoke during the first session, nor did he in any other way commit himself on basic Church matters. Whether he was for or against, he always maintained toward Pope John XXIII an attitude that at most could be called one of respectful reserve.

The Curia's real candidate, in any event, was not Agagianian but Benedetto Aloisi Cardinal Masella, elected treasurer of the Holy Roman Church immediately after the death of Pius XII, who had allowed this post too—which was vital in the event of a papal hiatus—to remain unfilled for many years. This selection of Masella as treasurer, in other words, as provisional ruler of Catholicism whose regency would continue until the election of a new pope, was significant because Masella was perhaps the most typical representative of the old Roman ecclesiastical society, which was drawn from the academy of noble men destined to be the diplomatic representatives of the Holy See. A member of a prominent Roman family, himself the owner of huge tracts of tobacco land round Pontedorvo, in the Liri Valley, he had in his own ancestry many splendid examples of services rendered to the Church. A great-uncle, Gaetano, also a cardinal, had negotiated with Bismarck for the end of the *Kulturkampf* and achieved success in a most difficult undertaking. The current cardinal, in his capacity as nuncio in Portugal, Chile, and Brazil, had conducted himself skillfully and shrewdly in various delicate religious and political situations. If Pius XII had called him "the nuncio of the storms," in recognition of the many obstacles that he had had to overcome or get round in the domain of relations between Church and State, the Vatican was also cognizant of the great praise due him for his exemplary behavior on the occasion of the famous miracle of Fatima.

In 1917, when the throng that had gathered round the three shepherd children who had spoken with the Madonna in the Cova da Iria saw the sun spinning in the sky, Masella was the chargé d'affaires in the nunciature in Lisbon. At that time he was young—thirty-eight—but he had the astuteness of the classic Roman prelate, and he was careful not to go to Fatima; this prudence earned him the lavish praise of Benedict XV. In fact, Masella did no more than to send two trusted agents to the place and then, on their return, report to Rome that one of the two stated that he had seen a remarkable meteorological phenomenon and the other insisted that absolutely nothing had happened.

In 1946, however, Masella had occasion as a cardinal to visit Fatima; he served as Pius XII's legate to the coronation of the statue of the Madonna in the huge sanctuary erected on the plateau; and there and then he himself saw two poor cripples, whom physicians had pronounced hopeless, rise completely cured from their litters. As successor to Pius XII, therefore, Masella would have had the proper credentials with respect to testimony as to miracles, and so the Curia cardinals' desire to make him pope might have indicated a desire for a certain continuity. The limited possibilities of this maneuver, however, were obvious, if only because of the candidate's age—seventy-nine. Actually the Curia cardinals wanted an interim pope who could maintain the status quo in the Vatican for no longer than was required to restore order to the confusion bequeathed by Pius XII.

All the power of the Curia men, nonetheless, was not enough to assure the election of a pope. Their strength was exceeded by that of another group, which was known in the Vatican, in a reference to old traditions, as the French party. In 1958 the French cardinals numbered five—Eugène Tisserant, Georges Grente, Maurice Feltin, Achille Liénart, and Clément Roques—and they constituted the largest non-Italian national bloc; the Italians at that time numbered eighteen. The French, however, had the advantage over the Italians in that they could assume the leadership of a multinational coalition made up not only of other countries linked to France by language or cultural tradition but also of Germany and South America. In addition they could count on the votes of a few Spaniards, apparently, and in any event as an electoral or pressure group theirs was unquestionably the most tempered by experience and the most capable of maneuver. Furthermore it was loyal to the old insistence of the French party in the Vatican on having a pope who would be, if not French, at least a friend of France. "The Italians always demand a pope of their own kind," it has been said *ab antiquo* in the Vatican, "and the French insist on a pope after their own style."

The most famous of all the leaders of the French party throughout history is still the noble and extremely rich fifteenth-century Guillaume Cardinal d'Estouteville, who when he went to a consistory ordered that he be followed by a train of thirty carriages in testimony to the importance of the Church of France. The party's modern leader in 1958, Cardinal Tisserant, who was less ambitious, not at all wordly, and less arrogant, was utterly different from Estouteville in habits and style, but the influence of the Church of France was in no way diminished on that account. "Its representative among the Curia cardinals," the most prudent Silvio Negro said, "is unquestionably what politicians call a good Frenchman."

A very robust man, Tisserant enjoyed a remarkable reputation because of his unlimited erudition as well as his character as a leader. He symbolized the authority of the Church, which he personified in a modern manner with his highly varied experience as a scientist, an explorer, and even a soldier (he was an officer on the French General Staff during the expedition in the Near East in the First World War). A master of the five Semitic languages—Hebrew, Arabic, Syrian, Amharic, and Assyrian—in addition to Greek and Latin, he spoke Persian, Russian, German, English, and Italian. "One of the finest minds in the Church, a living witness on earth to the wisdom of the creator," Wladimir d'Ormesson said of him in a speech welcoming the cardinal into the *Académie française.* As librarian of the Church, he had made the Vatican a library that in its equipment could stand as the equal of the most modern in the United States. That was why some in the Curia even spoke of him as "Tisserant the American," thus demonstrating their rustic provincial uneasiness in the presence of a mentality utterly remote from the Curia, above its pettinesses and its terrors.

Speaking of fear, there was a famous letter written by Tisserant on June 11, 1940—the day after Italy entered the Second World War—to the archbishop of Paris, Emmanuel Cardinal Suhard:

It is disgraceful. Here everyone is relying on the fact that Rome has been declared an open city and no one in the Curia will have to suffer, all the more in that the Secretariat of State and the Nuncio have persuaded the religious not to leave, in order to provide hostages for Italy. . . . I am in a state of the utmost uselessness, nailed down here, although I have asked the Holy Father to assign me to France.

Pius XII had refused to grant permission for Tisserant to leave, but even worse conflict raged between pope and cardinal:

Ever since the beginning of December I have been insistently asking the Holy Father to issue an encyclical on the individual duty of following the dictates of conscience, because this is the vital point of Christianity, whereas Islam supplants individual conscience with the duty of blind obedience to the orders of the Prophet and his successors.

Perhaps it was just this blind obedience on the Moslem model that Pius XII prized, and Tisserant drew his conclusion: "I am afraid that history will reproach the Holy See for having adopted a policy of its own convenience and nothing more."

When this letter became known (it was found in a library, after the death of Pius XII, by German historian

Eberhard Jaeckel of the University of Kiel), Tisserant asserted that it must be viewed in relation to "the particular moment in history that had evoked very special reactions in my mind as a Frenchman and as a priest." In every respect, he added as a good Catholic, the pope's attitude thereafter was beyond cavil: "My comments were directed not at his person but at some components of the Curia."

It is common knowledge, besides, that Tisserant never let pass an opportunity to range himself in opposition to Roman prejudices, the factions in the Curia, the power groups. When he learned that Pius XII was ill, he at once cut short his vacation, which he was spending in his country house in Lorraine, and burst into the papal palace in Castel Gandolfo with the zeal of a Christ driving out the money-changers. Immediately after the pope's death he ordered the ouster of the chief physician, Galeazzi-Lisi. A businessman as well as a healer, the doctor had crowned his career by selling photographs and descriptions of his patient's last days to the daily press and the weekly picture papers, and he was stricken from the rolls of the medical society.

Having got rid of Galeazzi, Tisserant ordered the immediate expulsion of Sister Pasqualina, born Josephine Lehnert, a Bavarian nun who for more than forty years had managed the pope's private life, not without occasional excesses in the way of intrusions into the domains in which the government (and the subgovernment) of the Church were conducted. Astounding stories had always been told about her: that it was her job to fix the order in which the papers placed on the pope's desk would come before him for examination; that she was in a position to determine the duration of audiences, including even those granted to persons of the highest station. Sister Pasqualina would enter the room and say to the visitor: "It would be well if you would leave. His Holiness is tired and must rest." John Foster Dulles, United States secretary of state during the early years of the Cold War, had his own personal experience of this, and later reported it to a newspaperman. One day when Dulles and Pius were in the pope's private study, the little nun entered and said in German: "Holiness, it is time for lunch." Thereupon the pope rose and, with the utmost indulgence toward her, said to Dulles: "There is no power on earth that could sway our good mother Pasqualina when soup is on the table." Meanwhile Sister Pasqualina had not moved an inch, as if she were trying to force a quick dismissal. It was said too that the importance, the influence, the authority of everyone in the Vatican was measured by the degree of favor shown to him by Sister Pasqualina, so that those few who, for example, were privileged to telephone her directly were extremely powerful. One such was Monsignor Fiorenzo Angelini, general adjutant of Catholic Action, and precisely as a result of these remarkable telephone privileges of his Fernando Tambroni, the Italian minister of the interior, had placed a police inspector at his disposition.

The problem that was raised for the French party by the choice of Pacelli's successor was very straightforward. The new pope should be another Italian, provided that he was not a member of the Curia, and, in addition, he should be a friend of France. The number of acceptable candidates was therefore quite limited, since, apart from the thirty-seven foreign cardinals and the Italians who were of the Curia, as well as those others who were precluded by their age, there remained to be considered only the archbishops of Palermo, Genoa, and Bologna and the patriarch of Venice: respectively, Ernesto Cardinal Ruffini, Guiseppe Cardinal Siri, Giacomo Cardinal Lercaro, and Angelo Cardinal Roncalli.

It was unlikely, however, that the foreign cardinals would be able to agree on Ruffini, who was notoriously reactionary and perhaps overly "Sicilianized" by reason of his twelve years' residence in Palermo, where he had earned the title of King of the Two Sicilies—the ecclesiastical and the political. Archbishop Siri of Genoa was known to be of a thorny character and hostile to all human contact, and in addition it was possible that his youth would count against him—he was fifty-two. Archbishop Lercaro of Bologna was admired for his exemplary pastoral character, but there had also been much discussion and disapproval of certain unusual actions by him that seemed highly inappropriate to many observers. It had been his idea to send the so-called "Flying Friars" into election rallies—that is, Capuchins who burst in and interrupted speeches by "red" candidates. And besides, as Don Lorenzo Bedeschi wrote, it was his habit to "sit at table with university students, to tolerate the wearing of hats if he saw that this was what those round him wanted, to sit over wine with a group of railway workers and listen to their extemporaneous songs, to circulate among costumed children during carnival and guess what comic-strip characters they were impersonating." All these acts were completely spontaneous and utterly natural for Lercaro, typical manifestations of his need to communicate; but in addition they brought down unfavorable judgments on him, such as that rendered, even though with affection, by one of his intimates, Luigi Santucci: "Cardinal Lercaro is—how shall I put it?—an afterschool cardinal, a holiday-excursion cardinal, standing outside the gate next to the ice-cream man's cart at the streetcar stop with a packet of sandwiches and a slingshot." He could not be made pope.

So there remained Roncalli, and not merely by elimination. Indeed he was more than acceptable to the Church of France, which had learned to esteem him in the difficut early years of his nunciature in Paris, when he had courageously assumed the defense of the French bishops against de Gaulle, who demanded that they be purged. Immediately after his entry into Paris the general had begun by placing Cardinal-Archbishop Suhard under virtual arrest and forbidding him to attend a *Te Deum* in gratitude for the liberation on August 26, 1944, at Notre Dame. Then de Gaulle had demanded that the Vatican withdraw its nuncio, Monsignor Valerio Valeri, on the pretext that none of the diplomatic representatives who had been accredited to Vichy could be accepted by the new government. Finally he had requested the replacement of more than thirty residential bishops, all accused of collaboration with the Germans.

It was precisely those Catholics who had been members of the Resistance or who were now members of the government—such as Georges Bidault—who were goading de Gaulle to take a strong stand against Rome. The Vatican, of course, sought to resist, pointing out that during the German occupation Monsignor Valeri had been distinguished for his unremitting efforts to restrain the French bishops from excesses of zeal with regard to Pétain and the Germans. This was indeed true, for the extremely mild Valeri, known in the Vatican as "a tin angel but one with a brain," was actually endowed with excellent judgment;

but for de Gaulle what was involved was a matter of principle on which he had no intention of giving ground. It was Pius XII who had to yield after four months of passive resistance that perhaps he would have much preferred to continue longer, as was his custom in difficult cases. It appears, however, that, since the end of the year was at hand, the Vatican had also to consider a ceremonial problem: the age-old tradition that it was the papal nuncio, in his capacity as dean of the diplomatic corps, who presented the corps' New Year greetings to the chief of state. If de Gaulle refused to admit Monsignor Valeri into his presence, the New Year greetings would have to be presented by the next diplomat in rank, in this case, Ambassador Aleksandr Y. Bogomolov of the Union of Soviet Socialist Republics; this, apparently, would have been a humiliation for the pope. So it was that at the end of November the negotiations between Paris and Rome were accelerated. Pius XII sent Tisserant to Paris to investigate and the cardinal was overwhelmed with honors by the new French government, which was enthusiastic in paying tribute and extending invitations to him, if only in order to emphasize the difference from its treatment of Valeri and Suhard, who were methodically ignored and virtually under a ban.

De Gaulle sent Monsignor Pierre-M. Théas, bishop of Montauban, to Rome. The prelate had served time in the German concentration camp in Compiègne because of his outspoken attacks on the anti-Christian character of Nazism. As a pastor, in fact, Monsignor Théas had always rejected and even contemned exhortations to caution. He would say that, when pastors, who are the sentries of God, prove blind and dumb, the curse of Isaiah (LVI:9–10) would be fulfilled: "All ye beasts of the field, come to devour: yea, all ye beasts in the forest. His watchmen are blind; they are all ignorant, they are all dumb dogs, they cannot bark; sleeping, lying down, loving to slumber." This amounted to a portrait of the Curia prelates during the German occupation, as Tisserant too had observed them, and Monsignor Théas had no desire to be associated with them: "I do not wish to be a dog that does not bark. When danger comes, I bark: that is my duty. Silence would be betrayal. 'Woe is me! . . . because I am a man of unclean lips' (Isaiah VI:5). I do not wish to be one of those who 'be blind leaders of the blind. And if the blind lead the blind, both shall fall into the ditch' (Matthew XV:14)."

All this was very fine—no exception could be taken to the concept of the pastoral duty incumbent on the bishops as God's sentries to stand firm against the beasts of all the fields and the predators of all the forests that threaten the flock—but it was tantamount to a condemnation of the bishops (they formed the majority) who had kept silent, and above all of the pope himself. Indeed, after he had yielded on the question of the nuncio, Pius XII wanted to stand firm on that of the bishops: "We dedicate all our supreme pontifical authority to the defense and protection of the bishops' authority and rights. Go, and repeat this statement *verbatim* in public when you return to Paris," he said to Monsignor Théas by way of dismissal.

In any event, as soon as the Vatican had agreed to recall the nuncio, de Gaulle received him in solemn audience and presented him with the Grand Cross of the *Légion d'honneur;* and, in token of respect to Valeri personally, Tisserant accompanied him on the whole journey from Paris to Rome. Valeri was a victim; and, too, because customarily a nuncio leaves France to become a cardinal, and he had had his red hat for nine years. His patient bearing, however, was such as to arouse admiration. "You have had to suffer much because of France," Tisserant observed to him on the journey. Valeri replied: "But I feel nothing of the sort, Your Eminence; say rather that I have suffered with France."

The matter of the bishops was still unresolved, and the whole problem was turned over to the new nuncio, Monsignor Angelo Giuseppe Roncalli, unexpectedly raised from his modest duties as apostolic administrator of the vicariate of Constantinople to the highest diplomatic responsibility of the Church at that time. Generally regarded as a man of less than the first rank, and completely unknown in France, Roncalli was chosen because, Father Ernesto Balducci said, the Holy See "had had proofs of his utterly absolute docility, combined with the resources of a good-natured and imperturbable character, which were most necessary in Paris at that period." Roncalli himself has described how he was informed of his new appointment by a top-secret coded telegram that he received in Istanbul on December 6, 1944. He deciphered it himself, but then he was certain that he had made a mistake and he had his secretary decipher it independently. At this confirmation he could no longer contain himself: "Someone must have lost his reason!" Then, repentant over his irreverence, he sighed more meekly, though not without irony: *Ubi deficiunt equi trottant aselli*—Where horses fail, asses get through."

He spent Christmas in Turkey and then left Ankara on December 27 aboard an American military plane that took him to Rome by way of Cairo, Bengazi, and Naples. He was received by the pope, who told him, perhaps by way of encouragement: "It was I myself, Monsignor, who thought of you, and I made the decision, no one else." It was a viaticum, but it increased his obligation: "To find myself suddenly taken up like Habakkuk and immediately flown from Istanbul to Paris was a kind of magic for me too," Roncalli said. "I could not deny to myself that the move was a serious one, and all the more because it would have seemed improbable to me; and certainly I should have had the courage neither to imagine it nor to wish for it."

He went on to Paris aboard the same military plane, and, when he was received by de Gaulle in order to present his credentials, he could not get a word out of the general. He made various attempts; he pointed to a mass of roses in a vase on a table. "How beautiful!" he said, in the hope of spurring the general into a conversation. "I love all flowers," Roncalli told de Gaulle. The silence persisted, and he tried again: "I love all flowers and all the beautiful and pleasurable things that God has created." With frozen insolence de Gaulle cut him short: "So do I."

It was an omen of the difficulty that awaited the nuncio in his mission. Bidault, who was then foreign minister, turned over to him the formal plea for exoneration presented by the thirty accused residential bishops among the eighty in France. In evidence of their collaboration, Bidault gave Roncalli a huge file of documents and press clippings that called for a purge of the episcopate. Roncalli pretended to see only the press clippings: "Newspaper articles, Monsieur le Ministre, do not constitute proofs," he said urbanely. Later he himself had occasion to tell a French visitor: "When I arrived in Paris it came to me like an enlightenment from the Holy Spirit: 'Dear old Angelo,' I said to myself, 'in the light of the circumstances you have only one way of coming out ahead, even though it may offend your vanity: play stupid, Angelo, play stupid.' " Thus he evaded replying to questions that were too specific, and he allowed conversations to wander. "I employ the crawfish's tactics," he explained one day. "If I am attacked, I retreat. I retreat, but I turn round and I am still in the same place."

In any event he had confronted Bidault from the very first day with a difficult question. If the charges of collaboration lodged against the bishops arose solely from the fact that they had recognized and supported a government like Pétain's that was a creation of legality, the Holy See would not have agreed to the removal of even one of them. Proceeding from the question of principle to that of merit, Roncalli pointed out in a more softly persuasive manner that the request for the removal of as many as thirty bishops was excessive. It was an insult to the Church of France as a whole, which should rather have been praised for the contributions that it had made to the Resistance. "Thirty bishops are too many," Roncalli insisted again and again, "to permit the continued presence of a nuncio. I too should have to leave."

Between his crawfish tactics and his technique of pretended stupidity, his efforts at persuasion and his threats of a rupture, the negotiations went on for a year and ended with the retirement of three bishops, who were prevailed upon to submit their resignations, rather than the thirty accused by de Gaulle. "We managed to eliminate the zero from the number of banned bishops," Roncalli remarked subtly, without claiming any further credit for a diplomatic success that represented the salvation of the Church of France.

Nothing less, moreover, would have been able to overcome the coldness and the aloofness that had greeted Roncalli in Paris. "It is not easy to determine," Nazareno Fabretti wrote, "whether Roncalli's contacts with the Church of France were more or less difficult than those with the government. Unquestionably they were more delicate and more complex." During the eight years of his mission, he visited seventy-eight of the eighty French dioceses, either on formal occasions or privately, and apparently all this traveling was a departure from the traditional style of a nuncio. Pius XII disapproved of it, perhaps because he was suspicious of possible compromises of his representative with the always dangerous Church of France, and the pope sent word to his nuncio to reduce his public appearances. Pius "kept him under close supervision and finally went to the extent of forbidding him to walk in the streets," Father Robert Rouquette, a Jesuit, wrote. Leone Algisi, Roncalli's biographer, confirmed this: "He received word from Rome that the Holy Father desired that his presence in the nunciature be uninterrupted." Roncalli decided to reply with his usual quiet self-confidence: "Holy Father, a mere remark becomes a rule of life for me. As far as my goings and comings in France are concerned, I go only where the bishops insist that I be present. And with my presence, as I did in the East, I attempt to be the eye, the heart, and the helping hand of the pope."

He left France with the rank of cardinal and Patriarch of Venice. Making his official farewell to President Vincent Auriol, Roncalli told him very politely that he hoped to be remembered by the French as "an honest and peaceful priest, always a sure and sincere friend of France on every occasion." He had in fact built up a great fortune in affection and respect, as much among the clergy as among the laity, and to French Catholics there was no doubt that Roncalli—that honest, peaceful priest, that sure and sincere friend of France—would one day be pope. He himself, for that matter, was thinking of it. Henri Daniel-Rops went to visit him in Venice and copied into his diary their very relaxed conversation on the subject. It was Roncalli who first raised it, as they were going through the apartment that had once belonged to Pius X. "Cardinal Sarto went from here to become pope," Roncalli said. "He did not expect that, poor fellow! Did you know that he had bought a round-trip ticket to Rome?"

"On your next journey, Your Eminence," Daniel-Rops replied, "will you buy a one-way ticket?"

"Hush, be quiet—God save me from such a misfortune!"

Daniel-Rops accompanied Roncalli then on visits to various relatives and fellow townsmen of the cardinal, who said to them with laughing simplicity: "See? Battista Roncalli's little Angelo is a cardinal and a patriarch! All that is left now is the papacy. But this is out of the question because the next pope will be the archbishop of Milan."

Roncalli's work as Patriarch of Venice—one of the most glorious offices of the Church—also contributed to the enhancement of his reputation as well as to his opportunities for further contacts with colleagues of his own rank. "During his time in Venice," Algisi wrote, "a dozen cardinals passed through the city, and he met as many more in his own numerous journeys inside and outside Italy." In confirmation of the hypothesis that during the last years of Pius XII there must have been various signs of what was to come, Fabretti suggested that as early as 1954 Roncalli must have certainly given thought to Pacelli's successor, and nothing could have "prevented him from imagining himself, even for a brief moment, as the potential candidate." Algisi remarked that on October 12, 1958, the evening when he left Venice for the conclave, Roncalli's "face was visibly filled with trepidation: he knew that he was known to everyone and that he enjoyed the esteem of so many, too many of his colleagues among the cardinals."

In Rome he, like many others, established himself in the Domus Mariae, the institute belonging to the women of Catholic Action—a large, modern, semi-monastic structure on Via Aurelia. At ten thirty every morning, punctually, he and the other cardinals in the general congregations presided over by their dean, Tisserant, gathered in the consistory room of the Vatican; Fabretti asserted that Roncalli "must have also been aware that even in the very earliest days of the consultations he had been encountering increasing manifestations of esteem, even among men who could not have known him very well." Algisi emphasized: "Little by little, as the days went on and the date of the conclave approached, Cardinal Roncalli was clearly aware of the sympathy that many cardinals felt toward him." Alden Hatch, a third biographer, wrote: "He would have had to be blind and deaf not to have known that he was on the final restricted list of eligibles."

Roncalli's letters of that period, furthermore, are the proof. He wrote an appeal to Monsignor G. B. Montini, archbishop of Milan, in tones of the most unmistakable meaning: "I am very much in need of the saints. Therefore I turn to you who are so close to the saints to whom I am especially devoted. . . . I commend my soul to Saint Ambrose and Saint Charles Borromeo," both of whom are buried in Milan. In a letter addressed to Monsignor Giuseppe Pazzi, bishop of Bergamo, he said:

A brief note just before going into the conclave. . . . The mind takes comfort in its faith in the new pentecost that may instill new vigor into Holy Church through the replacement of her leader and the reconstruction of the ecclesiastical organism. . . . It is of little importance whether the new pope comes from Bergamo. The prayers of all must cause the choice to fall on a man of wise and gentle governance, a saint and a sanctifier. Excellency, you will understand me. I greet you and embrace you.

He was even more explicit, and indeed wholly objective, with a French cardinal—Feltin or Roques—who asked him whether he considered himself eligible. He replied: "If they want a conservative, they will elect Ruffini. If they want a diplomat, they will choose Montini, even though he is not a cardinal. As for myself, I shall be elected only if they decide simply to look for a man with common sense."

As is the custom in conclaves, the first ballot, on October 26, was what is called the courtesy vote. The French endorsed Tisserant; some of the Italians voted for Ernesto Ruffini, archbishop of Palermo, the leader of the most conservative group; the English-speaking cardinals backed Stepan Cardinal Wyszinski, archbishop of Warsaw, the illustrious victim of Nazism and Communism who had also been the hostage of the Curia and a butt for Pius XII. Only a few votes went to Agagianian, of whom the ill-informed

51

continued to assert that he had entered the conclave "already halfway to the papacy." Thus the complimentary vote also served the purpose of establishing the numerical strength of each faction. Roncalli himself voted for Valerio Cardinal Valeri, his predecessor in Paris, in token of affectionate compensation for the bitterness that Valeri had had to endure in those days. Having become prefect of the Congregation of the Religious, Valeri could not be described as the spokesman of any specific tendency in the Curia; in fact, he was regarded as the "spiritualist" in the Sacred College because, in addition to praying, it was said, he also behaved like one praying. It is thought for that matter that Valeri received only this one vote from the first through the last of the eleven ballots; and it is also believed that Roncalli's election appeared certain, or, at the very least, extremely probable, from the first day of the conclave. In addition to the unwearying support of the French party, Roncalli is supposed to have enjoyed from the start the backing of Elia Cardinal Dalla Costa, archbishop of Florence, his old friend and colleague in the purple, and Maurizio Cardinal Fossati, archbishop of Turin, who occupied the cell next to his during the conclave. The cells were assigned by lot, and Roncalli had received No. 15, which had been set up in the quarters of the Pope's Noble Guard—in fact, in the office of its general. The door still bore the inscription: "The Commander."

Those who conducted Roncalli to his cell pointed this out to him with such meaningful winks that he was moved to reply urbanely: "Are you among those who believe in omens and presages? I am not." The next cell, No. 16, was assigned to Cardinal Fossati, who later wrote: "I do not think that I am violating the obligation of secrecy, from which, moreover, I should feel certain of being absolved by the great and kind goodness of the Holy Father, if I say that at a certain point a friend felt it necessary to enter his friend's cell *confortans Eum* (by way of comforting him)." And too, Roncalli's secretary, Monsignor Loris Capovilla, recalled that between ballots many cardinals and the secretaries and servants closeted with them in the papal palace competed with one another in "delicate attentions" to the patriarch of Venice as if to "sustain him with the warmth of their filial piety and the promise of devoted attachment." There exists, too, a diary, not yet published, which Roncalli kept in a big office-style desk-calendar, and which contains traces of the preoccupations that troubled his sleep during the nights of the conclave. He succeeded in mastering them, as he himself recounted subsequently, by asking himself: "But who is it that rules the Church? Is it you or the Holy Ghost? Well, then, Angelo, go to sleep!" And again on the same subject, with a variation: "I feel as if I were an empty bag that the Holy Spirit unexpectedly fills with strength."

Having thus sought and found sleep during those nights, he wrote simply in his diary on October 28: "This morning I was made pope." At the top of the page, however, there was a remark that seemed like a cry from the heart: "O Papa and Mama, would you have thought that your Angelo would become the successor to Saint Peter?" He told Monsignor Capovilla too what his first impression had been: "I thought of my home in Sotto il Monte: my father and mother." And again in a note for *Il Giornale dell'anima: "Vicarius Christi?* Oh, I am not worthy of that designation—the poor son of Battista and Marianna Roncalli, certainly both good Christians, but so modest and humble!"

That night for the first time he did not sleep. Later he told Daniel-Rops: "I spent the entire night in prayer. It was burdensome, you know, such a burden. But the Lord wished it. You remember the words of the prophet Jeremiah: 'You have conquered me, o my God, you are the stronger, and I have submitted.' One must always be ready to obey God's will." But the next day, October 29, he was still in the grip of dismay, as a note in his diaries shows: "Today the whole world is talking and writing only about me, my name and myself. O Mama, o Father, Grandfather Angelo, Uncle Zaverio, where are you? Who brought you to such honor? Continue to pray for me."

III

From Sotto il Monte
to Rome

Roncalli family origins:
"not lowborn but honored and respectable."
Studies and military service.
Secretary to the bishop of Bergamo:
the strike at Ranica, teaching, war.
Diplomatic experience.
Patriarch in Venice.
"Vocabor Johannes."

Roncalli is a highly honored family name that is quite widespread in Italy. A Count Luigi Roncalli, a composer in Bologna, was well known for having published pleasant caprices for the lute in the early sixteenth century. Cristoforo Roncalli was the name of the painter called by his pseudonym of Pomarancio because he was born (in 1552) in Pomarance, near Pisa. He defeated Caravaggio in a competition and he is still famous for his frescoes in the sacristy of the shrine of Loreto, a baroque triumph of declamatory and acclamatory prophets and sybils. In the late sixteenth and early seventeenth centuries one Francesco Roncalli of Brescia was court physician in Spain and the author of a treatise on the diseases and therapeutic methods then known in Europe. Another Francesco Roncalli, from Bergamo (1795–1875), was the head of that city's provisional government during the revolution of 1848, a member of the communal council for fifty years, president of the provincial council, and a senator of the realm after 1860. He was a marquis and of a rich family not unrelated to that of the "good Christian," Giovanni Battista, the father of Angelo. Knowing that Cardinal Roncalli was from Bergamo and remembering the name of the local nobleman, an old French diplomat in quest of information asked him one day, in French: "Are the Marchesi Roncalli related to Your Eminence's family?" It was the day on which Roncalli was elevated from nuncio to cardinal, and he recognized immediately that the old gentleman's inquiry was intended to be complimentary, even if it was not altogether immune to a most evanescent suspicion. Roncalli's reply, however, was of an angelic irony: "No, not thus far, to the best of my knowledge. But I feel somehow that from now on they will be more and more closely related."

He himself, however, asserted with rightful pride, in his hand-written *Notes for a Biography of Pope Roncalli:*

So much is certain, that Pope Roncalli's family came not from lowborn but from honored and respectable origins, stemming from the beginning of the fifteenth century and from the first *Martinus* Roncalli *dictus Maytinus de Valle Imania,* and from this first Roncalli of Sotto il Monte going back still farther to a certain Bonadio in the middle of the thirteenth century, followed by one Reubaldo whose dates were 1257–1285.

That Martino or Maytino came from Roncaglia, a district of Cepino in the Imagna Valley, and established himself in Sotto il Monte, a little settlement at the foot of the slope between the plain of the Po and the Pre-Alps, on the eastern arm of Lake Como, where the view begins to descend from the Canto Bassa toward the Adda. There he built a house, which was called Camaitino and which is still in existence; from 1925 until 1958 Monsignor Roncalli rented it as his summer home.

Just when I began to live in it, [he wrote in his notes], it happened that restoration work brought to light on the wall, which must have been the outer façade of the first structure, some fifteenth-century frescoes or pictures showing images of Saint Anthony the Abbot, a Madonna with the child, and Saint Bernardino, the great saint of that time: the whole was crowned

58

by a family crest: a tower on a field of red and white fesses: the exact crest of the Maytinos of Sotto il Monte, which, from the date of this discovery and with some additions, became the arms of the archbishop, then patriarch and cardinal, and now Supreme Pontiff, Angelo Giuseppe Roncalli, who has assumed the name of John XXIII. Just as it is, and quartered with the crest of Saint Mark, this papal coat of arms matches his passionate interest in and study of the ancient history of the land that gave him birth, and assuredly it does not arise out of any desire to claim noble origins.

Nevertheless he was deeply attached to his family name. Writing to his brother Saverio on December 3, 1961, he began, as if jokingly, by obeserving that it was remarkable that the Lord had seen fit to choose his vicar right in their own extremely modest house, but then he added at once, with apparent satisfaction: "As a result of this summons the name of Roncalli was brought to the knowledge, the affection, and the respect of the entire world."

He was born on November 25, 1881, the third child of a modest peasant family destined to become unusually large: there were to be thirteen children. Their father, Giovanni Battista, was an overseer for Count Ottavio Morlani, and through hard work and stubborn thrift he managed to purchase a small dairy and thirty square rods of land—about seven and a half acres. The future pope's mother, born Marianna Giulia Mazzola, was remembered as a silent woman "sparing in caresses but strong in consolation," which is a most excellent tribute. From his earliest years Angelo seemed a model child, the most intelligent in the family, the best endowed for schooling; and in fact, since he was the eldest of the sons, the family had some reluctance about assigning him to manual work, preferring to allow him to complete his school work.

He had been sent as a pupil to Don Pietro Bolis, the energetic parish priest of Carvico, who taught him logical analysis between slaps, making him stay on his knees for hours if he was guilty of a mistake. Then he was enrolled as a day student in the academy of Celana, another small town about four miles from Sotto il Monte, and ten-year-old Angelo made the round trip on foot every day, although without learning very much in this school. The marks that he brought home at the end of the first quarter were so bad (five in arithmetic and four in each of the four other subjects—the best mark would have been one) that Angelo hid the report. The headmaster of the academy gave him a bad-conduct mark and ordered him to report this to the parish priest. Believing that this mark was undeserved, Angelo tore up the note on his walk from Celana to Carvico, and, when Don Pietro Bolis learned of this, the boy was beaten again. But Angelo's conscience was clear. He knew that it was not his fault that he was gaining nothing from his studies, since those teachers did not know their jobs.

Later, when he entered the seminary, he did better. The Bergamo seminary has a great tradition that goes back to the earliest years of the history of priestly seminaries, the age of Saint Charles Borromeo, and it had maintained a high cultural and religious level when young Roncalli entered at the age of twelve, after he had passed the entrance examination for the public high school. Here he found his niche, once he had overcome the initial bewilderment attendant on his first encounter with real study. He quickly became a leader in his class, and his strong, pleas-

ing voice soon made him an expert singer as well. Then
he won a scholarship to the noblemen's academy, Cerasoli,
attached to the Roman papal seminary of Saint Apollinaris, and he studied theology in Rome until 1904, except
for the interruption of a year of military service. He was
conscripted in 1902 as a "one-year volunteer" and served
in the Lombardy Brigade of the Seventy-third Infantry
Division, stationed at Bergamo. The so-called one-year
enlistment was a privilege that cost a thousand lire and
that was reserved to university and seminary students,
who could choose the branch or unit in which they wanted
to serve for only a year instead of the usual three years
of the ordinary conscript; at the end they were discharged
as sergeants.

In the regiment (the motto of which was *acerrimus
hostibus*—overwhelming, merciless, irresistible to the enemy), life seemed to him to be no different from the
Babylonian captivity, as he wrote to his own spiritual
mentor, Father Francesco Pitocchi, and to Monsignor Vincenzo Bugarini, the rector of the Roman seminary: "Mine
is a life of the greatest sacrifice, a true purgatory." The
requirements of discipline and military discipline were
"very wearing and quite hard, principally in the beginning: suffice it to say that this miserable letter of mine
was begun perhaps a week ago without my ever being able
to finish it." He conceded, however, that in this situation
that was by nature painful to a cleric there were also certain consoling factors:

I have excellent officers who make it clear that they like me
very much; they show me great respect and they see to it that
others respect me as a religious, and above all they make certain
that I have the utmost freedom to fulfill my religious obligations.

Among my comrades in the ranks, most of whom are from Bergamo and Bresica and who also know my background, I have observed thus far only marks of reverence and affection; they vie
with one another to perform for me those little services that, if
they accomplish nothing else, spare me many irritations.

Even then it was a characteristic of his to find positive
aspects to every situation, and this habit was solidified
and strengthened as the years went on. In his autobiographical notes, in fact, the period spent in the army is
recorded with pleasure. The notes tell of "good military
service"; they describe the advances in his career (". . .
promoted to corporal on May 31, 1902, and to sergeant
on November 30 of the same year"), and they contain as
well an overall appraisal that is on the whole favorable:
"These were twelve months of which he was to retain the
fondest memories, as an experience of manly discipline
and as an initiation into the knowledge of the youthful
spirit of Italy's sons and the most practical means of
winning them over to what is good." A contemporary
photograph shows him looking very proper and almost
elegant in his black uniform, complete with collar and lapel
insignia, gleaming buttons, padded shoulders, silver pip-
ing, starched necktie; and his appearance is that of a
sturdy, open-faced soldier with splendid military-style
mustaches and regulation crewcut.

Discharged as a sergeant of infantry, he returned to the
Apollinaris seminary for two further years of study until
he was ordained as a priest and celebrated his first mass
on August 10, 1904, in the Church of Santa Maria in
Monte Santo, on Piazza del Popolo. On that same day he
was included in a pligrimage and taken to an audience
with the pope, who was then Pius X. "Your Holiness,"

Pius was told, "this is a young priest from Bergamo who celebrated his first mass today." The pope congratulated him more or less as a matter of routine: "I bless you and I urge you to do honor to your aims. May your priesthood be a consolation to Holy Church." Here Pius paused; then he asked: "When will you sing your first Mass in your own town?" Roncalli replied: "On Assumption, Holy Father," and the Pope repeated: "On Assumption. What a feast day. And those Bergamo bells, how they peal, how they peal."

Don Angelo returned to Bergamo as secretary to the new bishop, Monsignor Giacomo Maria Radini Tedeschi, who had paid a visit to Apollinaris specifically in order to choose as his assistant a young priest from Bergamo. There were two: Don Guglielmo Carozzi and Don Angelo Roncalli. The new bishop had both of them speak, judged their efforts, and then said to the rector in confidence: "If I were looking for a secretary who would keep my spirits up, I would take Don Carozzi. But I prefer Don Roncalli, who has great discretion." Monsignor Radini Tedeschi was a progressive prelate with an open mind; he came very close to trafficking with conceptions that at that time were condemned on the ground of "modernism." He had been assigned to the conference staffs, the first major training ground for Italian Catholics who were preparing for public life, and Pius X had selected him in that very summer of 1904 in view of the dissensions that were raging between the young progressives and the reactionary conservatives. Radini Tedeschi, who was a member of the former group, was sent to the Diocese of Bergamo. "It was suggested that you become archbishop of Palermo, but I said no," the pope told him. "Then Ravenna was suggested, and I said no again. Then it was Bergamo, and I said yes. Go there," Pius concluded, with a gesture of affection: "for such consolation as a bishop can find in the fact, Bergamo is Italy's first diocese."

Under the tutelage of Monsignor Radini Tedeschi, Don Roncalli learned to blend pastoral solicitude and understanding of social problems. "Good should be done well," the bishop taught him. "Good should be free, untrammeled by any servitude toward him who wishes to direct its fruits." In his book *Monsignor Giacomo Radini Tedeschi*, Don Roncalli recalled having always seen the Gospels and Leo XIII's social encyclical *Rerum Novarum* lying open on the bishop's desk: "These two texts were sufficient for him; in them his own great heart throbbed, ever alert to give himself and overexert himself for the beloved of Christ"—that is, the poor. Combining the Gospels with the social sciences, Monsignor Radini Tedeschi engaged in trade-union activity precisely because he was moved by religious concerns. "It is the workers," he said, "who are most tempted by sects; through their work and their day-to-day economic conditions they are most driven to rise against God, the government, and the laws."

Organized by a Catholic labor official who enjoyed the bishop's sponsorship, a textile workers' strike broke out in 1909 in Ranica, a little community near Bergamo. It was called in protest against the dismissal of a foreman, Pietro Scarpellini, who was vice-president of the Catholic Workers' League and who in the eyes of his employers had "compromised" himself by requesting the renewal of a labor contract, a reduction in the working week (it consisted of six ten-and-a-half-hour days), and some rise in wages. Above all, however, the question was that of asserting the workers' right to organize. As Don Roncalli wrote later:

> . . . what was at issue in Ranica was not a specific question of wages or individuals but a principle, the basic principle of the freedom of Christian organization of labor in defense against the powerful organization of capital. To take a firm stand on the side of the strikers in this instance was to perform a highly Christian duty, a work of justice, of charity, of social peace.

Don Roncalli therefore called out the young men of Catholic Action to help, and Monsignor Radini Tedeschi was among the first and the most generous contributors of money for the unpaid strikers.

> There was a great shocked outcry from many quarters [Don Roncalli recalled in his book] and reports of an unkind nature were sent to high places. A number of persons, even among men of good will, believed that a cause lost the right to be helped solely because the use of certain means might incur the risk of some intemperances. Monsignor Radini did not embrace this philosophy.

The unkind reports that were forwarded to high places were answered by Pope Pius X on October 20 with full support of Monsignor Radini Tedeschi and the statement that Pius "could not disapprove what he had wisely thought should be done in his full knowledge of the place, the persons, and the circumstances." The strike, the first example of a work stoppage defended from the height of an episcopal chair, involved eight hundred workers and continued from September 21 until November 8—fifty days. On the fiftieth day the employers capitulated.

Don Rocalli seemed to be a born organizer. The bishop had appointed him diocesan assistant to the women of Catholic Action, and soon the work of education and wel-

fare reached into all categories of women in nonagricul-
tural employment: nurses, sales clerks, office workers,
telephone operators. It would appear that in that lofty Bergamo inhabited by good middle-class people it was the
custom to remark with a mixture of protest and suspicion:
"That fine Don Angelo has tried to organize even the telephone operators. Couldn't he have been satisfied to organize
the sacristans?" This is the normal kind of antagonism that
recurs whenever a priest enters the fields of labor and politics unless he does so to the benefit of the preservation of
the existing order. While in actuality Don Roncalli was not
a revolutionary or even, to be honest, a progressive, the
punctiliousness with which he insisted on performing his
duties was enough and indeed more than enough to make
him an embarrassment.

He was "cautious and moderate" also in teaching the two
subjects—apologetics and church history—to which he had
been assigned in the episcopal seminary—two subjects that
in those years of anti-modernist struggle were to be treated
with extreme circumspection, to say the least. That very
meticulous biographer, Leone Algisi, said that he had been
filled wth "extreme interest and perhaps some other feelings" when he pored over the notes that the then Professor
Roncalli dictated to his students.

Unquestionably [Algisi wrote] they could not be described as
other than prudent. They reveal mature and measured knowledge.
Throughout they demonstrate rigorous respect for the thinking
of the Church, the effort to consider the most modern theological
conceptions in the light of the masters' views. At the same time
Roncalli's lessons could not be described as timid; they are
concerned not to stir up unnecessary dust storms of doubt, but
at the same time they are fair, impartial, and honest.

As for his prudence, it will be enough to mention that, when Roncalli was a seminarist in Rome with Ernesto Buonaiuti, he had refused even to read the mimeographed commentary that his companion had written on *l'Évangile et l'Église (The Gospel and the Church)*, the basic text of the doctrines of Alfred Loisy, the excommunicated exegete of biblical modernism. Not out of lack of courage but out of honest conviction, Roncalli in fact rejected all theology that had burgeoned and developed outside the control of the Church, and specifically with respect to Buonaiuti, moreover, he had to pronounce an extremely severe condemnation many years later—in 1947:

I have read his book, *Pio XII*. It is an *unjust and bad* book. Ever since Urban VIII, supposedly, the government of the Catholic Church has followed the wrong course, even with those most recent popes of our priestly life, from Leo to Pius XII. Poor Buonaiuti—we were students together in Rome, and he has gone so far astray ever since his self-aggrandizement first darkened and then completely quenched the light of faith! What an end for the poor man. And to think that this very man assisted me in my ordination as a priest.

None of this affected the impartiality and the honesty of the lessons that he taught to his seminarists. Monsignor Giuseppe Angelini, who was one of them, recalled that he would come into the classroom in a raging hurry, almost always late and breathing hard like a man who has run up many flights of stairs. He would begin to speak as if he were among friends, conversationally, without any trace of the lecturer's manner; gradually, as he continued, his enthusiasm became excitement: except for some unexpected interruption, possibly humorous but more likely merely relaxed, always extremely human—for example, devoted to describing the sufferings of the martyrs. Then in somber tones he warned the seminarists of Bergamo: "Be ready always to answer anyone who asks you the reasons for your faith."

Monsignor Radini Tedeschi, the great bishop and his protector, died in 1914. Then mobilization and the war emptied the halls of the seminaries; first the students went off to fight and then it was their teachers' turn. Recalled to the army in 1915, Don Roncalli put on his sergeant's uniform—he was assigned to the medical corps and detailed, at first, to a hospital in Milan, then to one in Bergamo. He let his mustaches grow again, and now they were more luxuriant than during his term as a conscript. In March 1916, like all priests serving in the army, he was made a lieutenant in the chaplains' corps; so he went back to his ankle-length cassock, with the insignia at the collar and the designations of rank on his sleeves and his cap; and he shaved off his mustaches. "I thank the Lord," he said years afterward, "that I was a sergeant and an army chaplain during the First World War. How much I learned about the human heart in that period, how much experience I gained from it, what great grace I received . . ." It was an experience that made him tremble: "Many times it happened . . . that I had to throw myself on my knees and weep like a boy, all alone in my room, unable any longer to contain the emotion aroused by the spectacle of the simple, holy deaths of so many poor sons of our people. . . ."

When the war ended he returned to teach in the seminary and, as was his passion, to organize the youthful members of Catholic Action. But he was soon interrupted. Early in 1921 he received a letter from Wilhelm Cardinal van Rossum, prefect of the Congregation for the Propagation of the Faith, a most eminent prelate and one of the most powerful men in the Roman Curia; he was known in jest as "the Red Pope," just as the father-general of the Jesuits is called "the Black Pope." The letter summoned Roncalli to Rome to manage what was called the farthing collection— the agency that collected the small weekly offerings made for missions. He might have felt flattered by this, since it was beyond question a sign that attention was being paid to him in Rome, but he was very sincerely dismayed. To give up the fine things that he was doing in Bergamo in order to go into an office that organized collections annoyed him and embarrassed him. He turned for counsel to the archbishop of Milan, Andrea Carlo Cardinal Ferrari, who was already very old and who in fact was dying of a throat cancer that had deprived him of speech: Roncalli asked whether, in Ferrari's view, he could leave what he was doing in Bergamo to go and vanish in the mazes of a Roman Congregation.

Cardinal Ferrari replied with a very cordial letter, ascetic and fatherly at the same time:

My very dear Don Angelo: You know how fond of you I am; and too this is an obligation to Monsignor Radini. For this very reason, here is my frank, unhesitant opinion. The will of God is more than manifest. The *Red Pope* is the echo of the *White Pope*: the *White* Pope is the echo of God. So this is an advancement. Where God calls, one goes without hesitation, abandoning oneself utterly to his loving Providence. Thus you will gain serene peace. Pray for him who blesses you with all his heart and is yours most affectionately *in Corde Jesu* [in the heart of Jesus].

Roncalli left everything and departed. In Rome he was also made a domestic prelate of His Holiness, a distinction

69

that, among other things, includes the wearing of a purple cloak; in it he appeared at Sotto il Monte on June 24, the feast of Saint John, to honor his father's name day. The women of the village, who had always viewed him with affection, addressing him intimately as "Angelino the priestlet," were stupefied and asked his mother, Marianna Giulia: "But what is your son doing with a habit like the bishop's?"

"Oh, those are things priests arrange among themselves," she replied. In her old age she had grown no more prodigal of speech. Her son was made a bishop four years later, in 1925, when he was appointed apostolic visitor to Bulgaria, and he was raised to the episcopate with the archiepiscopal title *pro hac vice* of Areopolis, which is the modern Petra *in partibus infidelium*.

The transition from teaching and organization to diplomacy was a major change for Monsignor Roncalli, and as well because the first assignment that fell to him was not easy. Relations between Bulgaria and the Vatican had been consistently very strained ever since old Tsar Ferdinand, even though he had been born into the Roman Catholic faith, had insisted that reasons of high policy made it necessary for him to have his eldest son and heir, Boris, baptized in the Orthodox rite. Ferdinand went to Rome and requested an audience in order to justify his action; Leo XIII allowed him to appear, but he had barely begun to speak when the pope rose from his throne, pointed to the door with an imperious gesture, and commanded: "Depart!"

With such precedents there could be little hope of success for a monsignor serving his apprenticeship in diplomacy. Boris, who had come to the throne after the First World

War, had confirmed his adherence to the Bulgarian national church, and his Roman Catholic subjects, although they were not persecuted, were nonetheless disquieted by the official attitude of aloofness. Furthermore, Boris as a man could not be trusted. In 1929, when the terms of his marriage to Princess Giovanna di Savoia, the fourth child of King Victor Emmanuel III of Italy, were under negotiation, he pledged first to Monsignor Roncalli in Sofia and then to the Vatican directly that he would permit the wedding to be performed according to the Roman rite and he promised that his children would be brought up in the Roman faith. And indeed the wedding was thus celebrated in Assisi on October 25, but, as soon as Boris was back in Bulgaria with his bride, he had a second ceremony staged according to the Orthodox ritual in the Cathedral of Saint Alexander Nevsky. Children were subsequently born and he had them baptized into Orthodoxy, thus breaking his word again.

"He duped me," Roncalli said simply. "But one must go on living still, and above all strive for peace. I am consoled by the hope that out of this evil there may one day come a greater good." When, after his appointment in 1934 to be apostolic administrator of the vicariate of Constantinople, he went to make his official farewell to Boris, he was stunned to find that he was received cordially and almost with friendship. "Apart from the business of the wedding and the baptisms, etc.," he wrote of the king, "he is a good soul. What a mystery human life is, though!"

Roncalli's appointment to the vicariate made him, even though he was not officially accredited as such, the pope's representative in Turkey and Greece, countries that were even more difficult than Bulgaria. The Orthodox in Greece are famed as the most anti-Roman in all the East, and, as for Turkey, Mustafa Kemal Ataturk had made it a fiercely anticlerical country. On the eve of his departure, Roncalli wrote to Monsignor Bernareggi, bishop of Bergamo: "In that country it will be necessary for me to hug the wall when I walk, as if I were out in a downpour, and do the best I can. I want to go slowly. Who knows whether I may not be able to go far?"

To get anything from the Turks was difficult if not impossible. Catholic schools were languishing for lack not only of funds and facilities but also of pupils. The practice of Catholic worship was becoming increasingly difficult in anticipation of a law that would prohibit the wearing of any religious habit in public. This prohibition came into effect on June 13, 1935, the feast day of Saint Anthony of Padua, and in the church named for the saint the apostolic delegate gathered all his clergy for the observance. Afterward a procession of priests and religious in civilian clothes—they were somewhat constrained by this unaccustomed garb— moved out of the church and through the main street of Pera under the curious stares of the Turks. In the van was Monsignor Roncalli, good-natured, smiling, and almost amused, as he appeared in photographs that show him very cheerful in a sober, well-cut, dark double-breatsed suit among his priests and the Capuchin brothers, some of whom concealed the prohibited "Roman collar" behind their long full beards in the place of the prescribed necktie. Moreover, Roncalli had not even given orders what colors or styles were to be worn. The style should be conservative and the color dark, he had recommended, but he had gone no further. "It will become apparent," he said patiently, "that clothes do not make the monk." Thus re-

stricted by the harshness of the law and the hostile aloofness of the authorities, Roncalli could cherish no illusions
of dramatic success; but he had his consolation: Each of
us has his own cross, and every cross has its own individual
form. Mine is certainly a twentieth-century model. Prayer
helps me to bear it with honor and with a certain good
taste that does not displease Our Lord either."

Life was difficult for him in Greece also. That country
was ruled by a dictator, General Joannis Metaxas, who,
during Roncalli's mission there, promulgated a law that
reiterated the religious nature of marriage and required
that it be entered into in the presence of an Orthodox priest
as an official of the state. In other words, even Roman Catholics, if their marriages were to be valid, would have to
adopt the Orthodox ritual. Thus it came to pass that, once
they had been married by their parish priest, the faithful
had to go before the Greek priest for a new ceremony, and
in this fashion a good half of the Roman Catholics in
Greece wound up lapsing more or less knowingly into
schism. Roncalli recognized that any change of the Greek
laws in a liberal direction was absolutely out of the question for the moment and that in addition the way in which
to obtain satisfactory and lasting results was not that of
diplomatic understandings, still less that of concordats,
but rather that of the union of the two churches in a Christian ecumenical point of view. The likelihood of such a
union seemed remote, as he was prepared to admit quite
frankly:

And yet this is our duty—that is, to insist on it constantly,
even against all the probabilities. All of us are guilty to some
extent, and we Latins—I say Latins in the East—have had and
still bear our share of responsibility in the matter. If some

effort is not made to overcome our sloth and look ahead, our decay will follow the same path as that of the East—the Greeks, the Slavs, and the Arabs.

This too was a sign, one of the many that might be recorded, of his typical attitude of understanding before judging and of his continuing dedication to the effort to understand the arguments and motivations of others. In this domain, even before his election to the papacy, he had amassed a very broad experience, and in part because it seemed to be his destiny to be assigned only to difficult undertakings. After Bulgaria, Turkey, and Greece, he faced the even more arduous task of Gaullist France. He wrote later:

> But I took everything calmly: one step after another, one appearance after another: negotiations, visits, talk, silence, and patience, quiet waiting and above all the constant influence of a serene, mild, and even, when necessary, slightly smiling spirit.

This was his way of being genuine, and he recommended its advantages to everyone. In the last speech that he made in Paris as dean of the diplomatic corps, on New Year's Day of 1953, he took his text amusingly from a fable of La Fontaine—one of the last, which contains the lines:

> Troublez l'eau, vous y voyez-vous?
> Laissez-la reposer,
> vous verrez alors votre image.*

"May it please God," Roncalli added, "that this doctrine, already stated in the 'Know thyself' on the pediment of the temple at Delphi, and in its fullness and its universality transcending any individual application, be under-

---

* If you make ripples in the water, can you see yourself in it? Let it subside, and then you will see your reflection.—TRANSLATOR.

stood and broadly put into practice wherever there is a responsibility to be met in the service of the common good."

In Venice too, where he arrived on March 15, 1953, as the forty-third patriarch, the situation was difficult. One of his predecessors had been Giovanni Adeodato Cardinal Piazza, later secretary of the Congregation of Consistories and a man of strict conservative austerity—almost reactionary, according to many accusations. Piazza was followed by Monsignor Carlo Agostini, known as an indefatigable worker but also extraordinarily demanding and even more nervous and easily irritated. Introducing himself to the faithful in April 1949, he declared: "What I intend, and ask of Our Lord, is to exhaust myself for you, Venetians!" But he at once created the impression that he was extremely authoritarian and that he lacked patience. He had laid down plans for the construction of churches, the creation of parishes, the initiation of various pastoral endeavors that could not have been brought to fruition in twenty years; but he was consumed by the lust to move quickly and he conceded no rest to himself or to others. "He never managed to be gentle," it was said of Agostini in a masterpiece of understatement when he died after long-drawn-out agonies on December 28, 1952, at the age of only sixty-five, exhausted by his labors and eroded by nervous tension after four years of feverish activity in his office.

So Roncalli was apprised that in Venice he was awaited with the hope that he would be "the quiet after the storm," and he was told of all the gossip that was circulating in the city and the entire diocese, all of it intended to draw comparisons and contrasts between him and his immediate predecessor, and to his advantage. He felt obliged ostensibly to ignore this, saying that he was not much impressed: "This is all talk. Still, to me it is an indication how the 'crew' feels. We shall see how much credence it is to be given, and let's leave the rest to Providence." He paid attention to it, one might say, from the very first day, for, in his introductory speech in St. Mark's to the municipal authorities and the faithful he began by saying: "Things have been said and written about me that go far indeed beyond my merits."

He continued with an excellent choice of words that at the same time provided an autobiographical sketch and a program of action:

I humbly present myself to you. Like everyone else who lives on this earth, I come from a specific family and place; I have been endowed with the grace of good physical health and a little common sense, enough to make me quick and clear in what I have to do: with a tendency to love my fellow men that keeps me faithful to the law of the Gospels and observant of my own and others' rights, that prevents me from doing evil to anyone, that inspires me to do good to everyone. I come from humility, I was educated to a contented and blessed poverty that makes few demands, protects the flower of the highest and noblest virtues, and prepares one for the highest elevations in life. Providence took me from my native village and sent me along the world's roads in the East and the West, placing me among people of diverse religions and ideologies, in contact with acute and threatening social problems, and maintaining me in the tranquility and the detachment of the student and the examiner; always concerned, apart from firm adherence to the principles of morality and the Catholic credo, more with what unites men than with what separates them and provokes conflicts. . . . Unquestionably the post that has been entrusted to me in Venice is great and far surpasses any merit of mine. But above all else I commend to your good will the man who seeks simply to be your brother—

76

affectionate, accessible, understanding. It is my firm purpose to continue in the course that has gained me honor thus far and that has perhaps prepared the way for this sojourn of mine in Venice among a noble population especially sensitive to voices that come from the heart, to simplicity in speech, in tone, in deeds, to that respectful and happy sincerity in all dealings that marks, even if only to a limited degree, the man to whom it is proper to refer as a gentleman in every respect, a gentleman without stain, deserving of respect and trust. Such is the man, such is the new citizen whom Venice has deigned to welcome today with such festive demonstrations.

Such too was the new pope, one might have said on the night of his election, October 28. "From certain indications I already knew that I would be elected," he confessed later, and he had even prepared the response that he would make to Tisserant, the dean of the cardinals, when the Frenchman should ask him whether he accepted his election: *"Tremens factus sum ego, et timeo* [I have been thrown into a tremor, and I am afraid]," he said very aptly. "What I know of my own poverty and smallness is enough for my confusion. But, seeing in the votes of my most eminent brothers the sign of God's will, I accept the election and I bow my head. . . ."

He had already thought, too, what name he would assume —John—and how necessary it would be to explain the choice, which might astound many because for more than six hundred years (except for Baldassare Coscia, who reigned as antipope from 1410 to 1415 under the name of John XXIII) no pontiff had borne that name. The last to have assumed it legitimately was Jacques Duèse, who was born in Cahors in 1244, was elected pope as John XXII in 1316, died in Avignon in 1334, and left the worst possible reputation behind him. Gregorovius wrote that

... his long reign had no purpose other than that of accumulating wealth; nor did he take counsels except from unchristian hatreds and lusts for power, by reason of which he filled the whole world with war. This old man seated on the Supreme Pontiff's throne, inspiring repugnance and antipathy, pettifogging of mind, inquisitorial in spirit, threw the Empire into a perilous conflict with the papacy and gave rise to a schism in the Church.

The fortune that he amassed, according to Giovanni Villani's *Cronache (Chronicles)*, amounted to eighteen million florins' worth of precious objects, so that Beatrice in Paradise cursed the pope from Cahors together with his predecessor, the Gascon Clement V: *"Del sangue nostro Caorsini e Guaschi s'apparecchian di bere* [The men of Cahors and Gascony prepare to drink our blood] . . ."* (*Paradiso* XXVII:58). As for the "pettifogger's mind," John XXII had given evidence of that when he proposed a "senseless dogma" on the state of blessedness in heaven that smelled of heresy and that he was compelled to retract; and for this Dante reviled him: *"O tu che sol per cancellare scrivi* [O thou who writest only to strike out] . . ."* (*Paradiso* XVIII: 130). He would have liked to put into practice the rules of Saint Thomas' *Regimine Principum (The Rule of Princes)*—that is, arrogate the temporal power to himself —but Gregorovius wrote that "the theologians, the scholastics, the learned monks, the experts in jurisprudence all devoted themselves to seeking out the essence of Church and State, of monarchy and papacy . . . and they drew the conclusion that the merger of the two powers in the pontiff must be condemned."

Roncalli's papacy, then, was to be in every detail the exact opposite of that of his remote predecessor of the same name; but it is certain that, if omens were to have been taken from that predecessor, they would have been the worst imaginable. In any event, apart from the fact that only a few days earlier, when he went into the conclave, Roncalli had remarked that he did not share the superstition of signs and portents, the explanation that he gave for his choice to the attentive cardinals in the Sistine Chapel was disarming in its simplicity: *"Vocabor Johannes* [I will be called John]. This name is dear to us because it is our father's. It is sweet to us because John is the patron saint of the humble parish in which we were baptised."

They cloaked him in white, in the largest of the three sizes of habits that had been prepared by the official tailor, but even this was too tight for him. "I feel completely bound," he said. Thus he went out on the balcony overlooking St. Peter's Square to bless the throng, and from the piazza he could be heard through the public-address system replying to some overzealous expert in protocol who was telling him how to behave: "I know, I know"—as if he had been pope all his life. The cardinals, who had left the Sistine Chapel, were in the windows, and John teased them for this: "You have risked excommunication because you have left the conclave without our permission. But we will exert all our influence to save you from excommunication." In any case he urged them to remain through that last night in the conclave's quarters instead of departing at once as had been traditional until then.

IV

"Pope" Means "Father"

What a pope should be.
John unlike Pius: austere, conservative,
father of all, and friend of none.
Merciful, not kind.
Among the convicts in Regina Coeli.
His eloquence.

ON November 4, 1958, when he had barely been enthroned as pope, John XXIII spoke in Saint Peter's. Those who were present at the ceremonies that morning said that they had observed a movement of surprise among the cardinals, the *monsignori*, and the dignitaries when, after the Gospel had been intoned, the pope began to speak from the throne in a loud, firm voice: "*Dilectissimi fratres, Sacrae Romanae Ecclesiae Cardinales, Archiepiscopi, Episcopi . . .* (Most beloved brothers, cardinals of the Holy Roman Church, archbishops, bishops . . .)." A speech by the pope had not been envisaged in the program laid down the night before, and hence there was no mention of it in the little printed schedule with the detailed description of the ceremony that had been distributed to all in attendance. According to the program, after the Gospel had been intoned, the Offertory would have followed immediately out of respect to a traditional procedure that prevents the pope from speaking during the pontifical mass of coronation. Even Pius XII, who was certainly not lacking in eloquence, kept silent on the morning of March 12, 1939; only a day later, when the Sacred College was presenting its congratulations to him, did he make a few appropriate remarks.

Contrary to custom, John delivered an address that was in fact a statement of a program. First of all he made it clear that he would be a different pope from his predecessor. To those who might suppose that he would have continued to behave as "a statesman, a diplomat, a scholar, an organizer of collective life, or one whose mind was kept open to all the forms of progress in modern life," he pointed out, not without severity, that they were all wide of the mark because they had an erroneous notion of what a pope ought to be. John took his inspiration from a thought expressed by Saint Bernard and copied by John, with annotations, into one of his private notebooks: *"Papa dicitur quasi amabilis pater*—One is called pope by reason of one's fatherly love." Then, in his first sermon of his pontificate, he pointed out that the pope is a good shepherd, as Christ wishes him to be and as Saint John reports in his Gospel in the words of the Master (John X:2–17, 26–28). The pope is the shepherd who is ready to give his life for his lambs, who hurls himself into battle against the wolf, and who, above all, guides his flock until the horizon broadens and still more sheep arrive; they too must be led: " 'They shall hear my voice, *et fiet unum ovile et unus pastor* (and there shall be one fold, and one shepherd).' "

Thus the commitment to ecumenism was already stated, in advance of the convocation of the Council. Again in his message to the world on October 29, the day after his election, John listed some of the criteria that provided the inspiration for his actions and that were later to be developed in subsequent encyclicals such as *Ad Petri cathedram* (June 29, 1959), *Mater et Magistra* (May 15, 1961), and *Pacem in terris* (April 10, 1963). In a word, he made his program public immediately, as a man can do when he has clarified his ideas on a subject and let them ripen with time. He spoke of peace, of course, as a pope might be expected to do, but in so doing he accentuated the concept of peace inseparable from justice, and in addition he gave voice to a sense of grief and pity, of all-embracing charity.

For the first time in many, many years, there was a return by Peter's successor to the use of language that was not that of a crusade, even with respect to the so-called Church of Silence—the clergy and the faithful subjected to persecution, or at least not permitted to enjoy full religious freedom, in the countries behind the iron curtain. John wanted this freedom to be restored in the name of civilization and the rights of man: *"Humanis iam diu acquisitus iuribus*—civil rights long since established." He spoke as a humanist, quoting together Cicero, Saint Augustine, and Saint Thomas Aquinas, but above all paying tribute to culture, which is undivided (*"civili nostrae huius aetatis cultui*—the civilized modes of this our time"), and affecting no disdain of modern civilization and its problems. Indeed, he manifested concern for the physical well-being of the peoples, calling for a kind of justice "that at last combines the reciprocal rights and duties of all classes" so that out of the harmony of a peaceful social order "a true prosperity" might finally arise with the fruitful increase of "public and private riches." He made it clear that he intended his pastoral activity to include the service of the just material demands of men: let the pope show his capacity to conduct himself with Christian meekness and humility, and from this all would derive the greatest profit (*"plurima emolumenta"*), and there would come "a vast gain as well in the field of human needs of a social and earthly character."

By way of illustrating the function that was incumbent on the pope, he quoted the Gospel according to Matthew

(XI:29): "Learn of me; for I am meek and lowly in heart." The exhortation was addressed to the great ones of this earth, beginning with the tyrants who shackled the liberties of peoples. He did not hurl anathemas, however, but he resorted to prayer to the eternal: "May God illumine the minds of the leaders of those nations and forgive the persecutors."

On the basis of the program that was thus set forth on his first day—and that was to be applied punctiliously as his pontificate went on—it could be expected that John would be different from Pius. Perhaps, however, he feared that this might not have been made sufficiently clear, and he was concerned to give it explicit confirmation. Carefully stressing his words, he said:

Every pontificate acquires a physiognomy of its own from the figure of him who incarnates and represents it. *Ego sum ostium ovium*—I am the gate of the fold. The function of pastor to the entire flock occupies a very special place in our heart. Other human qualities—knowledge, shrewdness, diplomatic tact, organizational capabilities—may succeed in embellishing and adorning a pontifical government, but in no way can they take the place of that function."

It was well known that John had much admired his predecessor's eloquence. Even during his time in Paris Roncalli had had occasion to discuss it in an article ("The Pope's Presence in the World"):

With miraculous eloquence, rarely equaled until now by any pope and difficult of achievement by those who will come after him, our Supreme Shepherd, Pius, ceaselessly offers these heavenly treasures of doctrine and grace not every month but every day, in various languages and in accents of the highest and most felicitous inspiration, to the spiritual healing of the whole world: *ad sanitatem gentium.*

The praise was genuine, and it was not divorced from a certain astonishment at this ability to speak every day in many languages on any subject: this was indeed amazing. One day, in fact, John had frankly said as much to Pius XII himself: "Holy Father, you will leave a difficult legacy to any successor who may want to try to follow you in your quality as a master of speech."

Now himself become a successor, he gave no thought to becoming a master of words. Receiving in the Clementine Hall several hundred Italian and foreign newspapermen who had covered the conclave, he spoke to them in French, the only foreign language that he knew acceptably, but, when he became engrossed in what he was saying, he mingled his French with Italian and Latin words, and the effect was splendid. He was rehearsing the story of Joseph, who was minister to Pharaoh and who made himself known to his unlucky brothers, the same story (Genesis XLV) that he had quoted in the unexpected address at the time of his coronation: "And he wept aloud . . . And Joseph said unto his brethren: I am Joseph your brother." John wanted to translate the Latin of the Bible into French, and Italian crept in: *"Et alors Joseph, scoppiando en pleurs* [And then Joseph, bursting into tears] . . ." but, totally unperturbed, he went on promptly: "And I too want to re-iterate to you that I am your brother, I am the eldest brother before God, to whom, as a shepherd, I must guide you; and I cherish feelings of love for all: to help you to see what is good in this world and especially what is in heaven."

The obligation stated in the enunciation of these holy matters did not make him forget his lapse of a moment earlier, or his use of the first person singular, almost un-heard-of on the part of a pope. He apologized for not yet having become versed in the use of the royal plural, and he also conceded that his French was rather *"comme-ci-comme-ça,"* although he pointed out that the lack was of no great importance: "The pope can speak in Italian, in French, in German, to the best of his ability and knowledge, as long as his real language is Latin, the idiom of the universal Church." Being a man with a sense of the practical, however, he understood quite thoroughly that it would have been useful to him to be able to express himself in some other modern languages as well in order to reach everyone better. In the early years of his pontificate, in fact, he made great efforts to learn a little English. "It is not that I want to make speeches in English," he told his confessor, Monsignor Alfredo Cavagna, "but it makes me feel that I am not a father when I meet so many people who speak only English and I cannot say even one word to them." So he began to study the language under the tutelage of Monsignor Thomas Ryan, now bishop of Confert in Ireland, but it would appear that he made poor progress. Almost as if by way of excuse, Monsignor Ryan has said that often the lessons were transformed almost immediately into discussions of far different matters in Italian.

When he received the late President Eisenhower in audience on December 6, 1959, the pope made an address to him in English after having very painfully memorized it. At one point he lapsed into a glaring error of pronunciation and he was immediately aware of it, perhaps because of a glance from his mentor, Monsignor Ryan: *'Oh, che bello* [what a beauty]!" he burst out in Italian, and in such a way that Eisenhower, even though he did not understand, burst into a hearty laugh, and the photographers were delighted to be able to show both men in a flash of ordinary merriment.

In a very short time John became popular as no pope had ever been. When he first went out into Rome he was overwhelmed, although by no means convinced, by the tremendous cheers that greeted him. Loudly hailed by a crowd on his visit to the Basilica of Santa Maria Maggiore on December 8, he said to a prelate: "I ought not to feel pride. Pius IX came here too one day, and everyone shouted: *'Viva Pio IX! viva Pio IX'*; not too much later everyone was shouting: 'Down with Pius IX! down with Pius IX!' " He visited a children's hospital on the Janiculum and the nursing sisters presented him with a white skullcap on a cushion so that he would give them his. This was a custom from the days of Pius XII, whose habit it was to give and receive ten or twenty caps merely in his progress through the nave of St. Peter's: he would accept a new one, wear it a few minutes, then give it to the donor of the next one.

John, however, refused to follow the precedent. "I will not give you my cap, for two reasons," he told the sisters. "One is that I do not wish to create a need for a capmaker who will have nothing else to do but make caps for me; the other is that this kind of thing can lead you into superstition." He was surrounded at the time by still and motion-picture and television photographers, and the pope urged moderation on them: "When one talks about the fourteen works of mercy, one must add a fifteenth: the toleration of bothersome people. I am very fond of photographers, but I mean by this to say that I like to be let alone now and then." One day, when he was seated on the throne of the lower basilica in Assisi and delivering an address to the fathers general of the various Franciscan families and other officials, he was irritated by the blinding glare of the television cameramen's lights. "Turn out the lights!" he thundered in a commanding tone, interrupting his speech. The lights were extinguished, but the still photographers' flashbulbs did not slacken, and once more John broke off his speech and glared almost threateningly in the direction of the cameramen.

On another occasion he had gone to visit the village of Quarticciolo, one of the most populous communes in the vicinity of Rome, and he was trapped in a huge throng that would not stop shouting and cheering. He tried to speak from a platform, but in all the clamor it was difficult for him to make himself heard because the crowd's enthusiasm was growing steadily louder. "If we want to communicate," he scolded the throng harshly, "it will be necessary for you to mortify your tongues when I speak. I have made a long journey in order to come here and talk to you. But now you alone want to speak. Very well, then, understand that I am going back to the city. Absolute silence is essential. Try to mortify your tongues if you wish to bring satisfaction to your hearts."

Regarded as a modernist pope, an innovator at all costs, John was, rather, rooted in tradition. But he was not a rhetorician, and therefore he was looked on as a populist and a subversive. A certain shock ran through the editorial offices of *l'Osservatore romano* on the receipt of the request from Monsignor Capovilla to modify the style of writing that had been customary in references to Pius XII. There was to be no more of such usages as "the Holiness of Our Lord" or "we present the text of His Holiness' speech as we recorded it from His august lips." Monsignor Capovilla suggested instead the use of simpler terms, such as "His Holiness," or "the Supreme Pontiff," or, best of all, "the pope."

This was merely a question of taste, however, because John was the most assiduous in respect for formal institutions, and, even though he was a man of the greatest simplicity in his own life, he accepted and indeed revivified all the princely pomp that surrounds a Roman pontiff, out of regard for the office and reverence for tradition. So too he endured the gestatorial chair, which made him physically uncomfortable and almost seasick, resigning himself to it as to a venerable symbol, that of God's will that "sustains and bears up" men.

He had a feeling for authority, and more than any other of his recent predecessors he admired Leo XIII, "a star of the first magnitude." But he shunned authoritarianism, "which stifles truth with rigid outward discipline, blocks any legitimate action, prevents broad views, and confuses intransigence with strength of character." Yet he knew how to keep his distance, and it very quickly became apparent that he was anything but easily influenced or readily adaptable, as might be imagined of a country priest, "all jolly and friendly like a nice family party at home or in school: quite the contrary," Don Giuseppe de Luca wrote; "while no one could have expected a more open smile and a more festive greeting from even his dearest friend, no one will ever make anyone believe that [Pope John] was so easily induced to talk." Monsignor Capovilla too said aptly that "Pope John was a father to everyone but a friend to no one."

He performed his function as pope, however, with "ready

inspiration," as everyone observed at once, almost as if he had been apprenticed to it for a long period, and so every morning when he awakened he had at hand a finished new idea. But he was not an innovator in his aims, and actually he introduced fewer reforms into the Church than did Pius XII or Saint Pius X. He did not attempt even to reform the Curia, and it was remarked that he never dismissed anyone from a post or stripped anyone of authority in order to facilitate the achievement of his own ends. On the contrary he showed by example that new structures could grow freely and even luxuriantly until they suffocated the old that had begun to decay. Nevertheless he succeeded in instilling into the Church the full potential of dynamism that modern times would permit, restoring to a degree the internal freedom and justice that had been altered by Pius XII, and turning somewhat for inspiration to more Christian eras but above all looking to the contemporary age not with the fearful aversion of his predecessor but with warm human affection.

"The world moves," he said on one occasion. "One must approach it from the right angle with a spirit that is always youthful and confident, and not waste time creating conflicts. I prefer to keep pace with those who move ahead rather than hang back and allow myself to be outstripped." This was fundamental Christian orthodoxy without the slightest taste for modernism. In fact John was incapable of conforming to fashions—even those that had made their way into the Church and the clergy during the time of Pius XII—and he was adamant in his austerity. He did not like television, for instance, because he found its programs too worldly and also "too effeminate." As patriarch of Venice, he spoke out from his pulpit when he saw girls

in shorts going through St. Mark's Square: "I do not say
that the women of Italy should be dressed in furs and
woollens. But they can wear those silk dresses that keep
them cool and also cost very little. Besides, Italy is not
on the Equator, although even there the lions are covered
with thick hair and even the crocodiles are protected by
very thick armor.

He called on film producers, directors, and actors to
give thought "to the problem whether the beautiful can
exist independently of the good," and he informed them
that, as far as he himself was concerned, he had resolved
the question: "Spiritual beauty is also an element in formal
beauty, because the spirit should always prevail, even in
the forms of entertainment. The world is oppressed by a
stifling atmosphere. Purify it! Let the fresh air in!" When
he was informed that "obscene and irreverent" paintings
were on display in the Biennale in Venice, he ordered his
priests not to go to the exhibition, and similarly he also
forbade them for several years to buy television sets or
even to watch the programs on other persons' sets. Visiting
a seminary, he expressed his disapproval of the secular
music that the students were playing in his honor: "I should
prefer it to be of more devout character," he told the rector.

Even the radio must have been unpleasing to him, in
view of the fact that he could not bring himself to mention
it by its name. On August 15, 1961, he noted in his diary
that he had made a broadcast: "Yesterday I had a summons to all Catholics transmitted over the whole world's
telephones . . ." Unlike Pius XII, he was not fascinated by
technology. When he was patriarch of Venice he did not
like to use the telephone, and he did so only very seldom

during his pontificate, and then only for inside calls to the Secretariat of State and his private secretary.

Harsh in his encounters with the press, he had no scruples in calling for laws that would restrict its freedom. Receiving Premier Antonio Segni, who headed a delegation from the Union of Italian Catholic Jurists, on December 8, 1959, Pope John said that the exercise of press freedom should not be left "to the mercy of improvisation, the feeble self-censorship of which there has been so much talk, or, worse, disingenuousness and pandering." The law, he said, should step in, and thereupon the pope laid down a set of recommendations for the guidance of Italy's chief of government:

> Let there be no fear of being taxed with excess scruple or exaggeration in the condemnation of certain publications. No one should buy, give credence to, foster, or indeed even mention by name any corrupt publication. Let no one be afraid to avail himself of all possible means of bringing this sector under merely human, civilized discipline, to say nothing of Christian.

He was distrustful of persons who made public claims to intelligence; he called them "know-it-alls." Nor did he like "progressives," for he was made suspicious by their inability to smile even slightly at their own theories. He did not like overly stern faces, or persons who gave evidence of taking themselves too seriously; as for himself, he took pains not to fall into error but rather was always instructing himself, as is apparent from one of his notebooks of reflections: "this feeling of my own insignificance that is with me always and that preserves me from vanity . . . and spares me from making myself ridiculous."

He was also distrustful of any overzealous critical undertaking, of the tortuous labors of the new Catholic intelligentsia, of the *théologie nouvelle* of the French school. He had made no secret of this when he was nuncio in Paris, and a French Jesuit, Father Robert Rouquette, has since acknowledged that at that time he judged the future pope harshly: "We thought that he had a tendency toward integralism, but we understood nothing; in his peasant wisdom he was following a balance of his own of which we saw only one side." Roncalli was suspicious of Teilhard de Chardin: *"Ce Teilhard, il ne pourrait donc pas se contenter d'enseigner le catéchisme et la doctrine sociale de l'église, au lieu de soulever tous ces problèmes* (Couldn't this Teilhard be satisfied to teach the catechism and the Church's social doctrine instead of raising all these problems)?" He is reported to have put this question to Father Rouquette, and it shows that he did not understand very much of Teilhard. But perhaps too he was not wrong.

On the other hand, he had a high opinion of Giovanni Papini for his *Lettere di papa Celestino VI (Letters of Pope Celestino VI)*, a fictitious pope who sent messages of peace and brotherhood to mankind, and this is easily explained. By any standards John was never what might be called a great consumer of culture; as Cardinal Lercaro said, "He was, rather, a producer of culture," and that is something quite different. He respected the discipline of study, however, and deplored its decadence. "Unfortunately," he said sternly one day, "there is little love for study; superficial skimming is much favored because it requires little effort. There is no more Latin, no more classical learning. Everyone alters the liturgy to suit his own tastes. Granted, there is a need for great forbearance and also for broad standards and understanding. But *sunt certi denique fines* [in the end there are certain limits]. And, when the limits are left too far behind, as Porta used to say, the least that is required is a box of the ears."

This too was further evidence of that wisdom that Father Rouquette would have called peasant wisdom. A native of the countryside, John naturally favored rural people. He would not have liked, however, to be called a peasant priest—not because he repudiated his own origins but because it would have seemed a way of narrowing the range of his priestly vocation. It was for this same reason that he did not approve the worker-priest experiment; he believed that an incident that he liked to describe was sufficient to discredit it: " 'You are a priest,' some workers said one day to one of those good, upright priests working beside them in overalls. 'You don't belong here. Look, there is a vacant lot. We will help you to build a temporary chapel. We will send our women and children to it, and —who knows?—perhaps one day we too will come. This is what we need: your Gospel and your altar, and nothing else.' "

This was what Pope John wanted of the priests, and in a direct appeal to the clergy of Venice on April 25, 1959, intended to restate the paramountcy of religious effort over all the rest, he found it appropriate and necessary to recall: "Christ engaged in neither sport nor politics, but his word touched every man's heart." Yet he wanted the priests to be light of heart as well: "A sad priest is a bad priest" was one of his basic maxims, which he himself obeyed by always maintaining a smile and an even temper. He disparaged the "colorless, wearisome senility" of those who live in the Church "with the minds of bureaucrats," and he spoke with sorrow of certain forms of laxity in the clergy when confronted with alluring temptations: "Comfortable jobs and duties, a tendency to a certain passive tranquility, with little zeal and little attraction for the spirit. They allow themselves to be overcome very quickly by weariness; they speak only in tones of self-pity, in mutterings that are neither charitable nor merciful toward others. Oh, what a penitence!"

Much more profound was his contempt for those priests who broke their vow of chastity: not so much because of the sin itself as for the impious pretense of overcoming it: "It is especially grievous to us that in order to salvage some scrap of their vanished dignity some of them can rant about the possibility, and its convenience, that the Catholic Church might forswear what has been for centuries and centuries and what is still one of the noblest and purest glories of its priesthood: the law of ecclesiastical celibacy."

Austere and sober, in the ancient manner, he was anything but fittingly described by that adjective that was most generally and most frequently applied to him: good. He was spoken of as the good pope, the pope of goodness, the pope with the smile, "the pope who has managed to bring goodness back into style in the world." In addition to being called good, with that tender goodness that one is pleased to descry in children, John was also described as simple, with the simplicity that is attributed to the poor in spirit who shall inherit the kingdom of heaven, and who are all the more certain of paradise if in addition they can boast peasant origins and family poverty, as John himself could. Perhaps he himself had unwittingly provided the springboard for these trite descriptions because he had said with great sincerity, like a child at his first communion: "I want to be good to everyone, at all times."

And so he became known as "the good pope," and, while the term was used with respect and gratitude by simple souls and poor people in general, there were also others to whom the adjective was moribund and by whom it was employed in a restrictive sense, pejoratively, as if to show that John was "good and no more." In any case he was accustomed to such forms of judgment, and many years earlier he had already had occasion to note in his diary: "Not without a certain ironic thrust they call me the good Monsignor Roncalli! If only I really were!" It pained him somewhat, but at the same time he dedicated himself to the cultivation of "meekness, patience, charity. And all this regardless of consequences, at the risk of seeming or being regarded as of little or no account."

Certainly he was good by natural inclination, but above all through an effort of will, and by no means was he good in the loose sense: he was merciful, rather, and this is a very much greater virtue. And he was anything but simple; on the contrary, he was endowed with humility and he further cultivated it inwardly—one of the few aspects of true heroism, which require unremitting effort, control, and intelligence. "Ever since I have been in Rome in this service," he said one day, explaining that the office of the pope was true "service," *servus servorum Dei* (the servant of the servants of God), "I have observed a general amazement at what I do and the way in which I do it. But I seek only, within the limits of my capabilities, to apply the teachings of the Gospel." On another occasion he revealed: "When I first became pope, everything seemed natural to me in the beginning. Then I began to look not without trepidation, which was overcome through intense prayer, at the duties to be performed and the decisions to be made." He rejoiced that he had been able to preserve "this personal serenity that so impresses the world," and he was insistent on reassuring the faithful during public audiences: "Do not believe that the pope spends sleepless nights. No, the pope sleeps very well."

He was fond of the table, too, and he preferred to eat in company rather than alone, in the custom of popes. He surrounded himself with people as much as possible, for he had a strong wish for personal contacts. He learned that, when he took his walks in the Vatican gardens, tourists were forbidden to go up to the dome of Saint Peter's, from which, he was informed, they would have been able to watch him. "Why should they not see me?" he demanded. "I am not doing anything shameful." He had no fear of being caught off guard in any circumstances, nor did he make any effort to seem other than what he was. Piero Bargellini wrote that, while all of us have a kind of reserve about certain actions or details of our daily lives that are neither culpable nor exemplary, John, on the contrary, "knew nothing of certain proprieties because nothing in him was improper. If he was tired he said he was tired, and he let himself fall heavily into an armchair, resting his hands on his knees. 'We are more or less in private here,' he would say, stretching. 'Here we are all men together.'"

One day, during his patriarchate in Venice, he was present, with President Giovanni Gronchi of Italy and Giovanni Bovetti, deputy speaker of the Chamber of Deputies, at the dedication of a bridge. John fell asleep in his chair while the official orators were droning through their official oratory. When he awakened he felt regret but not shame at his human failing. He made it a point to show himself undisguised, as he was, and to conceal nothing, "not even what might have caused some impairment of his supreme dignity in the eyes of some prig." He was the incarnation of innocence, to quote Bargellini again, and "on one occasion he told me with endearing sincerity how much he had enjoyed some scenes from a comedy by De Filippo on television the previous evening. This was understandable enough, but I think that in the fact that the pope made no mystery of it there was something sublime."

Thus he admitted too that at least to a certain extent he had become reconciled with television, which in the past he had regarded with aversion. There could be good in everything, and he would not hesitate to recognize it. "My temperament," he said of himself, "is inclined to indulgence and immediately accepts the good in people and things, rather than criticizing and judging hastily. Therefore, and also because of the considerable difference in age and its fruit in greater experience and deeper understanding of the human heart, I find myself not seldom in painful inner conflict with the environment that surrounds me." He had suffered from this in his youth as well, for to him any form of intolerance was displeasing to the ultimate degree.

If we had more grace and more forbearance at times [he wrote in one of his notebooks in 1917], how many more victories there would be in so many souls! One does something, but one soon tires; above all no one is too capable of comprehension, compassion, patience. And to think that Saint Paul's praise of charity begins, indeed, like this: "Charity suffereth long, and is kind; charity envieth not; charity vaunteth not itself, is not puffed up" (I Cor. XIII:4).

He placed great price also on courtesy, "which too is a branch of charity," as he wrote. His habit of rising to greet the entering visitor, his removal of his papal cap, the cordiality of gesture with which he melted the rigidities of protocol, his warm regard and friendly speech of introduction were all signs of the gentility of his spirit. When he went to the Quirinal to attend the ceremony at which the Balzan Peace Prize was awarded and President Antonio Segni of Italy urged him to sit in the armchair under the canopy that had been prepared for him, he replied with a spontaneous gesture of genuine concern: "Won't you also be seated?"

In private audiences he was most cordial, and in fact he preferred to speak rather than to listen, in contrast to Pius XII, who was often a mere listener and who therefore embarrassed his visitors. John, on the other hand, when a question was asked, could quickly resume the conversation on his own without leaving much opportunity for others, and hence it often happened that only at the end, after much lapse of time, could the purpose of the audience be recalled to his attention. "Every now and then," Bargellini recalled, "a monsignor would appear at the door and kneel. This meant that the audience was running too long. Pope John would make a gesture not expressing impatience but urging calm, as if to say: 'I will be there in a moment.' And he would go on talking." As a result, there were often long delays in scheduled audiences while the pope concluded his probably extemporaneous conversations with earlier visitors; so John became notorious among formalists for unpunctuality.

He was essentially a gentleman, however, and it was his sincere ambition to behave "with courtesy and indeed with real courtliness" to everyone. Probably, but wrongly, the Roman nobles of the "black aristocracy" did not appreciate him: they did not like attending at the court of "a peasant pope," and they were nostalgic for the pope of the new social-climber plutocracy that Pacelli had been. In actuality John excelled his predecessor in delicacy, sureness of taste, and discretion. He was the pope whom no one ever saw kissing babies on the pattern of candidates to every office who seek to win the most easily influenced votes at the lowest cost. One day when an audience was marred by a baby who showed "some signs of restlessness," John interrupted what he was saying to interject aptly: "See, the little one too wants to join the conversation with the pope: he would like to discuss, but he cannot yet manage to make himself understood. Who knows with what devotion he will come back here when he is older! But now it would be better to try to ease him, though of course not right here in the audience chamber." Actually John preferred that children, as they should, remain at home: "When you go home," he told the faithful at one audience, "you will see your children. Give them a kiss and tell them that it is the pope's kiss."

Simple, just, and above all not demagogic. And no one ever saw John distribute charity with his own hands or look on as it was bestowed, even if it was he who had ordered it. Indeed he deplored paternalism, "which places its subjects under care solely in order to assure the dominance of its own power and its own authority. It seeks to make everyone aware of its own generosity, but it never respects the rights of its own subordinates. It speaks in a tone of protection but it refuses to permit collaboration." John was certainly not paternalistic and he did not like to display his power, and still less his beneficence. This was not only modesty and a lack of vanity but also a manifestation of respect for others and himself.

It was in just this spirit that on the day after Christmas, 1958, he went to visit the convicts in the prison of Regina Coeli in Via della Lungara in Rome. When Guido Gonella, the minister of justice, told him that his visit was an act of evangelical charity that "the whole world" admired "with pleasure and emotion," John looked up at the ceiling as if irritated by this exaggeration. He did not look at the minister again until Gonella began discussing plans. "It is our desire," the minister asserted, "to continue on our open-hearted road to the improvement of our whole penal system in order that punishment may become progressively more humane and more rehabilitative."

These were honest words, fine words, but typical of bureaucracy; contrast those of the pope to the convicts gathered in the rotunda, the center from which the four cell blocks radiated (the prisoners who had been there longest, as the deans of the establishment, were marshaled round an altar; the others were grouped in the galleries of all four floors. "My dear sons, my dear brothers, we are in Our Father's house here *too*," John said, and the emphasis with which he said *too* made a tremendous impression. The prisoners burst out into a cheer—"*Viva il papa!*"—that sounded fierce but was only a surge of hope. "Are you glad that I came? are you glad?" John asked as he proceeded with his very amiable little talk.

"On my way here from St. Peter's," he said, "I remembered that, when I was a boy, one of my good kinsmen, who had gone hunting one day without a license, was arrested by the *carabinieri* and locked up. Oh, what a feeling! Oh, the poor fellow! But things like this can happen

103

sometimes, even if one's intentions are not wicked. But, if one makes a mistake, one pays for it, and we have to make our sacrifices to the Lord." As he spoke he raised his arms and gestured with his hands, but suddenly he stood still as if struck by a sudden thought. "What a great thing, what a beautiful thing Christianity is!" It was a cry of real enthusiasm, and from above the prisoners shouted cheers and applause through the bars of all four cell blocks. John concluded in the manner of a man among friends: "Are you glad that I came? are you glad? I knew that you wanted me to come, and I too wanted to see you. And so here I am. To tell you what is in my heart as I speak to you would be impossible, but how else would you want the pope to talk to you? My eyes look into yours: no, why are you weeping? Be glad that I am here—are you not glad? I have pressed my heart against yours. The pope has come, here I am among you, and with you I am thinking of your children, who are your poetry and your sorrow, of your wives and sisters and mothers." Then he agreed to pose for the photographers, surrounded by a group of convicts, and it was an unprecedented addition to the inconography of the papacy. As he left the prison, he blessed the inmates with his three fingers spread, but, after this sacred gesture, he made another in response to the ensuing cheers: he took off his papal cap, raised it high, and waved it vigorously.

This was true mercy, not tearful good works; but that speech in the prison was notable also as an example of John's characteristic felicity with words and his capacity to find the unexpected cue: a pope's telling convicts of his uncle's arrest by the national police for hunting without a license leaves us speechless. On other occasions John was remarkably reserved, but in the sense of understatement, which can also be a tendency to humor. One day he received a delegation of the association of Italian business executives, and, when his visitors had told him about the activities of their group, he said: "Of course you have to work toward a certain end, as you have just explained to me. But remember that there is always Providence, on which everything that can happen in life depends. Look what happened to me."

There were times, too, when he was lyrical in a simple fashion. On the night of the Council's inauguration, October 11, 1962, he was so happy that at one point he could only attempt to share his rejoicing with the Romans who had thronged into St. Peter's Square. He pointed his finger toward the sky and said: "It is as if the moon too were in a hurry tonight. See her up there, looking down on this spectacle. This evening is the conclusion of a great day of peace." Perhaps the finest speech, at least from the point of view of John's typical felicity in improvisation, in contrast with his predecessor's laborious efforts, was the one that he made at Loreto on October 4, 1962, recalling that he had been a seminarist there during the jubilee year that had been proclaimed by Leo XIII.

"It was September 20, 1900," John said. "At two o'clock in the afternoon, having received holy communion, we were able to plunge our soul into profound and heartfelt prayer. What can be sweeter for a young seminarist than to converse with our beloved Heavenly Mother? But unfortunately the tragic circumstances of that period, which had polluted the atmosphere with a subtle odor of mockery of anything that had to do with spiritual values or religion or Holy Church, turned that pilgrimage into bitterness as soon as we heard the loose talk in the streets."

In other words, Roncalli as a young seminarist had been jeered at in Loreto on September 20 by the turn-of-the-century anticlericals. "We remember too," he added, "what we said that day as we were about to start our journey home: 'Madonna of Loreto, I love you so much, and I promise to remain faithful to you and a good son of the seminary. But here you will never see me again!' "

V

The Pontifical Legacy
of Pius XII

When the Church took sides: Pius XII,
Don Luigi Sturzo, Alcide De Gasperi, Luigi Gedda.
Patriarch Roncalli's welcome to the Socialists
and disciplinary action by the Vatican.
The specter of Masonry.
Clerical meddling in Italy.
Strained relations between Church and State.

PIUS XII had left John the unhappy legacy of a Church involved in the controversies of Italy's political parties. As a result there had been a resurgence of anticlericalism, as in the days when the Holy See had demanded temporal power. Pope Pius had never hesitated to interfere in Italian affairs with heavy pressures, illegitimate interventions, and violations even of the terms of the Concordat. His had been a period of overpowering control extending even into matters that might have seemed minor, such as certain instances of administrative elections or the creation of communal councils.

In the spring of 1952, for example, Pius XII had proposed that the Christian Democratic Party form an alliance in Rome with the neo-Fascists and that the two groups offer a single slate of candidates. He ordered Don Luigi Sturzo * to prepare a formal resolution to this effect, and it is said that Sturzo wept as he obeyed an order that revolted him. Alcide De Gasperi, then premier, had attempted to persuade the pope of the lack of wisdom in the move, writing him a carefully reasoned letter that Monsignor G. B. Montini, then deputy secretary of state, undertook to deliver to the pope. It was an excellent letter, and, among other things, it said respectfully:

* An anti-Fascist priest who had spent many years in exile during Mussolini's rule and who had become the leader of the Christian Democrats after the war.—TRANSLATOR.

I ask forgiveness that in this letter I deal with political activities that are so far beneath the lofty spiritual concerns governed with so much wisdom by Your Holiness, but I do not wish to hide the fact that, if the current daily troubles persist and grow worse, in the end even the defense of the cause of religion will suffer as a result. . . .

It was a courteous request to the pope to confine himself to the spiritual concerns of the cause of religion, but, in view of the fact that on the contrary Pius XII made it clear that he was also occupying himself with the communal councils of Italy, De Gasperi explained:

These are the alternatives: either to concentrate on the most reliable and active Catholics a broad front that can resist the enemy's array, which is still extremely strong, or to consider the creation of a kind of more programmatic and systematic Christian Labor organization, which, rationalizing its methods, its doctrines, and its actions, would proceed with social reforms on the broadest scale. . . . I can assure you, Most Holy Father, that we are not guided by political expediency but inspired by love for our nation's civilization.

Pius XII, however, probably understood the nation's civilization differently, and indeed the reply to De Gasperi's letter was the repeated order to prepare a single candidate list in Rome that would include Catholics, Liberals, Monarchists, and Fascists. Father Riccardo Lombardi, a Jesuit and an integralist propagandist who in those days used to describe himself, with considerable irreverence, as "the microphone of God," was assigned to put on the conclusive pressure. *De Gasperi, uomo solo (De Gasperi, A Man Alone)*, a biography by the premier's daughter, Maria Romana, tells stories that seem reminiscent of the Spanish Inquisition:

On the morning of April 19 Father Lombardi came to Castel Gandolfo to talk to my mother. In ninety minutes of conversation he managed to go from flattery to threats, insisting that the Christian Democratic Party broaden its front by means of an electoral list ranging into the extreme right. He used arguments such as this: "Rather than see the Communists win the Campidoglio in an election the pope would prefer to have Stalin and his Cossacks in St. Peter's Square." Then, alluding to my father, he added: "Understand, if the elections go badly, we will force him to resign."

"Operation Sturzo" failed because of a last-minute error made by the Fascists and skillfully exploited by De Gasperi and his minister of the interior, Mario Scelba; but subsequently, from any point of view, the elections came out equally well because, contrary to the pope's fears, the Communists did not conquer the Campidoglio. Nevertheless this was not enough to placate Pius XII, whose stubbornness was clearly epitomized in an observation by Maria Romana: "The pope did not want to listen, or perhaps he did not know how to reply to political inquiries that did not match his own thinking." It was indeed for this reason that, when De Gasperi asked in June for an audience for himself and his family (it was the thirtieth anniversary of his marriage and at the same time his daughter, Lucia, had just taken her perpetual vows as a nun), Pius XII, with whom it was always easy to obtain an audience, refused to receive the De Gasperi family.

"It was a surprise to us," Maria Romana wrote, "and a great sorrow to my father." The announcement that the audience had been refused was conveyed to De Gasperi by the Italian ambassador to the Holy See, Francesco Giorgio Mameli, to whom De Gasperi replied in a grieved but very dignified letter characteristic of his personality:

111

As a Christian I accept the humiliation, although I do not know how to explain it; as premier and foreign minister, I am required by the dignity and authority that I represent, and of which I cannot divest myself even in private affairs, to express my amazement at so exceptional a refusal.

There was nothing exceptional about it for Pius XII, who did not hesitate to elevate into a theory the notion that the Church ought to take sides. Receiving Christian Democratic provincial government officials of various ranks on July 22, 1956, some four thousand persons in all, Pope Pius actually asserted with stunning frankness: "Certainly, if everyone were inspired in his civic and political action by Christian faith and morality, establishing Christ and his doctrine as the foundation of every system, . . . then the Church would be able to remain outside every conflict, avoiding any alignment with any of the competing sides. But today there are men who want to build a world on the denial of God, and others who demand that Christ be kept out of the school, the factory, the Parliament. And in this battle, more or less open, more or less declared, more or less bitter, the enemies of Christ are sometimes assisted by the votes and propaganda even of those who continue to call themselves Christians. Nor is there any lack of those who seek impossible alliances, deluding themselves as to the variety of changing tactical expedients and on the other hand forgetting the unacceptability of the unchanged final goals."

In that summer of 1956, therefore, the Church opposed its veto to a coalition of Christian Democrats and Socialists in the municipal government of Milan. An article by Professor Luigi Gedda, general chairman of Catholic Action and of the so-called Civic Committees, in which he characterized as absurd "any collaboration between Catholic functionaries and the servants of those who persecute the Church in so many parts of the world," was enough to make the Christian Democratic Party's national council abrogate its agreement with the Socialists. The obedience of the party, which was Catholic, was natural enough, but the special climate of those years might be better conveyed by the commentary of a more or less liberal Milanese newspaper, *Il Corriere della Sera,* which itself saw nothing at all out of the way in the fact that it was the pope who made the decisions for the city of Milan:

> The Church tolerates no dialogue with the governments behind the iron curtain, where far more important issues than the formation of a municipal government are at stake. If the Church excludes any compromise where the clergy is subjected to such harsh persecutions, how could it have indulged the mad notions of those who want to set up councils at any cost? One cannot help wondering what kind of impression would have been left with the Catholics of the whole world by such a concession on the part of the supreme authority in Rome. Are the martyrdom of the priests and religious freedom worth less, perhaps, than the councilors of the large cities?

John's attitude was quite different. He had no intention of taking sides: he was fundamentally convinced, as his *Giornale dell'anima (Spiritual Diary)* shows, that "any consideration or intervention by human effort is worth very little in these matters of worldly interest." He sought to be friendly and benevolent toward all, without any distinction among parties, and above all without making prejudicial judgments against anyone, as he had already demonstrated when, as patriarch of Venice, he had exhorted the faithful to welcome the Socialists of all Italy, who were holding their thirty-second party congress there.

It was an appeal without precedent in episcopal usage, except perhaps for one set by Andrea Carlo Cardinal Ferrari, archbishop of Milan, one of the leaders of the Church who was most aware of worldly problems and whom Roncalli regarded as one of his preceptors. Following Ferrari's example, he spoke of the Socialists to the Venetians in terms that were both respectful and courteous on February 1, 1957. In a speech that came from his heart, he began:

This month of February is still wintry with its intense cold, its sudden fogs that seep into bones, attack the organism, and make for torpor, except that now and then there are fleeting periods of benign sunshine to encourage us back to life, to joy, and to fruitful work. So the month that is beginning now appears to us from our lagoon in its physical and spiritual aspects. During these first weeks Venice already is in part, and in part is becoming, an important point of convergence for the whole of Italy.

Then he alluded to an appeal that was then in progress in the Venetian courts in connection with the mysterious death of a girl called Wilma Montesi, a mystery that had fascinated and indeed perturbed, if not stunned, all Italy; and therefore, having paid the requisite compliments to "the great judicial system of our country," which was preparing to do justice "without distinction or privilege for anyone," the patriarch went on to announce:

Another gathering of much greater dimensions, if not of equal importance, will be held in the next few days in Venice, and every part of the peninsula will be represented: the congress of the Socialist Party. Inasmuch as I am taking the liberty of mentioning the matter to you, respectfully and without anxiety, and speaking as a good Venetian who holds hospitality in high esteem, as indeed one should according to Paul's precept, which says that the bishop should show himself *hospitalis et benignus,* you will understand the unusual importance that I place on this event, which seems to offer great hope for the immediate future of our country.

In saying this the patriarch was alluding to what then seemed probable: that the congress in Venice might lead to a reconciliation and possibly even collaboration between the Socialists and the governmental majority. Even then, in fact, notwithstanding the contempt and derogation expressed by Pius XII, an opening to the left was regarded by Italian politicians as a practical possibility. Such a conclusion seemed desirable to the patriarch, who said:

It is certainly inspired, I should like to think, by the effort to arrive at a system of mutual understanding of what is most important in the sense of improved living conditions and social welfare. Such an endeavor is founded on sincere good will, on honorable and generous intentions.

The difference between his position and that of Pius XII could not have been greater. Certainly it was a source of sorrow to the patriarch that the Socialists were atheists:

It is always with some pain, and sometimes with acute pain, that a shepherd of souls is obliged to recognize the fact that many upright and lofty intelligences stand deaf and mute as if before an empty sky even though it forever radiates the truths of religion; they do not know or they apparently have forgotten the fundamental principles of that divine message that even among the frailities of men and eras was the pulse of twenty centuries of history, of scholarship, and of art, that was the glory of the nations of Europe, the glory of the world; and it is painful to reflect that such men think that they can solidly rebuild the modern economic, social, and civic structure on any foundation that is not Christ's.

115

This was an appeal to the Gospels, not to the so-called Christian social doctrine (which itself might have been set off against Socialist doctrines, but without any claim that its superiority would be unchallengeably apparent), and indeed the patriarch proceeded in a purely spiritual vein:

But, having said this by way of a frank statement of spiritual position, as is the usage among honorable souls, I still cherish in my heart the wish that my children of Venice, as hospitable and friendly as in the past, will make their contribution toward the fruitfulness of this congress of so many brothers from all parts of Italy for a common progression toward the ideals of truth, good, justice, and peace. And it is to this wish that I add the call to everyone who believes, who hopes, who loves, especially for the duration of this congress, to pray more intensely and more purely to all-powerful God for the profit, the consolation, and the encouragement of all to greater understanding, to good will, and to good deeds. For every devoted, faithful Christian, February is filled with high summonses to consolation and rejoicing: the rays of blessed sunshine among the chills of winter, of which I spoke to you.

This was a statement that should have seemed beyond cavil to every man of good will, even from the point of view of doctrinal orthodoxy; but in that era a witch-hunt was raging even among priests, and, in fact, the transcript of the patriarch's speech was immediately read over the telephone to Rome as if by way of accusation. According to Carlo Falconi's account in *l'Espresso,** the call was made by a Venetian Jesuit and received by Father Giacomo Martegani, deputy for Italy to the general of the Society of Jesus. He immediately submitted the matter to his superior, Father Johann Baptist Jannsens, and then, it

* An independent and reasonably liberal semi-intellectual weekly.— TRANSLATOR.

116

was reported, he went to the Vatican to turn over the transcript to Monsignor Domenico Tardini, at that time undersecretary of state for extraordinary ecclesiastical matters.

The question was judged to fall within the jurisdiction of the sacred consistorial congregation, one of the duties of which is to keep the bishops under surveillance and *ipsorum periclitari doctrinam*— that is, examine and evaluate their doctrines. The secretary of that congregation at the time was Giovanni Adeodato Cardinal Piazza, one of Roncalli's predecessors in the Diocese of Venice, where he had acquired a reputation for speeches of a very different nature. Indeed, he had been full of public adulation for Mussolini, the man sent by providence who had saved Italy from the peril of becoming the "prey lusted after by savage, atheistic Communism." Patriarch Piazza had said too that on behalf of "growing, needy Italy" Mussolini had not hesitated to challenge the forces of the Negus of Ethiopia and the combined enemy powers, and, as the unconquered Duce, he had legitimately and laudably "sought conquest and approved an imperial peace."

Sometime later, after September 8, 1943, Patriarch Piazza breathed more easily when the Germans had established direct control over Italy: "The Church is aware that the strings of Badoglio's government * are pulled by Masonic and Jewish quarters, so that the situation of the Church is now gravely endangered," he told Koester, the German consul in Venice. In a report to Berlin on December 3 of the same year, the consul added:

* After Italy's capitulation to the Allies a provisional government was headed by Marshal Pietro Badoglio, who until then had loyally served Fascism.—TRANSLATOR.

The patriarch informed me that the manner in which the Jewish question was being handled in Venice was causing him serious concern. The night before, extremist Fascists had arrested poor, aged, and ailing Jews in their homes, while such rich and privileged Jews as had not fled from Venice were allowed to move about unmolested. This injustice very much perturbed him, and in his view the only possible solution was for the German authorities to institute measures against the Jews because then at least justice for all would be guaranteed. It is well known that the patriarch's chief desire is that all Jews and half-Jews be confined in a ghetto.

If these were the desires and the convictions of Cardinal Piazza, it is possible that some trace of them had survived, and in any case it was certain that he would hand down a formal canonical condemnation of the doctrines of good will espoused by Cardinal Roncalli. A brief comment was made by the Vatican radio, and *l'Osservatore romano* published an article of disavowal; Roncalli's name was not mentioned, but he felt it necessary to clarify the significance of his statements. He felt compelled to make it clear that he had never intended to initiate a dialogue with the Marxists, and to this end he had to write in the *Bollettino diocesano* of February 28:

No dialogue between Catholics and Marxists has ever been opened in Venice. Recent explicit documents of my own and of the episcopate on this subject are absolutely explicit and authentic. Finally, it is a source of great regret to me to have to take this occasion to deplore the bad habit of certain newspapers of inventing and fabricating intentions, attitudes, and utterances attributed to a bishop and to ascribe political signficance even to his mere appeal to his flock for prayer, good will, and courtesy.

Quite apart from prayer, courtesy and good will were out of use in those days, and in fact the language then

employed in the Church of Italy tended rather to the trucu-
lent. One of the most powerful cardinals in the Curia,
Alfredo Cardinal Ottaviani, undersecretary of the Holy
Office, for instance, wrote a book called *Il Baluardo (The
Bulwark)*, made up of some thirty of his articles, sermons,
homilies, speeches, and exhortations:

> A kind of cannibalistic insanity disguised as social redemption,
> clad in the robes of politics and diplomacy, wearing the yellow
> gloves of legitimate authority and with a train of espionage
> dragging everywhere behind it, is wrecking mankind with im-
> punity, utterly unmolested; it is destroying civilization and it
> seeks to make and is making this world into a desert of fear, a
> Sahara of the spirit.

One day in 1954, speaking to a group of French religious who had gone to the Holy Office to plead the cause
of the worker priests, the same cardinal remarked sneer-
ingly that the saints of the Church had never taken it
upon themselves to initiate reforms and yet all of them
had turned out to be vigorous reformers:

> Today, however, on the pretext of going out to deal with men
> panting after the goods of the world, they as reformers of the
> apostolate speak more of earthly than of heavenly bread: I mean
> certain pygmies who make it appear that a theology can be put
> together as one puts together a crossword puzzle and who invent
> a new theology. Not at the feet of Jesus, like Mary, but face to
> face with the serpent, like Eve, they allow themselves to be be-
> witched in order that they may be the more easily snared and
> devoured.

Ernesto Cardinal Ruffini, archbishop of Palermo, distributed a pastoral letter in the same vein to the Sicilian
episcopate:

Our doctrine is that of the Gospels, and, if all Catholics were thoroughly familiar with it and were solidly united for its application without even once paying heed to false prophets who seek to confuse and divide them, then it would be possible to hope that within a short time—at least as far as our own country is concerned—there would be the greatest progress in secular life. Furthermore [the cardinal concluded, having just returned from visits to Salazar's Portugal and Franco's Spain], a quite recent double experience confirms what we have just stated. There are nations that do not tolerate Communism and that have achieved tremendous progress; whereas here among us absolutely nothing has been gained by having accepted the support of the organized Marxists.

It was not only the Communists, however, who were the targets of Italian bishops' fulminations. Monsignor Beniamino Socche, bishop of Reggio Emilia, a "red" diocese that was described in Catholic circles as "a labororatory for scientific experiments in Communism and its practical effects," offered his flock an *Address on Communism* that examined its origins, causes, and contributing factors and that concluded with a universal condemnation:

All those who are not Communists—illuminationist laymen, the backwash of nineteenth-century anticlericalism, the new radicals, with all their shared antireligious and anti-Catholic venom . . . all these are playing Communism's game. Even more: we may say that secularism is the father of Communism.

If such judgments could be handed down from the most elevated episcopal pulpits, it was hardly surprising that they were echoed by the Catholic press in the lesser provincial dioceses. *La Voce delle Marche*, the weekly organ of Monsignor Norberto Perini, archbishop of Fermo, asserted that the members of the lay parties were all masons, anticlericals, libertines in the guise of decent men, exploiters of misery, schemers, money-changers . . . people who, devoid of any moral scruple, seek to foster loose living, irreligion, paganism, and so many more social diseases, well aware that all such things will favor their base instincts, their unavowable interests, their poisonous hatred of the church . . .

"The symbol of such people," the archbishop's organ concluded by way of comfort, however, "is a rat trying to gnaw away Mont Blanc."

The publication of the archbishopric of Chieti, backed by the authority of the local ordinary, Monsignor Giovambattista Bosio, seemed more pessimistic, however. Following Cardinal Piazza's example in leaving aside the Communists, it seemed, like him, consumed by fear of the Masons, "sectarians possessed by demons and held in slavery by the chains of the most terrible of tyrants: the devil." In Italy the devil had apparently returned to the disguise of the Masonic serpent, leaving Catholics "confounded, as a man who awakens from a terrible dream, by the discovery that once more Masonry has risen again and thrown off its mask, returning as the cancer of Italy to every vital ganglion of the nation's government."

It was absolutely untrue that Masonry amounted to anything in Italy during the years of transition between the pontificates of Pius XII and John, but in these episcopal frenzies one could see traces—indeed, almost an incrustation—of the clerical mentality of the time of the Syllabus in the late nineteenth century, when it was the custom of Pius IX to call the liberals "emissaries of Satanas," "the phalanx of hell," "the servants of Belial," "steeped in the most poisonous filth of hell." Employing the same phraseology almost a hundred years later, the organ of the archbishop of Chieti in 1958 denounced them as "servants of the green dragon that thrusts forth its hundred heads without any further hesitation or caution."

Nor was it merely a question of language. The verbal bellicosity was matched by the incursions of the hierarchs and the priests, who, during the pontificate of Pius XII, and in emulation of his example, frequently poured across the borders of the area reserved to the Church in order to deploy themselves in the domain of politics and to profit thereby. Since the Italian state was feeble, and, furthermore, governed for the most part by a party of Catholics, the business was easy enough, even if it could not be approved from a religious point of view.

There were shocking instances of the involvement of ecclesiastical authorities in financial deals and worse, such as those uncovered by Luigi Preti, the Social Democratic finance minister, in the summer of 1958. Giovanni Battista Giuffré, an enterprising swindler, had worked out an ingenious method for plundering the savings of the peasants of Emilia and Romagna, promising them fantastic interest and indeed paying it initially. As an unscrupulous private banker he at once had archbishops and bishops on his side, especially those of Montefeltro and Cesena, Monsignor Antonio Bergamaschi and Monsignor Augusto Gianfranceschi, followed by the governing fathers of convents, mitered abbots, parish priests, curates, and religious. Notwithstanding the extremely harsh penalties prescribed by the code of canon law, which excommunicated clerics who, under their own names or others', engage in business or commerce, bishops and priests joined Giuffré in looting the peasants' savings.

There was a revolving fund of tens of billions of lire in

direct contravention of the public law on the use of credit, which Giuffré blandly went on violating, consoled by the approval, if not the exhortations and encouragement, of *monsignori* of the Curia and the papal welfare agencies. With these savings, which, of course, the peasants of Emilia and Romagna would never see again, Giuffré had built a number of churches, a large number of offices for Catholic Action, asylums, and other works of piety: canon houses and convents. It was all a fraud, but his activity was spoken of as a miracle of Christian piety and Giuffré was called "the banker of God." In fact, *Mondo cattolico*, a pious publication, declared in December 1956:

> There have even been some who have attempted to accomplish conversions in his name and to make propaganda for his work; consequently he has found himself compelled to impose a curb on an excess of zeal that might have compromised the soundness and effectiveness of his good works or enticed religious to neglect that ecclesiastical obedience that constitutes the core of the organization of the Church.

A tempest of financial folly had swept over priests and monks in many provinces, and, in addition, extremely high sources were frequently setting bad examples. Prince Giulio Pacelli, a nephew of the pope, had prevailed on Giulio Andreotti, the Christian Democratic finance minister, to exempt him from the payment of all taxes on the ground that he enjoyed diplomatic immunity as the representative of the republic of Costa Rica to the Holy See. The same service was made available to another papal nephew, Count Stanislao Pecci, the minister of the Order of Malta to the Vatican, as well as to Marchese Filippo Serlupi Crescenzi, who was also a member of the Vatican aristocracy as a representative of the republic of San Marino. Actually all three of these men were rich Italian nationals whose diplomatic capacities were not only apparently but really mere honorary titles.

But at that period the Italian government yielded and yielded again to the requests of the Holy See or of Catholic organizations. Even in the field of law it appeared that the principle had now been established that, in the event of conflict or discrepancy between canon and civil law, the canon should prevail, and, similarly, the Concordat between Italy and the Holy See * was paramount to the Constitution of the republic. The Italian Ministry of Justice, for instance, was requested to initiate a prosecution against Roger Peyrefitte, a French author, because *Paese Sera,* a daily newspaper, had published his article, "The Pope's Rome," in which he had written, quite truthfully: "Being the pope's nephew is a fine trade because of the great avails that it brings not only in the churchly but also in the worldly sense."

Arrigo Benedetti, publisher of *l'Espresso,* was convicted of defamation of the pope because of an article, "The Pope's Party," in which he had said that by going out into the streets and meddling in Italian domestic politics, as Pius XII wanted it to do, the papacy was naturally assuming the risks of any political group: that is, of being challenged on a basis of equality by others, contradicted, opposed, even attacked in vulgar fashion, because there was a point beyond which it was impossible to make a distinction between the spiritual head of Christianity and the source of a given political course. If such a course was publicized, counseled, and possibly imposed in the name

* It dated back to 1929, when it was arrived at by Mussolini.—TRANSLATOR.

of the head of the Church without any disavowal of clerical activists by that head of the Church, divorcing his own responsibilities and salvaging the good name of his Church, the worst could happen in the political arena. Benedetti was convicted by a court that set forth a disturbing principle of jurisprudence: that in a country bound by a Concordat the pope enjoyed the privilege of an extraordinary state of immunity: regardless what he said, did, or decided in politics, the Italian citizen could only accept and obey with the same kind of mandatory submission that the faithful Catholic owes to the head of his Church.

A punishment of another kind—irrevocable expulsion from any teaching post in the public educational system —was imposed on Giovanni Radice, a teacher of English in the Pietro Giannone Academy in Benevento. At the instigation of Don Ferdinando Grassi, the instructor in religion, Radice's students had signed a protest accusing him of having flaunted and propagated atheism. Don Grassi, in actual fact, had heard that Professor Radice had written a commentary and criticism of John Milton's *Paradise Lost,* which was not included in the official curriculum and, even worse, which had been written by an Anglican poet who was an enemy of Catholicism. Don Grassi had therefore prevailed on some twenty students to denounce the teacher for atheism, and the boys were delighted to vie in their testimony, embellishing and enriching the evidence.

They said that their teacher had even drawn a comparison between Jesus Christ and Socrates, and Don Grassi provided the gloss: "This constitutes an implicit and indirect denial of the divinity of Christ." The students charged that Radice had praised Milton's sublime courage in the

125

face of the problem of death: "This is clearly an attempt to cast doubt on the immortality of the soul." They said that he had spoken highly of other authors, including Giovanni Boccaccio, Geoffrey Chaucer, and Voltaire: "A glaring offense to Catholic morality and an insult to purity." Finally the students said that it was not their teacher's custom to make distinctions between Catholic and non-Catholic writers and that he had discussed he wars of religion without stating his adherence to either side: "But this is a denial of every revealed faith from the throne of philosophy, and therefore it is atheism!" Consequently Radice, in a proceeding that ran from 1959 into 1960, was dismissed from his position in the national school system.

By that time John was already pope, but it must not be assumed that his accession had made an overnight change in the atmosphere of a country that was certainly among the most irreligious and un-Christian but that was also deeply steeped in and rotted by clericalism. The State's progressive abdication of its prerogatives and even of its functions had opened the way for the Church to insinuate itself into positions of control and privilege that it continued to exploit secularly. All youth welfare activity, for example, had been contracted on a concession basis to a papal commission, the POA, which received funds from the state for the management of the whole establishment of the Commissariat for Italian Youth, known as GI (for *Gioventù italiana*), which in the beginning consisted of 340 gymnasia, 310 health resorts, 296 youth houses, 52 theaters and film houses, 154 parcels of undeveloped land, and 68 sports fields. Within the general sphere of assistance, two-thirds of the funds available to the Ministry of the Interior for this purpose wound up in the hands of the POA; this was ample justification for the charge that was current at the time and that was summed up in the title of a book by Carlo Falconi: *Assistenza italiana sotto banderia pontificia (Italian Assistance Under the Papal Flag)*.

It appeared that even the Italian armed forces were about to be transferred to the papal flag. It was customary that groups of officers be ordered to attend political-religious lectures delivered by Cardinal Ottaviani. Giulo Andreotti, then minister of defense, himself headed the delegations of generals and admirals who went to listen. Whenever there was a religious celebration, naval units were placed at the disposal of the bishops; on the occasion of the eighth eucharistic congress of the Marche, for example, the motor-barge *MTC 1102* was in good time "converted into a flower-decked altar," according to *Il Resto del carlino*, "on which the Monstrance was enthroned, followed by a procession of swimmers." On the 450th anniversary of the death of San Francesco di Paola, two naval tankers, the *Po* and the *Mincio*, alternated in carrying his relics from shore village to shore village along the Calabrese and Sicilian coasts for two days. In honor of the dogma of the physical assumption of the Immaculate Mother into heaven, two naval corvettes, the *Pomona* and the *Vormano*, served as escorts off Fiumicino to the tug *Gufo*, on the deck of which the Virgin's statue was displayed between two rows of honor guards of sailors and *carabinieri* in dress uniforms. On other occasions, air force helicopters were detailed to transport other saints' relics to various parts of Italy. At the air force academy in Florence, all the officers attending courses, all noncommissioned officers of the permanent garrison, and all the enlisted air personnel at the base were ordered to a two-day detail of religious ceremonies for the fulfillment of their Easter duty. A circular letter laid down their obligations in terse military parlance: "Part I: meditations. Part II: confessions. Part III: Solemn Mass."

While Ottaviani was indoctrinating the officers of the armed forces, Pius XII himself undertook the obligation of guiding the responsible officials of the Ministry of the Interior and the chiefs of police into the right path. One day in the autumn of 1955, Minister Ferdinando Tambroni led a regiment of his associates—undersecretaries of state, regional directors, prefects, inspectors, chief inspectors, and inspectors general—to Castel Gandolfo in a pilgrimage the size of which *l'Osservatore romano* contentedly calculated at nine hundred. The pope informed them that it was not his intention to descant to them on political problems or matters of bureaucratic practice, but he laid down a few directives, calling for vigilance, prompt action, and severe punishment against all offenders and "in particular against those who cherished or evidenced projects of violent subversion to the damage of the State." Not only "evidenced" but even merely "cherished" plans that had not been evidenced were therefore to be considered criminal. Further establishing his criteria for discrimination on the citizen's inner convictions, Pius XII added that on the other hand the police could regard practicing Catholics as beyond suspicion: "The State," he assured them with confidence, "has nothing to lose and everything to gain in those citizens who, because they are sincere and fervent believers, manifest the surest guaranties of respect for the public authorities, of observance of the laws, and of absolute honesty in their private and public lives."

It was a rather ingenuous standard by which to distinguish the good from the wicked among the citizenry, since it is impossible to descry any identity or equation between the observance of religious precepts and the observance of a nation's laws. Pius XII, however, serenely assumed this position, issuing specific instructions to the minister of the interior and his subordinates: "It is our ardent desire that whatever serves the preservation and the growth of religious values in Italy be the object of your special concentration. Facilitating as far as you can the difficult apostolic task of the church, you are at the same time advancing the welfare of the citizens and the good of Italy."

On the motion of a Catholic deputy to Parliament, Pia Colini Lombardi, the sister of a Jesuit preacher, the Church succeeded even in deleting September 20, the anniversary of Rome's reunification with Italy, from the list of national holidays. So it came about that the Italian government was known, with a certain contempt, as the vicar of the vicar of God, and its ministers were looked on as part of the secular arm, as in the days of confusion between the two powers. Naturally this did not result in any enhancement of religious fervor among Italians; it merely encouraged the injection of ecclesiastics into secular matters, and sometimes to the clergy's disadvantage. The reaction was inevitable: a resurgence and spread of anticlericalism, an unhappy phenomenon that is inescapable in all dark years of clerical arrogance.

Ecclesiastical brazenness had mounted to such a degree that it seemed irresistible, and it was at a point at which the self-satisfied Jesuits on the staff of *Civiltà cattolica* spoke of the Italian State habitually in language that no one else could have dared to employ without being accused

of sedition. Father Salvatore Lener, for instance, wrote in
No. 2586 for the third Saturday of March 1958:

This wretched State of ours, barely risen out of the abyss of
defeat in war, of occupation, and of the destruction of the former
monarchical and Fascist system—this newborn Italian republic,
so weak in comparison with the colossi that threaten its peace
from without and toward the domestic enemies of its independence
and freedom—this government that is so tolerant of everyone—
parties, trade-union organizations, groups and grouplets of opinion to whose shocking subversiveness no limit is set—this government and this Parliament that cannot manage, let us not say to
repress political strikes and strikes by its own functionaries and
employes, but even to discipline them legislatively, as the Constitution requires: this democratic state, in short, which is so extremely pacifist, tolerant, downright forgiving of everything and
everyone . . .

Having been reduced to such a level, according to the
Jesuits, the Italian State would ultimately have to yield to
the demands of the Church, abdicating even the last prerogatives of civil sovereignty. On one occasion, when Monsignor Giacomo Cannonero, bishop of Asti, was formally
accused before the courts on charges of improper interference in the election campaign of 1953, *Il Quotidiano*,
the Catholic Action organ, denounced the accusation as
"infamous and sacrilegious" and added that it was "simply
absurd" that there could be "any control in Italy over the
teaching of a bishop" or that "anyone at all should be able
to lodge accusations against a bishop or a priest."

This was tantamount to contending that the privileged
ecclesiastical courts had been reestablished in Italy, and
the outcry went up again in 1958 when another bishop,
Monsignor Pietro Fiordelli of Prato, was tried and convicted on a charge of having abused his spiritual attribu-

tions by sitting in judgment on the behavior of a private citizen and insulting him in public because he had been married in a civil ceremony only.

This bishop refused to appear in court, or to be judged by the authorities of his country. He repeatedly hurled insults at the Italian law, describing civil marriage with the mocking adjective *so-called*, which was evidence of his intent to disparage the nation's law. When at last he was convicted, Giacomo Cardinal Lercaro, archbishop of Bologna, arose to declare his solidarity with Fiordelli; and, in protest against the judgment, he ordered all the church bells in his diocese to ring the mourning knell.

The verdict against the bishop of Prato aroused not only the scorn of Lercaro but also the anger of the Jesuits of *Civiltà cattolica*. In their contempt for the Italian State, which was always so feeble with everyone, they saw fit to mourn that on the other hand the secular power was moved by a vestigial desire

... of manifesting every aspect of presumptuous omnipotence, an overwhelming ardor for the preservation of its sovereignty intact, only against the Catholic Church. Only against her can the government continually "behave like a savage," showing its teeth and banging its fist on the table, and even twisting the alleged interferences with its own jurisdiction into denunciations of the Concordat, attacks on continued diplomatic relations, the renewal of hostilities, and the restoration of the old oppressive jurisdictionalism camouflaged under the liberalistic principle of separation!

In substance, then, having observed that there was some tendency in Italy to defend the principle of the State's jurisdiction in the administration of justice, the organ of the Society of Jesus warned the State, in this same No. 2586, that the Church believed that it had justification for a declaration of war: "The divine rights of the Church, which have always been defended even *ad effusionem sanguinis* [to the shedding of blood], which are creating martyrs now in Communist countries, will be solidly upheld by the Church in Italy and everywhere." "Everywhere" was vague and therefore hardly binding, but the idea that in Italy, that docile submissive Italy, a crusade even *ad effusionem sanguinis* might be necessary was evidence of a truculent spirit from which John would have to suffer much before he could succeed in rectifying it.

VI

Gradual Corrections
in Course

The influence of Cardinal Ottaviani.
The political duties of Catholics.
John's own point of view.
Slow evolution among the bishops.
An opening to the Left?
Alarm among the conservatives.

AFTER John's accession, Cardinal Ottaviani continued to enjoy much credit and to exert an influence, even *extra moenia,* arrogating to himself the function and indeed the right of direct and always obfuscatory intervention in Italian political life. He continued, for example, to speak publicly whenever there was a Cabinet crisis, as in February 1959, on the eve of the creation of a Center-Right government that was to be headed by Premier Antonio Segni. Ottaviani backed Segni, attacking those Christian Democrats whom he held responsible for the so-called opening to the Left and whom he described as "sacristy pinks." For Fanfani and his followers the cardinal found another label: "adolescent musketeers of the national leadership of the Christian Democratic Party," and Ottaviani condemned without appeal all Catholics who "in positions of political authority dare to align themselves with those who not only offend but butcher the Church"— in other words, the Socialists.

Ottaviani also reproached President Giovanni Gronchi of Italy for his journey to Moscow. In a sermon in the Basilica of Santa Maria Maggiore in Rome on January 7, 1960, he asserted that it was "impermissible that a Christian could even contemplate shaking hands with an enemy of Christ, the leader of those who every day repeat the murder and crucifixion of Christ." This was also the period of the Russians' first great ventures in space, and Ottaviani vilified the Russians as atheists "who think that they can sweep clear the skies with their prowess in space." By way of more effectively terrorizing his audience, he then raised the specter of a possible visit to Rome by Khrushchev, hoping that John would follow the example set by Pius XI during Hitler's visit in 1938 and withdraw to Castel Gandolfo.

Bernard Lavergne wrote at the time in *La Tribune des Nations*:

This bizarre cardinal has made himself into a violent political demagogue and devastatingly doomed any possibility whatever of peaceful coexistence between the two blocs, thus demonstrating his own striking preference for the indefinite continuation of the Cold War and hence for a hot war, for it is inconceivable that an acute state of Cold War should not erupt one day into hot war. By uttering words so charged with hate Cardinal Ottaviani has succeeded above all in proving that a Roman cardinal can be the worst of Christians. Fortunately there are in all countries men who are inspired by sincere Catholic faith; but this does not compel them to admire the papacy, and therefore it does not change the fact that the Roman Curia is imprudent.

Given these examples, it was only natural that the lesser bishops too should have continued the custom of meddling in political affairs and in the activities of the parties in their respective cities. In April of 1960 the archbishop of Agrigento, Monsignor Giovanni Battista Peruzzo, issued a formal order to the Socialist mayor not to appear in church for the ceremonies of Holy Friday and Saturday "either alone or in the company of the members of the city council, because that council includes among its number many Marxists, who are open and bitter enemies of Catholicism." In the following month the archbishop of Bari, Monsignor

Enrico Nicodemo, ordered the mayor, Senator Giuseppe Papalìa, also a Socialist, to leave the pier in the port where the solemn ceremonies in honor of the city's patron, San Nicola, were being held. The mayor obeyed for the sake of peace, thus making it clear that he regarded himself as a guest of the prelate and not the first citizen of his own city.

Urbe, a Catholic news agency, declared, furthermore, that the episode in Bari confirmed the impossibility "not only of collaboration but even of the merest social and civic coexistence between Catholics and Marxists. The accession of the Socialists to the seat of power on the local and national levels would automatically revive the conflict between Church and State that was so happily resolved in 1929." More pertinently and more wittily, *Paese sera,* a Left-wing newspaper, drew a moral as fitting as it was bitter: "If you do not go to Mass you will be hooted at and called an unbeliever; if you do go, you will be told that your presence is not welcome and you will be thrown out; life is not easy for a Socialist mayor when the archbishop has sworn vengeance against him."

It is certain that John was grieved by these things. When he relaxed in genuine confidences to himself in his *Giornale d'anima,* in fact, he wrote in dismay:

The bishops are more exposed to the temptation to inject themselves beyond all proper proportions, and they should be all the more urgently warned by the pope to abstain from taking part in any kind of political controversy whatever and from siding with one or another fraction or faction. Let them preach justice, charity, humility, meekness and the other virtues of the Gospels to all parties alike and in a universal fashion, defending the rights of the Church when these are violated or menaced.

In his desire to effect a rebirth of the Christian sense of responsibility and to arouse pastoral zeal ("No other obligation or function should be incumbent on the bishops," he said), he deemed it his duty to issue a call for a synod in his diocese of Rome *(Prima Romana Synodus)* for January of 1960. By a synod was meant the lawful convocation of the priests and clerics of a diocese, on the order of the bishop, for the purpose of discussing and debating whatever dealt with the care of souls. The Latin says that the purpose of a synod is *"constituere quae ad vitia coercenda, virtutem promovendam, deparavatos populi mores reformandos et ecclesiarum disciplinam aut restituendam aut fovendam necessaria et utilia esse*—to establish whatever may be necessary and useful to the curbing of vice, the promotion of virtue, the reform of the depraved customs of the people, and the restoration or encouragement of the discipline of the Church." The Latin is extremely clear in its statement of the need to battle vice and exalt virtue, to curb bad morals and to exalt the Church.

This splendid precept having been transmitted by John to the administrators of his episcopal Roman diocese, the proceedings of the synod were compiled in three volumes comprising a total of 755 articles. It was a huge undertaking for the codification of standards, and in particular its Article DCLXIII set forth the civic duties of Catholics: "Let Catholics take an active part in politics . . . in order to cooperate in the material and spiritual prosperity of their countries . . . to further the principles of Christianity . . . to prevent the conquest of power by citizens who are enemies of religion." The following article stated that a Catholic should choose that political party that offers the greatest guaranties of inspiration from Christian principles. Article DCLXVII required that economic and social organizations and endeavors recognize "the authority and the teaching of the Church." Finally, Article DCLXXII forbade workers to join class-based trade-union federations.

During the first election campaign that followed the Roman synod—the local elections of the autumn of 1960 —Cardinals Clemente Micara and Luigi Traglia, respectively the Pope's vicar and pro-vicar for Rome, took the chair at the meetings of the capital's civic committees, which they baptized the assault infantry of the Catholic electorate. Putting aside the solemn and sometimes no more than allusive language of the proceedings of the *Prima Romana Synodus*, Cardinal Pro-Vicar Traglia told these valiant infantrymen of the ballot that they must beware "not only of the Marxist and atheist persecutors but also of the lying, lukewarm defenders of the Church: full trust is to be given only to those who accept and faithfully preach Christ's doctrine."

Once a free hand had been given to an episcopate that had been indoctrinated under the guidance of Pius XII in a program of constantly increasing interferences with political affairs, the results could not have been different. Going beyond the deliberations of the Roman synod, in fact, an announcement issued by the Curia in the name of the Italian bishops' conference declared:

The most eminent and very excellent archbishops and bishops of Italy, on the occasion of the election to be held on November 6 of the current year, regard it as their duty to inform all the faithful that for the illumination of their consciences the declaration made by the prelates under the date of May 3, 1958, remains valid and adequate.

Hence, at the start of the third year of John's pontificate the political instructions of the time of Pius XII were still in force; and in the declaration of May 3, 1958, they had been stated thus:

The most eminent and very excellent prelates of Italy, fully aware of their grave responsibilities, confirm in connection with the forthcoming elections the guiding standards that had already been laid down for such contingencies. They especially remind the clergy and the faithful of their obligation of loyalty to Christ and to the Church, and, consequently, their solemn obligation to vote, to exercise the right of suffrage in conformity with the principles of the Catholic religion and the decrees of the Church and in total respect for its just rights, to be united in their votes in order to erect a solid bulwark against the very serious perils that at this very moment menace the Christian life of the country. All parish priests will communicate the contents of this announcement in such manner as shall be prescribed by the most eminent and very excellent ordinaries.

It might well seem that there could be nothing objectionable in the bishops' claim to the right to instruct the faithful to vote for the defenders of religion and the Church; but, when the bishops ordered that Catholics "be united in their votes," they were implicitly taking a position on behalf of a specific party—in the instant case, the Christian Democrats—and hence they were engaging in propaganda in favor of one of the slates of candidates as against the others. This was a form of interference, and as such it gave rise to disputes like those that in Pacelli's time had unfailingly accompanied every election in Italy.

L'Osservatore romano had begun to publish a regular feature called *Punti fermi (Full Stops),* and it was known that the author, or at any rate the direct inspiration, was Cardinal Ottaviani. Jettisoning the last disguise, *Punti fermi* reiterated the principle that the individual believer was incapable of choosing between one political party and another. In every instance Catholics taking part in politics, it said, should practice

> . . . adherence to the teaching of the Church and rejection of any division between the conscience of the believer and the conscience of the citizen. . . . The prohibition on collaboration with the forces of atheist, anti-Christian Marxism is an act of moral authority. The Church hands down its judgment on circumstances of necessity that the individual believer, in contrast, is incapable of grasping.

This was a summons to blind obedience, in contrast to John's desire to revive the extremely rare virtue of Christian courage and responsibility. But Ottaviani and the Holy Office had also the support of Giuseppe Cardinal Siri, archbishop of Genoa and chairman of the commission of Italian bishops, which issued a pastoral letter to the faithful specifically dedicated to the notion that dangerous influences might be exerted on the Church through the spreading mentality of democracy, the growing practice of democracy, the rooted habits of democracy.

> The most painful agonies of the Church of Italy at this moment [the cardinal wrote] arise from the fact that a far from negligible number of her children, some of them indeed militants, behave toward her in such a spirit of criticism, of autonomy of principle, and of positive action in delicate matters as at times to rival the worst anticlericals of the past.

In fact, according to the cardinal, laymen engaged in politics were increasingly arrogating to themselves "a spirit of criticism and autonomy with respect to the same that is certainly irreconcilable with the various positions laid down by Jesus Christ."

Thus Siri, the chariman of the Italian bishops' conference, aligned himself with Ottaviani, Micara, and Traglia, all Curia cardinals, and, since this occurred during John's pontificate, it was quite natural that the pope should be held partly responsible for it. Consequently there was a tendency during this period to regard John as another interventionist pope, and indeed there was a typical fictitious story current on this score. One Sunday in March of 1960 Antonio Segni, who, after the fall of his Center-Right Cabinet, had assumed the responsibility of forming a Center-Left one, was coming out of the parish church in Via Sallustiana after Mass. A monsignor bundled up in an overcoat with upturned collar approached him and asked him to enter an automobile bearing Vatican plates that was parked at the corner of the street. "Where do you want to take me, Father?" Segni asked with a timid smile. The priest did not reply, but he showed his face; he was monsignor Antonio Samorè, titular bishop of Tirnovo and secretary of the scared congregation for extraordinary Church matters.

Stifling a sigh, Segni accompanied him. In the Vatican the premier was taken to the secretary of state, Cardinal Tardini, who began to make small talk until at a certain point one of the doors of his office opened and the pope walked in, absolutely by accident, so that when he saw Segni he exclaimed: "But what a wonderful surprise, my son!" In the conversation that followed, the pope did not refer to the problems of the Center-Left or to the Socialists, but Segni understood everything and understood it thoroughly; the next day, March 21, 1960, he abandoned his effort to form a Center-Left government.

The story is completely untrue but it is fascinating in

the same way as an installment of a serialized anticlerical novel of the nineteenth century that might have been written by Garibaldi. But it was a number of Catholics who put it into circulation, adding that it had been told to them by the premier himself, tempted to make an opening to the Left but prevented. Moreover, when Segni abandoned his attempt during the meeting held by the leaders of his Christian Democratic Party, there were quite matter-of-fact inquiries whether anyone "had come round to see him." That was the then current jargon phrase among the Christian Democrats to indicate that the Vatican had asked for something, had volunteered a warning, or had sounded an alert. One of the party leaders, Franco Evangelisti, had quite frankly asked during the meeting: "Premier Segni, has anyone come round to see you? My conscience as a Catholic compels me to think of such things. There is no sense smiling in this room when I say things of this nature. Premier Segni, has anyone come round to see you?"

Certainly the pope had not manifested himself in the sense imagined or desired by the antagonists of the Center-Left. It is definitively known that on March 14, exactly one week before Segni resigned his mission, John had spoken quite differently in a private audience granted to Monsignor Vincenzo Gilla Gremigni, archbishop of Novara, who reported the pope's words in an article in his *Diocesan Review:*

It was at about noon on March 14; the pope . . . deigned to converse with me for about three-quarters of an hour. . . . Paternally, he wanted to set forth his thinking in social affairs too, not to say political, cordially emphasizing the Center position that is naturally the Catholic's because of that equilibrium that he enjoys through his serene possession of the truth; and the pope ex-

143

plained: "Heart and mind should be firmly ensconced in the center, so that in Christian charity, as the need may dictate, the hand can turn to the right or the left and yet there is no impairment of the definitively center position from which neither heart nor mind ought ever to depart."

This explains why John in no way sought to prevent, but, rather, viewed with serenity the accession of the Center-Left in Italy. Fundamentally it was a problem that did not concern him, concentrated as he was on considerations of the interests and the universal needs of the Church. Pius XII, who had a lawyerlike and logical mind, started from the concept that Communism was an antireligious and anti-Catholic phenomenon, drawing the conclusion that it must be fought and that therefore every political opportunity, however trivial, must be seized with total commitment. John, on the other hand, who was more deeply engaged with much different matters, did not "send anyone round" to discuss Italian political developments.

This did not mean that he had not followed with real apprehension the unhappy political events that had afflicted Italy during the few months of Tambroni's government in the spring and summer of 1960. This Right-wing experiment had been openly espoused by the Curia; as late as July 13 Fernando Cardinal Cento, formerly papal legate in Portugal, where he had become a friend of Dictator Antonio Salazar, assumed Tambroni's defense and indeed magnified his virtues. He said that this man who had been premier during the bloody days in Genoa, Rome, and Reggio Emilia had demonstrated that he possessed qualities and virtues that made him worthy of admission to the sixth heaven of Dante's paradise. This is Jove's heaven, in which flies the imperial eagle in whose eye the upright sovereigns are: David in the pupil, and then, going from the eagle's beak up by way of the brow, Trajan, Hezekiah, and Constantine, in that order; moving downward from the pupil there are William the Good of Normandy and that Ripheus of whom Virgil said that he was the most honorable of the Trojans. As the sixth saintly illumination round the pupil and David, Cardinal Cento proposed to install Tambroni.

This was not merely rhetorical bombast; it was an expression of the reactionary politics that was dearest to the Curia and that the bishops' conference had appropriated as its own. Manipulated by the Curia under the chairmanship of Cardinal Siri and established as its heir apparent, the conference had come to duplicate the Curia's conservative characteristics in spite of the new pope's directives or, at the very least, his inspiration. Indeed, John, who was properly concerned with the bishops first of all, had already called on the Italian bishops' conference to revise its own bylaws in order to establish itself in a more autonomous fashion, on the model of the bishops' conferences of other countries. It was essential that the Italian conference too emancipate itself from the hypnotism of the Curia, precisely because it had become the custom not even to hold a meeting of the conference. The Curia assumed the responsibility of issuing announcements in the bishops' name, and the bishops first learned of them when they read them in the newspapers, as happened in 1960, when there was no conference. A regular session, however, was held from November 5 to 8, 1961, and John was quite pleased by the fact, frankly remarking to the prelates who had gone to render homage to him in the Vatican: "This is the first time that the Italian clergy has come together."

It might have been intended as a rebuke, and certainly it was interpreted as such. Whoever asked Monsignor Capovilla, the pope's secretary, for clarification received the highly emotional reply: "It is better, it is better." But there was no way of knowing whether the evaluation was Capovilla's own or the echo of the pope's. Things did in fact gradually improve. The official communiqué issued after the 1961 conference said—a dramatic innovation —that the Italian bishops felt themselves able to guarantee

. . . the unremitting understanding of the Church and its total devotion to all its always beloved sons whom an insidious propaganda seeks to lure away from its bosom by poisoning their spirits with doubts of the sincerity and efficacy of its maternal solicitude for their legitimate aspirations.

Until then the Italian bishops' conference had never employed such expressions. It had always been much easier to detect in its final decisions the repetition of old condemnations and old anathemas mingled with new maledictions elaborated from time to time in order to combat the new trends of political development. Without condemnations, and indeed with an invitation to those who had strayed far from the Church, the first "Johannine" conference was concluded in terms that had a precious signficance for those who knew how to interpret them.

They were fully understood, for instance, by Aldo Moro, secretary of the Christian Democratic Party. Two weeks after the end of the bishops' conference he spoke on television, and without any fear of error he said that the Church hierarchs would not attempt to prohibit any move toward the Center-Left that included a dialogue between Catholics and Socialists.

The phraseology was not fortuitous; Moro chose his

words quite carefully during a televised press conference. Eugenio Scalfari, editor in chief of *l'Espresso*, asked him: "In the event that your party laid down certain directives and at the same time the Church hierarchs through their episcopal channels challenged these directives, do you believe that your party would nevertheless be in a position to enforce them? I should like to hear your opinion." Moro replied with the tongue of an angel: "We believe that, because of its clarity, its prudence, and its firmness, our position is such that it cannot give rise to the hypothetical situation that Professor Scalfari suggests." Moro's confidence was too solid not to have its foundations in guaranties already obtained. Little by little the wind was changing, as a result of the patient tactics adopted by John in his dealings with the Curia and the Italian bishops. He was following a technique of his own, already profitably tested in France with de Gaulle, which was that of giving in on some points in order to reinforce his position on others that were more expedient or more important at the time, always prepared to return later to the counterattack on the earlier issues. He had made this his rule, as is shown by a letter written by him as early as 1921 to one Don Clienze, a priest of his diocese:

In the era of the conflicts of which even I heard the last echoes, the motto of our elders was *Frangar non flectar* [Break but do not bend]. I prefer the contrary device, however—*Flectar non frangar* [Bend but do not break]—especially in dealing with matters of everyday concern: and I believe that the whole tradition of the Church is on my side.

Acting on this example, even Cardinal Montini, archbishop of Milan, sent a letter to the clergy of his diocese that was a kind of discliplinary document calling for caution. He said that it was inadvisable "to foster the so-called opening to the Left at this time and in the form at present envisaged," but he concluded with a warning: "Should circumstances in our judgment be altered, we do not intend to refrain from giving you other instructions." This was already a step forward; and from many other little clues as well, symptoms each of which by itself was almost imperceptible but all of which together showed a coherent line, it was clear that there was a development that seemed to show that John was about to take the initiative from the Curia and the Italian bishops. Instances of "difficult city councils" were resolved through collaboration between Catholics and Socialists without any effort at protest by bishops. In Sicily on September 9 there was a genuine opening to the Left that was not denounced by Cardinal Ruffini. It was observed that institutions and persons once dominant were being eclipsed or even were vanishing from the political scene. There was no further talk of the civic committees, for example, or of their enterprising founder, Professor Luigi Gedda. Catholic Action, pastorally directed by John into purely spiritual endeavors, stopped interfering in the Christian Democrats' political activity, and even Father Riccardo Lombardi, who had functioned as "the microphone of God" for the mobilization of the mass of Catholic voters in the elections of 1948 and 1952, was restricted to the operations of the so-called Center for a Better World.

There was of course no lack of contrary indications to attest to the continuing struggle between the pope on the one hand and the Curia and part of the episcopate on the other. After a majority of the Christian Democrats, in the party's April congress, had voted approval of the

Center-Left in the form stipulated by Moro, Cardinal Ruffini declared the vote illegal. In *la Voce cattolica (The Catholic Voice)*, the spokesman for his See, he said that "the truest majority of Catholics stands with its own bishops and knows how fatal is this alms of support that is begged of the Socialists." Similarly, receiving the leaders of the National Federation of Small and Medium Industry on February 15, 1962, Cardinal Ottaviani described the chiefs of the Christian Democrats as "unthinking Christians" and accused them of shameful deals for personal profit. But the next day, February 16, the third Friday of the month, which was the normal day for the deputy secretary of the Holy Office to have his audience with the pope, John did not receive him. Some sources said that Ottaviani had not appeared but had gone away to rest in the abbey of Grottaferrata by way of further protest; others said that John had warned him not to appear.

Even if both hypotheses are purely speculative, they nonetheless demonstrate the intensity of the division; moreover, on the same day *Oggi*, a weekly picture magazine published in Milan, carried an interview with a "prominent figure in Catholic circles," described also as an "eminent layman" who could not disclose his identity ("his anonymity," the magazine pointed out, "must be preserved for reasons that are indeed dramatic"): he denounced "the new wound inflicted on the Church by the alliance between the Christian Democrats and Socialism." It was generally believed that the eminent layman was Professor Gedda, and *Italia*, the daily newspaper that spoke for the bishopric of Milan, launched an attack that showed that Cardinal Montini had found the circumstances altered and therefore he had issued new instructions concerning the Center-Left:

First of all, what is this melodramatic atmosphere that prevents the "prominent figure" and "eminent layman" from revealing his name? Here we tumble into the ridiculous because, thank heaven, we live in a democracy where anyone can discuss a political development whether he judges it favorably or harshly. In other words, we live in a country where neither the headsman's block nor the stake exists for anyone who wishes to express his own views.

Montini's newspaper then proceeded to humorous speculation to the effect that the eminent man did not even exist or that, if he did exist, he was in no way eminent or even worthy of credit, since everyone could be expected to know that the official voice of the Church was exclusively the pope and the bishops.

Expressions of the Church's joy and sorrow [*Italia* emphasized] have always been communicated to the world through the august voice of the Holy Father and the official statements of the ecclesiastical hierarchy. Now there has been no word that He Who alone is authorized to speak in the name of the Church has expressed the opinion that is dealt with in the article.

So John worked step by step to establish his own authority in a sense and a direction totally opposed to those that had characterized Pius XII. Even *Civiltà cattolica* fell into line, in accordance with the vow of obedience to the pope that is peculiar to the Jesuits, and in fact, when Italy began in 1962 to discuss the election of a new president, No. 2684 of the magazine contained a kind of placet for the selection of a candidate who was not a Christian Democrat, not a devoutly practicing Catholic, not even a militant soldier of the Lord, provided he was an upright man.

The magazine did take part in the discussions on the choice of the new head of state, and it very humbly lamented:

What is especially unpalatable is the secularist demand, which embodies the implied accusation that Catholics are deficient in their appreciation of the State and that they are incapable of defending its independence against supposed clerical interference. This accusation seems to us unjust, undeserved, and gratuitous, because it is not warranted but, rather, belied by the facts.

Whether the charge was just or unjust, *Civiltà cattolica* continued that the problem could not be stated in terms of secularism as opposed to Catholicism, but rather that it was one of suitability:

Let that citizen be chosen who has the greatest authority and who is most capable of fulfilling the task that the Constitution assigns to the president of the republic. This is what the Italian people expects of Parliament.

It was extremely well put, and, furthermore, it appears to have been inspired by John personally. A secret report from the armed forces' intelligence service to the president then in office, Giovanni Gronchi, said, in fact: "[Giuseppe] Saragat is supposedly the pope's candidate. Center-Left quarters in Rome believe that John would rather have a Catholic anticlerical like Saragat in the Quirinal than a Catholic atheist like Merzagora, Campilli, G. Martino, or Segni himself." Even if the secret service report was synthetic, its tone was unmistakably Johannine, so much so that it could be taken as an authentic product of a man in a position to invent the truth.

Reactionary episcopal circles and the Italian Right were plunged into the bitterest disappointment. This an-

guish reached its nadir when the Italian bishops' conference of 1963 issued a call for broader social views and
thus for alliances with the Left. Above all, when it spoke
of Communism, the bishops' conference emphasized that
Communists as such were not to be attacked but were to be
reproached only in so far as they were atheists. Next, it
denounced as conscious or unconscious inciters to Communism persons and groups who were easily to be identified with the Italian Right:

> We must be understood also by those who fear, indeed who
> oppose atheistic Communism but who so often, with their neo-
> pagan and materialist philosophy of life, and with their skepti-
> cal and corrosive criticism, accomplish in the end results that
> tend to defeat the moral resistance and spiritual rebirth of our
> people.

The outrage was great, and there were efforts at resistance outside the Church as well, but all, of course, in the
name of religion. The first source of anxiety was the bishops' own phrase, "atheistic Communism." It could give
rise to the inference that its target was atheism alone and
that perhaps it did not attack that social system that, even
though inspired by Communist economic doctrines, made
no professions of atheism. "Would it not have been better
to speak of Communism without restrictively qualifying
adjectives?" *il Corriere della sera* asked, as if in rebuke
to the bishops for negligence in the performance of their
jobs. Actually the bishops had adopted the expression
coined by Pius XI for his encyclical of March 19, 1937,
Divini Redemptoris, and it was not readily apparent why
they should have dissociated themselves from this authoritative and classic model. On another occasion, however, the same newspaper had pointed out, with quotations

from John Henry Cardinal Newman, Lord John Emerich Acton, Antonio Rosmini, and Alessandro Manzoni, that it was possible to be at the same time a paradigm of Catholicism and an impeccable liberal, provided that one preserved an inflexible anti-Socialism.

At this point one might also say something of the opposition, the rebellion, the indignation among the eminently respectable people who, faced with the pope's attitude, began to feel their own religious faith wavering. But to go into the details would be to descend to the ludicrous, and from every point of view that would be out of place in dealing with what in the last analysis is a religious subject.

Pope John blesses the crowd in Saint Peter's
Square on his way to the opening of the Ecumenical Council (October 11, 1962) UPI

Pope John waves from an open car in Loreto, where he visited a shrine dedicated to the Virgin Mary. The whistle-stop train trip was the first taken by a Pope in nearly a century WIDE WORLD

A surprise visit to the Vatican printing plant, which publishes *l'Osservatore Romano* and Church publications in seventy languages UPI

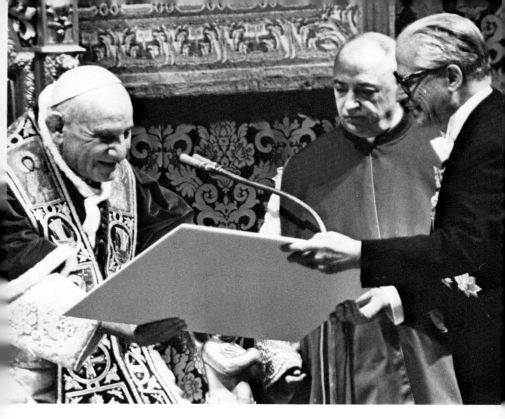

Pope John receives the $160,000 Balzan Peace
Prize (May 10, 1963) from Giovanni Gronchi,
President of the Balzan Foundation, while Msgr.
Mario Nasalli Rocca di Connegliano, Papal
Chamberlain, looks on   WIDE WORLD

When he paid a Christmas visit to the inmates
of Regina Coeli prison on December 26, 1962,
Pope John revived a custom established by
Pius IX, who visited prisoners every Christmas
during his papacy (1846–1878)   UPI

In the same tradition Pope John visited a different church in his diocese on each Sunday of Lent. Here he blesses the crowd at the Church of the Ascension, his first Lenten station UPI

On March 7, 1962, Pope John revived a tradition not followed for two centuries when he led the first of a series of Lenten processions. At left, Ash Wednesday, he leads a crowd on the first of the six "Roman stations" of Lent UPI

The Congolese delegation to the Catholic Rural Congress presents the Pope with a carved elephant tusk WIDE WORLD

A Papal audience for the sick on Saint Joseph's
Day (March 21, 1959) UPI

The last photograph of the Pope before his final
illness was taken on May 25, 1963, as he recorded an annual radio message to the faithful of
the Sanctuary of Pieckary, Poland WIDE WORLD

VII

The Total Neutrality
of the Church

Conflicts between John and Cardinal Tardini,
the secretary of state.
A rash observation on the situation in China.
God has not entrusted any
special mission to any nation.
Amleto Giovanni Cardinal Cicognani
becomes secretary of state.
Pacem in terris.
Defense of Poland, a martyred nation.

OUT of the confidence that he always placed in men, John, once elected pope, did not hesitate to keep Monsignor Domenico Tardini in office as acting secretary of state. Known as the Vatican's outstanding expert in his field, he boasted almost forty years' seniority in the Holy See, having been appointed secretary to the Congregation of Extraordinary Ecclesiastical Affairs in August of 1921, when Benedict XV was still pope. Under Pius XI Tardini had become deputy to the secretary of state and under Pius XII acting secretary.

John made him the titular secretary and announced the appointment when he received Tardini and his associates for their first business audience after John's election. When the introductions had been completed, he said very courteously: "At times we have to speak at some length and we feel hampered by prefixes and suffixes; therefore we have decided to eliminate as many of them as possible. Meanwhile we shall begin by omitting Monsignor Tardini's 'acting' and call him, more simply, secretary of state." In his first consistory on the following December 15 John raised Tardini to the rank of cardinal. Thereupon it was Tardini's turn to make a jest, explaining why he had accepted this elevation from John after having declined when Pius XII had offered it to him earlier: "I refused the red hat at that time because I wanted to be let alone. But one can refuse this pope absolutely nothing."

The complete outspokenness in the relations between John, the epitome of amiability, and Tardini, the rather unpolished modern Roman, dated back many years. They had first met in the Congregation for the Propagation of the Faith, where Tardini had for many years taught sacramental dogma before his transfer to the Vatican's Congregation for Extraordinary Affairs, and where his illustrious students had included such future cardinals as Gregory Peter Agagianian and Francis Spellman. John and Tardini had been fellow students in the seminary and had taken their state teaching examinations together—both passing with unanimous acclaim, a remarkable achievement for two clerics in those days—and ever since then they had remained friends. Both, moreover, had had typically Roman careers, attaining the highest positions of responsibility without ever once having been sent out of Rome—without ever having left the city, one might say. Essentially conservative, reserved in the manner of the older members of the Curia, a typical representative of that class of prelates who, apart from Vatican offices, know only some few Catholic Action headquarters or educational institutions in those areas that are their protectorates by virtue of their rank as cardinals, Tardini was at bottom hardly the most predictable choice as John's close and most direct collaborator.

In actuality they disagreed often, although John never lost patience on that account. "I know that he does not think much of me," the pope said of Tardini, "but I have a high opinion of him, and as well because he always speaks plainly to me. Besides, he knows what he is talking

about. As a rule, when we speak we begin from two opposite points of view. Then we begin to come closer together
and meet roughly in the middle, and this is fine." One day
the pope assured Father Giuseppe Tucci, the editor in chief
of *Civiltà cattolica,* that he had had no hesitation about
making Tardini secretary of state. He admitted that they
did not always agree on everything, but he urged Father
Tucci to follow Tardini's views in every instance rather
than the pope's: "It is he who is responsible for the secretariat of state; so . . ."

With that "so" John flung out his arms as if it were an
argument that put an end to all uncertainty, in tribute to
the principle of the division of labor and the recognition
of jurisdictions. In contrast to Pius XII, "Pope John never
tried to get along without those who might have different
opinions from his," Father Nazareno Fabretti wrote, emphasizing the existence of conflicts between John and Tardini. "Everyone knew and recognized that their two tem-
peraments, notwithstanding certain superficialities, were
very different; and particularly in the moments of decision
on and preparation for the Council it was not difficult to
be unaware of the bewilderment of a man in other respects
as pious and religious as Tardini." John himself one day
told Daniel-Rops, his old friend from his service in Paris,
how he had foreseen and feared Tardini's opposition to the
Council. Under the date of May 1, 1959, Daniel-Rops'
diary contains a confidence offered by the pope:

Suddenly it was the Council that had become the subject of
his monologue. It was not more than three months since he had
announced its convocation: obviously it was this that was the
prime subject of his concerns. He described how the inspiration
for it had come to him, how he had confided this to Monsignor

Tardini, what reactions he had feared, and what joy he experienced when he found that Tardini was so fully in agreement on it.

But, although initially Tardini seemed to favor the idea of the Council, he subsequently became convinced that it would be better to defer it to a later date. He cited the discouraging experiences of Pius XII, who for almost three years had given thought to the notion of convoking a council and who had even authorized the Holy Office to undertake preparatory work, which was later abandoned and interred in the archives. To Tardini it seemed that this precedent demonstrated the impossibility or the untimeliness of a council. John stood firm on his own idea, and it would appear that the controversy was finally resolved by a joking comment from Tardini, who muttered: "At least, Holy Father, let us cling firmly to the principle that only Latin will be spoken in it. In this way they will all have to be more brief."

On other occasions, however, it was John who was the loser, usually when the question was one in the area of major international matters, which Tardini tended to monopolize. John, moreover, seemed initially inclined to let him have his head, and gave the impression almost that he himself was not cut out or trained for such matters. "Never had anyone semed to me to be less given to thinking and planning than this Pope John to whom I was speaking," John Carmel Cardinal Heenan, archbishop of Westminster, remarked one day in amazement at the pontiff's apparent absent-mindedness, thoughtlessness, and lack of foresight.

There was also the further fact that in the Secretariat of State, as in the rest of the Curia, the atmosphere was still

160

that of the time of Pius XII, and here John found himself
in difficulties even with respect to the speeches that he had
to deliver. As long as it was merely a matter of voicing
hopes and wishes for peace or for the liberation of mankind from the terror of nuclear weapons, the traditional
generalities of the Vatican's diplomatic position remained
unchanged, so that John's generous appeals were easy.
Laments for the dead were equally legitimate and included
in the accustomed formalities: "Too many young men in
the prime of life have shed their blood. Too many ceme-
teries are already filled with the victims of war, and they
warn us harshly once and for all to arrive at harmony and
unity and a just peace."

It was more difficult, however, to maneuver in the domain of the concrete problems that arose from time to time
and that, in the initial period of the pontificate, might also
be snares set for the pope. A typical case was that of the
so-called bishops' ordinations in China in December of
1958. Impeded in their communications with Rome, Chinese Catholic priests left in isolation after the ouster of
Western missionaries had finally organized themselves into
a kind of autocephalous national church in order not to
lose the privilege of the religious toleration extended to
indigenous followers of any creed. It might have been regarded as an expedient in order to enable the Chinese
Catholics to survive and testify in anticipation of better
times, and so charity and pastoral understanding would
have been the proper attitude toward the Chinese Catholic
clergy.

Unexpectedly, however, on the occasion of the consistory of December 15, 1958, John made a speech that
could have been written by his predecessor and that was

actually from the hand of Tardini, who had that day been raised to the purple:

For some time the Catholics of China have had to endure unprecedentedly difficult and painful conditions. The missionaries have been calumniated, imprisoned, and finally expelled, peaceful messengers of the Gospel that they were, including a large number of bishops and archbishops. Zealous and fearless Chinese bishops have been thrown into cells, and not a few others have been placed under house arrest or in other ways prevented from freely performing their pastoral duties. . . . It should be no cause for wonder that, when the pastors are afflicted, the sheep entrusted to them should also be the object of temptations, of threats, of physical and spiritual vexations, all intended to induce them to abdicate their faith, to reject the foundation of their Catholic vocation, to break the chain of obedience and love that binds them to the chair of Peter. Unfortunately, we have to report with pain that there have not been lacking those who, more fearful of the orders of men than of the holy judgment of God, have bowed to the acts of the persecutors, going even as far as to accept a sacrilegious consecration as bishops from which they can derive no jurisdiction over the faithful because it was performed without the apostolic mandate.

This was all quite accurate, both from the point of view of historical record and from that of the validity of the protest and of the contravention of canon law; but it was all ill timed and sterile as well, as is so often the case with the documents that come from the Curia. It was indeed the Curia that had induced the pope to issue this denunciation, and the only personal note was John's addition of a very characteristic lament after his condemnation: "These errant brothers have opened the way to an attempt at schism: and we should never have wished to pronounce that word *schism* at the outset of our pontificate, for it burns our lips and anguishes our heart." He was always to feel regret over this act, as for an error committed in good faith but out of insufficient reflection. Years later he blamed himself for having acceded to the Curia without having first investigated: "It was a delicate situation and not clearly defined in its outlines; and I spoke without having taken sufficient thought because of what I had been told."

He did not forgive himself for having treated the Chinese as enemies at the moment, and thereafter he was extremely vigilant against any recurrence of such an error. When Ludovic Cardinal Stepinac, archbishop of Zagreb and metropolitan of Croatia, died on January 10, 1960, John was meticulously correct, remembering that the prelate had been tried and convicted on charges connected with the atrocities perpetrated by the Catholic Ustashi * during the Second World War: he mourned Stepinac, naturally, and even recalled that because of his imprisonment Stepinac had been unable to receive his red hat from the pope in Saint Peter's; but John was careful to avoid any disrespectful allusions to Yugoslavia or her government. With dignity and discretion he said only: "This simple, noble father and pastor of God's church was very dear to our spirit. His long suffering over fifteen years and the serene and confident dignity with which he bore it have entitled him to universal admiration and veneration." In Belgrade this comment was described as "austerely friendly" to Yugoslavia, and it served to open the way to the cordial conversations that finally culminated in the understanding arrived at between Marshal Tito and the Vatican.

* Croatian nationalists who collaborated with the German occupant.— TRANSLATOR.

In this same month of January 1960, there was another appearance by John on the international scene, but this one was characteristically his own, without any intervention by Tardini. Chancellor Konrad Adenauer of West Germany, a most fervent admirer of Pius XII, had been granted an audience with the new pope, and, on the basis of some mistaken information, there was a general expectation that the pope would make it the occasion for an important political statement supposedly elaborated by Tardini in three days of arduous labor in order to clarify the official point of view of the Holy See on such subjects as the thaw in the Cold War, relations between East and West, the reunification of Germany, and the Berlin problem. Adenauer, of course, arrived equipped with a suitable prepared reply.

John, however, was merely cordial. He began by complimenting Adenauer on his ebullient good health and "the fresh, vigorous energy with which he continued to devote himself to the high functions of his noble office." Then the pope rejoiced over the religious sentiments that distinguished the chancellor's family (his son, Paul, was a Jesuit), and finally John broadened his remarks to include the whole "generous" German people, recalling its history, its culture, its religious faith, its industriousness, its intelligence, its good heart, its laudable conquests in the worlds of art and science, its loyalty, its dignity, its love of country: "For our most beloved people of Germany we voice paternal wishes and hopes for an evermore prosperous future to be born of the good will of each of its sons."

Adenauer listened attentively as Monsignor Bruno Wüstenberg, the Vatican's German interpreter, translated phrase by phrase; and the chancellor recognized that any hint of politics had been kept out. In his reply, therefore, he had to cut short his prepared remarks, restricting himself to the statement that the good relations between the Bonn government and the Holy See were an aid to the cause of civilization and peace; but, rather than sacrifice the whole substance of the thoughts that he had intended to voice, he concluded by saying all in one breath: "I believe that God has given the German people in these disastrous times the special duty of being the guardian of the West against those powerful forces that press on our countries from the East."

Even though it was not an actual summons to a crusade, this Teutonic concept of the *Wacht in Ost*, the vigil against the East by the will of God, was far from welcome to John. Actually he did not reply to it directly but very subtly found some other, more neutral response. In kindly fashion he began by recalling his own German experiences: he pointed out that, unlike his holy predecessor, Pius XII, he had never served as nuncio in Germany but nonetheless he had many good friends who were Germans. As if he were consistently following the same line of thought, he then spoke of his days as papal nuncio in Paris, when he had occupied himself with the fate of the German political and war prisoners in France: "Above all we were concerned with the German seminarists who were able to assemble in Chartres. And last year many of them who are now priests came to Castel Gandolfo to offer us their filial thanks. The West German government, too," the pope concluded, with a smile of satisfaction, "was pleased on one occasion to show us its appreciation of our priestly and paternal endeavors by conferring one of its high honors on us."

The pope having refused to have anything to do with the

concept of the *Wacht in Ost* and Adenauer's attempt to
obtain his blessing for the rearming of Germany having
come to nothing, a newspaperman asked Adenauer the next
day where the chancellor had gotten the revelation that
God had appointed the German people to defend Europe:
"Perhaps from Hitler?" the journalist suggested. Adenauer had a ready answer: "Not from Hitler. Actually, I
spoke of a 'duty' of the German people, without meaning
by that that it was God's chosen people. If you want to
know my source, the phrase is contained in a telegram
sent by Pius XII to President Theodor Heuss of West Germany in November of 1957."

Even before it was learned that Adenauer was a liar (in
the telegram sent by Pius XII to Heuss on November 23,
1957, there is not a word that could be interpreted as an
allusion to a mission or duty of the German people to wage
war against the East), it was easy to understand why he
should have been at odds with the pope, because John was
far removed from the world of Adenauer and other Germans and in fact from that of all nationalists of whatever
race. His reply to the chancellor was no improvisation. He
had long since written in one of his journals, under the
date of November 26, 1940, what might be taken as a
presage of that reply:

> Some have contended and still contend that God should pre-
> serve this or that nation and make it invulnerable and victorious
> because of the upright men who live in it or the good that is
> accomplished in it. They forget that, if God has in some way
> established nations, he has left states to the free decision of men.

Nationalism was repugnant to him, and all the more as
he was obliged to recognize, during the war years, that

"we are all more or less infected by nationalism, and even ecclesiastics serve it." And again, in his private notebook, he wrote:

The world is poisoned by an unhealthy nationalism based on race and blood, in contradiction of the Gospels. Especially on this point that is of the utmost timeliness: *Libera me de sanguinibus, Deus* [Set me free of blood, o Lord]. Jesus died for all nations, without distinctions of race or blood.

He returned to the same subject on October 25, 1942:

The Holy Church that I represent is the Mother of the nations, of all the nations. All persons with whom I come into contact have to admire in the pope's representative that feeling of respect for every man's nationality, embellished with good grace and merciful judgment, that earns universal confidence.

He was at that time in Istanbul, and in another journal he commented on a religious ceremony during which, out of respect to the country that was his host, he had blessed the faithful in Turkish. With a pleasant touch of humor he noted:

When the *Tanre mubarek olsun* [Blessed be the Lord] was recited, many people left in resentment. Among the grumblers were the Italians. I am quite satisfied: on Sunday the Gospel will be read in Turkish in the presence of the Ambassador of Italy, who, for that matter, is quite broad-minded. The Catholic Church respects everyone and makes no exceptions for anyone. The apostolic vicar is the bishop of all, and he intends to do honor to the Gospel, which admits no monopoly of nationality, refuses to be petrified, and looks to the future.

If this was the Church as John understood it, there seems to be no doubt that he was less restricted in showing its true face to the world after the sudden death of the headstrong, obstinate Cardinal Tardini, who as secretary of state was too resistant to John's innovations. He died during the night of July 30, 1961, and the pope, who was at Castel Gandolfo, was informed shortly before dawn. John dressed hastily, hurried to Rome, and went immediately to the room in which his associate had died. In his grief he prayed for a long time, and at noon he appeared at the window of his private office to announce the loss to the pilgrims gathered in St. Peter's Square: "Very early this morning the angel of death came into the papal palace and carried off with him Cardinal Secretary of State Domenico Tardini, who was the pope's closest and strongest arm in the government of Holy Church. Think how our heart is grieved . . ."

He spoke of his grief to Monsignor Alfredo Cavagna, his confessor, too, calling Tardini an outstanding servant of the Church. "He was a precious associate. Even if we did not agree at times, we knew that both of us sought the good of the Church." He added that Tardini's sudden death left him "absorbed and distracted in many and grave cares" of his ministry as the servant of the servants of God: "By other paths of unanticipated inspiration we are brought together round the fundamental principles of ecclesiastical sanctification." Actually he had at once chosen a new secretary of state because he considered the post too important to be left vacant even twenty-four hours. Tardini's funeral, long-drawn-out like all ceremonies in Saint Peter's, had consumed almost a whole day. Peter Nichols, an English correspondent for *The Times* of London, wrote in his book *The Politics of the Vatican* that on that very evening the pope had a telephone call put in for old Amleto Giovanni Cardinal Cicognani, who was already in his late seventies and who for twenty-five years, from 1933 to 1958, had been the apostolic delegate in the United States.

Cicognani had to be coaxed before he would accept the summons to go back to the Vatican at that late hour of the evening, but, in the last analysis, he could not refuse to obey. Very simply John told him that, during the obsequies for Tardini, he had looked round at the cardinals present and examined their faces one by one in an attempt to determine who could succeed the secretary of state. The choice had fallen on Cicognani. Cicognani hesitated, he gave evasive answers, vacillating perhaps; he said that he was already too old ("but you are two years younger than I," the pope objected), and in any case he wanted time to think. John went on talking for ten minutes more, explaining that he needed the help of an expert on the world of the Americas since he himself had never left Europe; and then he concluded by saying that Cicognani had certainly by now had enough time to think. Cicognani accepted.

He was indeed old—seventy-eight—and the choice seemed strange, a sign of a tendency in John to prefer the talents of old age—which are not always remarkable for their enlightenment or their openness—whereas the tradition of the Vatican called for the appointment of younger prelates to the onerous post of secretary of state. Moreover, Cicognani seemed too closely bound to the United States. During his long tenure in Washington his home there had become what American Catholic high society called "the little Vatican." It was feared therefore that the Holy See's policy would be closely coordinated with Washington's, and confirmation of this was seen in the fact that, making his first journey as secretary of state, Cicognani did indeed go to the United States, appearing

169

in Dallas, Texas, as the pope's legate to a local Catholic federation's convention.

But John was a man whose destiny it was to astonish. He upset all the anticipations and calculations with his encyclical *Pacem in terris,* which was to remain as his masterpiece, and which he wanted to address not only to the bishops, the clergy, and the faithful, but also to all men of good will, even if they were not baptized, even if they were hostile to religion. He said on April 9, announcing the encyclical,

> Universal peace is a goal that concerns everyone without distinction. On the brow of the encyclical shines the light of the divine revelation that gives its true substance to thought, but the doctrinal lines spring as well from the inmost needs of human nature and fall for the most part within the sphere of natural law.

He explained calmly that false doctrines on man's nature and destiny (that is, materialistic doctrines like Marxism) should not be identified or confused with the historical and political movements that might have found inspiration in them:

> . . . for once elaborated and defined, the doctrines remain the same forever; while the aforesaid movements, acting on constantly evolving historical situations, cannot help feeling their influences and therefore cannot help being subjected to quite profound changes. Moreover, who can deny that, to the extent to which they are interpreters of human beings' rightful aspirations, such movements contain positive elements worthy of approval?

From this logical statement he proceeded to its political application: "Therefore it can be shown that a reconciliation or a meeting of a practical nature, which might have been regarded yesterday as inopportune or not fruitful, may yet become timely and fruitful today or tomorrow." Whenever, therefore, political and diplomatic occasions suggested that initiatives of this kind be taken, it should be quite clear that, contrary to what had been proclaimed from Peter's throne during the years of the Cold War, the Church would raise no objections from the point of view of faith and doctrine. Indeed, by virtue of its utter supranational neutrality, it would always be favorable toward them. In addition John recommended the unwavering employment, especially in politics, "of language that is dignified and respectful to all." Earlier, in his June 1959 encyclical, *Ad Petri Cathedram,* there had been a charming parenthesis, "We wish to offend no one," and all the repeated exhortations to disarmament, to peace, to the abandonment of the use of force were made in a deferential, serenely courteous tone.

This was the language of dignity, but it was so unaccustomed that international opinion was bewildered by it, as if struck from behind. This relaxing language of the pope's seemed almost a betrayal of the Church.

Many were amazed, if not downright stunned [Father Georges Jarlot wrote]. Was not the most urgent problem after all that of the Communist threat to the West and to Christian civilization? Russia had the atomic bomb, she was about to match and surpass the United States in the conquest of space; China, with an incalculable population potential, was entering the arena of technological competition. The defense of the West was now the defense of Christianity!

In Italy *il Corriere d'informazione* published a satiric cartoon beneath a headline that distorted the title of the encyclical, *Pacem in terris,* into *Falcem in terris (Sickle on Earth)*, as if the pope had become the propagandist of Marxism and its symbols. When he saw the publication, John sighed. "Oh," he said, in dismay, "they really do not understand me." Nevertheless he was not too much upset: "No, I do not grieve over what is written or said about me. It is all in good faith, I pray for those people and I love them more than the others. Besides, I am lucky enough to forget everything right away." While not everyone was prepared to give up the crusader rhetoric of the Cold War, John himself stood firm in his old-fashioned Christian thinking: "If we call ourselves and are brothers, if we are all summoned to the same lot in this life and the next, how is it at all possible that some treat others as opponents and enemies?"

Monsignor Pietro Pavan, a teacher of social economics in the Papal University of the Lateran and one of the pope's collaborators in the preparation of the encyclical *Pacem in terris,* wrote that John's views in international politics were straightforward and indeed ingenuous. Since both major camps, the Western and the Soviet, asserted that they had embarked on the arms race solely for reasons of defense, the pope had to take judicial notice of this. He explained to Monsignor Pavan: "I must not doubt it—who can ever tell? I cannot attribute bad faith to one side or the other. If I did so, there would be no dialogue and all doors would be closed."

This was a high degree of simplicity, which was not ingenuousness in the sense of meager acumen or a tendency to let himself be gulled. It was optimism, but not a superficial view or ignorance of evil; it was optimism directed to the discovery of the good that John open-heartedly sought even where it might be concealed. Translated into politics, these moral attitudes led to the complete supranational neutrality of the Church, which, however, John wanted to be active:

This neutrality should not be understood in a purely passive sense [he said on the day when he was informed of the award of the Balzan peace prize] as if the pope's function were confined to observing events and preserving silence. It means, on the contrary, a neutrality that conserves all its force of testimony. . . . We have said this on many occasions: the action of the Church is not purely negative, it does not consist solely in exhorting governments not to have recourse to force of arms; it is an action that seeks to contribute to the training of men of peace, of men whose thoughts and hearts and hands are peaceful. The men of peace called blessed in the Gospel are not inactive: they are those who construct peace: *factores pacis* [peacemakers] (Matthew V:9).

The Cuban crisis of October 1962, which coincided almost perfectly with the inauguration of Vatican Council II, put the pope on guard and inspired him to an appeal to which even Khrushchev was not insensible:

While the Ecumenical Council has barely begun amid the joy and hope of all men of good will, see what menacing new clouds arise to darken the international horizon, sowing fear in millions of families. . . . Let those who feel the responsibilities of power, with their hands on their consciences, heed the cry of anguish that rises to heaven in every part of the earth, from innocent babes and old men, from isolated individuals and communities: Peace! Peace! We implore all who govern not to be deaf to this cry from mankind. Let them do all that is in their power to save peace: thus they will spare the world the horrors of a war of which no one can foresee the frightful consequences. . . . Let them persevere therefore in negotiations. To encourage, foster, accept negotiations at every level and at every time is the rule of wisdom and prudence that gains the blessings of heaven and deserves those of men.

If peace among men had not been preserved, the Council itself would have been meaningless, even when John hoped that it would be able to open new horizons to mankind. He had taken the occasion joyously, speaking openly with the foreign delegations, the separated brethren, the diplomats, and even, in some cases, going well beyond the limits of political prudence, one might say, in order to pour out his sincere joy in a purely pastoral sense. Indeed, one day, October 8, 1962, receiving Stepan Cardinal Wyszynski and the Polish bishops who had gone to Rome for the first session of the Council, John greeted them warmly, calling Poland the eternal victim of aggressions from East and West, a people martyred for freedom. As an Italian, he found it admirable that compatriots of his had contributed to Poland's independence, and as a claim to honor for his native diocese he recalled that Colonel Francesco Nullo of Bergamo, who had fought for Garibaldi ("and who had also defended the Roman Republic of 1849"), had gone to fight for Poland in 1862 and fallen heroically at Kraykawka. "You tell me," he added, "that resurrected Poland has erected monuments to this noble colonel and that streets have been named for him, as for example in Breslau in those western territories that you have recovered after centuries." Having embarked on the theme of freedom, he continued: "I have followed the efforts of your people, which is fighting for the inviolability of its frontiers. I have followed with emotion all the heroic efforts of your people."

These remarks were taken down by a stenographer and

translated into Polish and German; ultimately, of course, they came to the attention of the German ambassador to the Holy See. At this time Adenauer was still in power in Germany. He ordered his ambassador to the the Vatican, Hilger A. von Scherpenberg, to lodge a protest with the secretary of state because the Bonn government believed that the pope's remarks were tantamount to recognition of the Oder-Neisse boundary, which West Germany did not accept, since she claimed the Breslau region as German territory. Von Scherpenberg was received on October 15 by the deputy secretary of state, Monsignor Angelo Dell-'Acqua, whose reply left him speechless: "All the Holy Father's conversations with the Council fathers are covered by absolute secrecy." Hence the Holy See could neither confirm nor deny the statements attributed to the pope and in fact could not even take the matter into consideration.

At this reply, which he considered to be impudence, the ambassador protested that the pope's remarks were being circulated on paper bearing the imprint of the Press Office of the Council and were thus enjoying its credit. Monsignor Dell'Acqua replied that Cardinal Cicognani had already launched an investigation into the matter and found that the stationery had been improperly used at the instance of Cardinal Wyszynski's secretary, who should instead have used, if anything, the stationery of the Polish Bishops' Conference. This would have made it even more authoritative, von Scherpenberg suspected, and he reduced everything to one specific question: "Apart from the secrecy of the Holy Father's conversations with the Council fathers, apart from the stationery of the Press Office and the Polish Bishops' Conference, what at this moment is the position of the Holy See with respect to the territories formerly belonging to Germany and now incorporated into Poland?" Monsignor Dell'Acqua replied with magnificent imperturbability: "It is unchanged."

In actuality the Holy See had some time earlier resolved on *de facto* recognition of the new status of Poland's western territories. At one time these regions belonged to the German Dioceses of Breslau and Warmia, the *nullius* prelacy of Schneidemuehl, and, in lesser proportions, to other dioceses. In any event it was necessary to assure spiritual assistance and religious government for these faithful, and the Holy See had entrusted the responsibility to Cardinal Wyszynski as metropolitan, establishing four new Polish dioceses: Opol, under Monsignor Franz Jop; Olszryn, under Monsignor Tomas Wilczynski; Breslau, under Monsignor Boleslav Kominek; and Gorzov, under Monsignor Wilhelm Pluta. Monsignor Dell'Acqua had no trouble reeling off all these names for Adenauer's unfortunate ambassador, but at the same time he pointed out that it was a matter only of *de facto* recognition, since the Holy See always follows the rule of "not making final changes in diocesan boundaries until possible questions of international law involving those territories have been resolved through treaties that have been completely ratified."

In the light of this formal, official statement, the ambassador had to concede that the Vatican's point of view had indeed remained unchanged: recognition of the state of fact, while still lacking the conditions (the peace treaty with Germany) that would make possible its transformation into recognition *de jure*. Later the pope inquired as to the effects of this little diplomatic mixup, which revived Adenauer's distaste toward him, and he was perhaps amazed but certainly very pleased to learn that the Bonn government, having taken note of the word "unchanged," declared that it regarded this as satisfactory in every way and thus the incident was closed. "God be thanked," John said to Monsignor Dell'Acqua. "We have told the truth, that we do not like nationalism, and we have been rewarded. May it please the Lord always to assist us so."

VIII

An Opening Toward
the East

"I am emulating Christ!"
Relations between the Vatican and the Soviet Union.
Khrushchev's congratulations
on John's eightieth birthday.
John's prayer for the Soviet cosmonauts.
Khrushchev's daughter and son-in-law visit the pope.
Khrushchev to go to Rome?

WHEN Pius XII was on the throne it was taken for granted in the Vatican that the Catholic Church must rely for its defense on the Western nations, not on the basis of treaties or concordats but for reasons of fact. The people's democracies were antagonistic to the clergy and restricted freedom of worship, whereas the Western democracies, even those with Protestant or secular traditions, showed respect for the Holy See and in addition were capable of gratitude if they received support from it. Hence the Vatican's doors were always open to the politicians of the Atlantic bloc and barred to those from the East. In other words, the Church took sides in international affairs as it did in Italian domestic politics.

John too was persuaded of the necessity for a Christian crusade, but he wanted it to have a religious authenticity of its own and not to be confused with political, to say nothing of military, campaigns. Moreover, he was in no doubt as to the outcome of any confrontation, and, as a fearless Christian, he was not given to dramatization. "Yes, we are face to face with Goliath the giant," he said one day to the pontifical missionary commission, "but perhaps we waste too many words that might better be used in prayer. We find ourselves confronted by someone who seems colossal: but he is not strong, he is not sound, for he engages in undertakings of error, of greed, of vio-

181

lence. Nor should we suppose that a victory for this Goliath must necessarily mean death and universal devastation, because even in his domains souls survive that are nurtured on the same illumination as ours; they remain faithful or they are close to us in their participation in the same Christian ideal."

On the other hand he was deeply distressed, to the limits of his sensibilities, by the thought that there were so many men of good will in the world whom the Church condemned or outlawed or rejected when in one way or another they could be brought closer to the Church. "But I am emulating Christ!" he cried one day, pointing to the crucifix on his desk. "I am emulating Christ, and I open my arms wide to them. I am their father and I love them, and therefore I am always ready to receive them." This was attested to by the archbishop of Cambrai, Monsignor Emile-Maurice Guerry, whom the pope had received for a confidential talk. "Monsignor," John continued, pointing his index finger at the archbishop, "not all the requirements of the Gospel have been understood!"

John's so-called advances toward the Soviet world had no other inspiration or purpose, but, for all that they were solely evangelical in the most exclusive fashion, they represented a politically arduous undertaking, given the fact that the atmosphere in the Vatican was what it had been in the time of Pius XII with respect to relations with the Eastern countries, which were still regarded as a kind of other world, the kingdom of Antichrist. Therefore there was great surprise when, John having become pope, one of the first actions of the papal diplomats was to "thank" (this is the verb employed in the Vatican by way of relieving someone of an obligation or releasing him from an offer) the ambassadors of the exiled Polish and Lithuanian "white" governments—respectively, Casimir Papée and Stanislas Girdvainis. They alone, among all the diplomats accredited to the Holy See, did not receive the ritual invitations to present themselves to the new pope.

Both protested, complaining that the Vatican was thus impairing its own resistance to Communism in Eastern Europe, as well as implicitly recognizing the annexation of Lithuania by the Soviet Union. The action with respect to Papée, however, had been requested by the primate of Poland himself, Cardinal Wyszynski, who argued that by maintaining relations with a phantom government the Vatican was injuring the cause of Catholics living in a country ruled by a government in being. Wyszynski, whom Pius XII had accused of surrender to the pressures of the Warsaw government, or at least of imprudent compromises, was certainly neither a coward nor yet an opportunist. Nevertheless he had no wish to identify the fate of his Church with the political ideals of Polish reaction; and, since in any case he had to maintain day-to-day relations with the government and the Communist Party of his country, he found himself in a position weakened, or, worse still, made equivocal, by the mere presence of Papée at the Vatican.

The foundation for the "thanks," or exoneration, extended to Papée and Girdvainis could not be faulted. Their accreditation to the Holy See dated from 1939, and in 1958, unfortunately, neither of them could present new, up-to-date accreditation that would be legally valid. They were informed that they could continue to come and go in the sacred papal edifices, where no one entertained the slightest doubt as to their personal merits, but they could no longer do so in their official uniforms in view of the fact that unhappily they were not in a position to "present documents," as *l'Osservatore romano* put it with admirable technical precision on January 5, 1956, "that could be recognized as diplomatically valid within the meaning of international law."

In substance, however, no change was made in the situation by this kind of formalism. When it became known during the summer that Khrushchev was about to visit the United States, the news was regarded as ominous in the Vatican. The Holy See was still distrustful of any policy leading to *détente,* and in any event it was hoped that the meeting between Khrushchev and Eisenhower would not produce any substantial results. *L'Osservatore* said on August 12:

> Day-to-day problems and the general interests behind them are what they are, and the positions of both sides are rigid: any possible agreement would presuppose major concessions on one side or the other, and there is no ground for believing that retreat is possible either by the United States or by the Soviet Union.

Actually the Holy See was still hoping that, for lack of an agreement, the two sides would continue in the existing state of tension, which the Vatican had always regarded as the lesser evil or at least the necessary evil in a world infested with ineradicable Communism. Nevertheless there was always a psychological danger, and indeed *l'Osservatore* declared that the improbability of an understanding between the United States and the Soviet Union in no way diminished the success of Communist diplomacy, which had succeeded in initating a dialogue with the greatest of the Western powers.

Dialogue was looked on at this time as a trap intended to snap shut on anyone rash enough to venture into it. Cardinal Tardini, secretary of state, continued with unremitting contempt to rebuff every such opportunity that offered, so that all the Soviet Union's attempts at communication were reduced to a kind of serenade beneath the windows of the apostolic palaces, which remained as tightly sealed as in the days of Pius XII. On January 14, 1960, for example, after Khrushchev had announced to the Supreme Soviet that the Soviet Union was about to make a massive reduction in its armaments, the text of his speech was distributed through diplomatic channels to every country in the world. Moscow wanted the pope too to have a copy, but, since normal diplomatic relations between Russia and the Holy See did not exist, the Soviet Embassy in Rome was instructed to request the papal nuncio in Italy, Monsignor Carlo Grano, to make certain that the document was carried past the bronze gate.

By virtue of the code established by the Congress of Vienna in 1815, the papal nuncio is always the dean of the accredited diplomatic corps in every country, and as such he is obliged to maintain formal relations with all his colleagues, even if they are the representatives of governments with which the Holy See does not maintain official relations. Monsignor Grano was certainly not derelict in his formal obligations, but the only reply that was made to the Soviet request, which, in the last analysis, was an act of deference, was a labored feature story in *l'Osservatore romano* in which, among the various jokes, witticisms, and suspicions inspired by the occasion, the author remarked that, speech or no speech by Khrushchev to the

Supreme Soviet, the Soviet Union would always be armed to the teeth in order to devour the universe.

This was the period just before President Gronchi's visit to Moscow, and there was also talk that Eisenhower was going to reciprocate Khrushchev's trip to the United States. So-called political circles asserted that the Vatican actively disapproved of Gronchi's journey although it was prepared to resign itself passively to the thought of Eisenhower's. The version put out by the supposedly well informed, the presumed intimates of the secretary of state, had it that the pope himself looked with favor on meetings among the highest leaders, those who really enjoyed authority and influence over the world's destinies; and it was pointed out that such a statement implicitly approved Eisenhower's visit and cast doubt on Gronchi's, since he had less authority and in every case less influence on the fate of the world.

It was specifically in anticipation of this second journey that Cardinal Ottaviani went to the Basilica of Santa Maria Maggiore and, in a speech after Mass, denounced it with the usual terrorist diction that was still being employed in the Vatican after John's accession, with the same instinctive naturalness as before.

The change did not come until September of 1961. Cardinal Tardini had been dead a month, and the Berlin wall had been erected a few weeks earlier. John was at Castel Gandolfo, and on the morning of September 10, at the conclusion of a Mass celebrated in invocation of peace, he made a speech that reiterated the ageless exhortations of all popes. For example, he said that governments should bear in mind the terrible responsibilities that were theirs "not only in the sight of history but also in the judgment of God." He urged leaders not to yield to deceptive and erroneous pressures, he reminded them that law was paramount to force, and he called for policy of disarmament, justice, and peace.

In this address, in a word, there was nothing remarkable, but Khrushchev attempted to take advantage of it for the initiation of communication with the Church, and his gamble was a success. He arranged for a press conference at which Soviet journalists would ask him what he thought of the pope's appeal, and his replies were prominently displayed in *Pravda* and *Izvestia* in addition to being distributed abroad by the Tass news agency. By way of a start Khrushchev said that he had read the pope's speech with interest, and this in itself was a major matter, since it was a public statement by a Soviet leader. What came next, however, was more important:

> The concern for peace that the pope manifests is proof that understanding is constantly growing abroad that impetuosity and adventurism in world politics cannot lead to anything good. Obviously the head of the Catholic Church takes into consideration the feelings of millions of Catholics in all parts of the world who are perturbed by the military preparations of the imperialists.

Unquestionably Catholics ought to have been concerned by worldwide military preparations, without distinguishing between imperialists and non-imperialists, but Khrushchev, who apparently had his own propaganda requirements, continued:

> John XXIII pays tribute to reason when he warns governments against a universal catastrophe and exhorts them to recognize their tremendous responsibilities in the sight of history. His appeal is a good omen. In our age, since man possesses the most destructive means of slaughtering people, it is forbidden to play

with the fates of nations. Fear of God's judgment, of which the pope speaks, has nothing to do with the matter. As a Communist and an athetist, I do not believe in divine providence. But, since we have always been and will always be in favor of a peaceful solution to conflicts, when a call comes from any quarter to negotiate in the interests of peace, we can only welcome it. And now I wonder whether fervent Catholics such as John Kennedy, Konrad Adenauer, and so many others will be capable of interpreting correctly the pope's warning.

This statement was not exactly a model of its kind, because it indicates an excess of smugness on the part of Khrushchev, who viewed the pope's message as addressed exclusively to the imperialist powers. Offense could also have been taken at the superfluous and gratuitous proclamation of atheism, and indeed *l'Osservatore romano* declared that John's message was directed to all governments and all nations and refrained from sitting in judgment on any specific situations. "By virtue of its apostolic inspiration and therefore of its universal application," it was impermissible to interpret it "in a single sense." In any event, for the first time in its history as the mouthpiece of the Holy See, *l'Osservatore* went as far as to say that there was a positive aspect to the Soviet statements, and that was the recognition of the peaceful and peacemaking function of the Catholic Church: "It is an admission that is in direct contradiction to the image broadcast by well-known propaganda—the image of a church guided only by political aims and subservient to the powers responsible for international conflicts."

This Russian admission was no novelty, since even during the reign of Pius XII the then Soviet Foreign Minister Andrei Gromyko had similarly if not indeed even more broadly paid tribute to the Catholic Church as a friend of peace. Hence, if there had been any change in attitude, the change had been the Vatican's, not the Kremlin's. The archbishop of Bologna, Giacomo Cardinal Lercaro, on the other hand, pointed out that notice must be taken of "a new fact, a significant fact, a change in attitude that seems to have occurred in the Kremlin with regard to the Church of Rome." Efforts were made to ascertain the factual basis for his discovery of the so-called change in the Kremlin's "attitude," but on this point the cardinal's response was not exhaustive. It was learned that he had been received by the pope a few days previously, but on the other hand all the intrepid *monsignori* of the Vatican's Secretariat of State, whenever they were asked on what John thought he could base his conviction, what new event had occurred in the Kremlin, replied innocently that the pope made his judgments with the simplicity of one who places hope even in the smoking of a slender wick, who looks anxiously for any sign, however minimal: "In that vast wall that seemed to rise like a fortress between the father and his millions of faraway children a chink has now begun to appear, even though it be of the smallest." Observers questioned what, concretely, were even minimal signs, what were the slender wicks: "For the present even the politeness, the good manners, the deference can be sufficient. These do not yet amount to cordiality, but, after so much display of indifference, they must be counted as change in a world that seemed even in its outward forms to have fallen back exclusively on the overbearing arrogance of its own strength."

The spirit of such words was very much John's, even if it is not permissible to ascribe them directly to that source. There was also the rumor that John had evolved a certain project of international politics that would have entailed new decisions to be made by Italy: supposedly she would have to free herself from bloc politics and show the world new paths of utter supranational neutrality on the model of the Church. In 1960, while Tardini was still alive, John had had this message conveyed to prominent figures in Italian politics, suggesting that it was time to adopt a new course in international affairs as soon as the fall of Tambroni's government had put an end to the hopes of the "nationalist" Right. The pope asserted that this would enhance Italy's international prestige, and, when it was pointed out to him that Italy would thus slip ultimately into the most obvious of political positions, neutralism, he retorted: "I understand. Neutralism is a very ugly word that does not adequately express what I am trying to say: neutrality."

Even if Italy was not inclined to take the course of neutrality, John's efforts toward a *détente* found other outlets. On November 25, 1961, the pope's eightieth birthday, Khrushchev sent him a congratulatory message by way of the Soviet Embassy in Italy. The next day—it was a Sunday—Gurgoyen Agayame, the first secretary of the embassy, asked to be received by the papal nuncio, Monsignor Carlo Grano, and gave him the message, thus creating for Grano a new problem that was diplomatically difficult of solution. According to custom, he could have refused the message: but, in contrast to the usual circumstances—since it was not a question of a political document—it would have been inappropriate to react with rudeness to a gesture of courtesy.

It appears that Monsignor Grano conducted himself with great talent, or so at least it was thought by experts in diplomatic virtuosity. He did in fact accept the Soviet message and even keep it, because he allowed it to remain lying on his desk when Agayame was making his farewell; but in reality, preserving what diplomats call the substance of the forms, he behaved as if he had not received it. With extreme subtlety, Monsignor Grano did not ask the secretary of state for an appointment in order to convey the message to the proper person: but, taking advantage of the purely fortuitous circumstance that he was expected to go to the Vatican that very Sunday evening for certain spiritual exercises, he put the Kremlin's message into his briefcase "and thus it wound up with the secretary of state and then on the pope's desk," as the ingenious Vatican spokesmen explained in their attempt to make it appear that everything fell into place through mysterious coincidences of fate.

In any event, fate was quite obliging. Indeed, John's reaction when he had read the message was instantaneous. Signed by Ambassador Semyon Kozyrev and addressed to Monsignor Grano, the document read:

In accordance with instructions that I have received from Mr. Nikita Khrushchev, I beg you to convey to His Holiness, John XXIII, on the occasion of his eightieth birthday anniversary, my congratulations and my sincere wishes for his good health and for success in his noble ambition of contributing to the reinforcement and consolidation of peace on earth through the solution of international problems by means of frank negotiations.

His Holiness, John XXIII, decided to reply at once to Nikita Khrushchev, and the next day, Monday the twenty-seventh, Monsignor Mario Cagna, counselor to the papal nunciature in Italy, rang the bell at the gate of Via Gaeta 5, the Soviet Embassy in Rome, to present the pope's thanks over the signature of the nuncio, Monsignor Grano. This note said:

His Holiness, Pope John XXIII, presents his thanks for your good wishes and expresses to the entire Russian people his sincere hope for the development and consolidation of world peace through happy concords of human brotherhood. To this end he offers fervent prayers.

In the light of the prevailing climate, this first contact—more or less direct—was of remarkable importance, and precisely because of its great novelty no one among the authorized official or semi-official sources felt competent to comment on it; on the contrary, all of them tried to keep it as concealed as possible from public knowledge. *L'Osservatore romano* and the Vatican radio, for example, were absolutely silent on the subject, and so, of course, was *Il Quotidiano*, the official journal of Catholic Action.

"It is still essential to proceed with caution," it was explained. "Many of the faithful, the simplest of mind, would not understand at all, since they are not yet prepared to grasp the meaning of these changes." In Moscow too, for that matter, the identical pattern of silence was maintained with respect to this gracious exchange of greetings between Khrushchev and the pope. The Kremlin decided to make no public disclosure of it because sending greetings to the pope was more or less the same as going to church: "And to church no atheist goes, for any reason. No policy, no diplomacy has anything to do with it. Atheists do not go to church." This was what Khrushchev had said in America by way of justifying his refusal to accompany Eisenhower to a Sunday religious service in the United Reformed Trinity Church near Camp David in September

1959. The remark showed that Khrushchev was well aware
of the political realities connected with religious activities,
and it was precisely for this reason that political significance ought to be attributed to the act of sending birthday
greetings.

A few months later it was John's turn to send good
wishes: for the success of the journey in space then being
undertaken by the Soviet cosmonauts Nikolayev and Popo-
vitch. During a general audience in Saint Peter's he said
poetically that the angel of God was consecrating the con-
junction of heaven and earth, of the divine and the human:

> At this time we should like to join in the intentions of our
> prayers the young pilots in space. Beloved sons belonging to all
> peoples, you are gathered here as good brothers while the pilots,
> in a virtually decisive and certainly determining fashion, are test-
> ing man's moral, intellectual, and physical capabilities, and they
> are continuing that exploration of creation that the Holy Scripture
> encourages in its earliest pages: *Ingredimini super terram et re-
> plete eam* [Go forth over the earth and replenish it] (Genesis
> IX:1–7). The nations, and in particular the younger generations,
> are following the progress of the marvelous launchings and navi-
> gations in space with enthusiasm. Oh, how we wish that these ven-
> tures might assume the significance of homage paid to God the
> creator and supreme lawgiver!

Perhaps for political reasons, but more probably out of
ordinary vulgarity, John's greeting was tastelessly returned
by the two young pilots, who, as soon as they were back
on earth, indulged themselves in more or less uncalled-for
assertions of their atheism. They said that they had
traveled the length and breadth of the sky and encountered
neither God nor the angels there. This was playing into
the hands of Cardinal Ottaviani, the belittler of the cosmonauts "who think they can sweep clean the skies with

their exploits in space." In any event, there was frequent repetition of a question that was also a reproach to the trusting pope always ready to see in everything providential auspices that were more than debatable: "Was it really essential that the pope give his blessing to such unworthy cosmonauts?"

This time the Vatican's reply was exemplary, even if it was not official in nature. *L'Osservatore romano* said that the very frequency and insistency of atheist propaganda proved the persistence of a strong religious sentiment in the Soviet Union. Then it pointed out that

> . . . the pope's greeting and benediction are understood in the spirit by which they were inspired—that is, the Christian spirit, the spirit of love, which is far above any political ideology, and, again in accordance with the Christian spirit, it matters little that they were poorly reciprocated by the brave but ill-bred cosmonauts (who, poor fellows, said what they had been ordered to say) even if many persons who do not think about these matters may still be perplexed by a benediction of persons who do not believe and who allow themselves to be the tools of antireligious propaganda.

There were still many prejudices to be overcome, however, and in fact, when it became known in the spring of 1963 that John had received Khrushchev's daughter and son-in-law, Rada and Alexis Adzhubei, at the Vatican, feeling ran so high that the Jesuits' publication, *Civiltà cattolica*, deemed it necessary to publish an article in explanation and justification of the pope's action. As the rule required, galley proofs were sent to the pontiff for his prior reading and approval; but John did not want the article published. This time, he said, such concern to justify the pope was uncalled for: "I have no need to be defended."

He felt that he had every right to receive Khrushchev's son-in-law, who had asked for the audience, and John was not afraid of any unpleasant consequences: "An athetist? what can he say to me, at the very worst? That the Church is finished, dead; and I will tell him that that is not true."

In the Vatican, however, efforts were made to disguise the audience in one way or another. It had been requested directly from Moscow at the time of the award of the Balzan Peace Prize to the pope on March 7, 1963. The prize committee had included four Soviet academicans, all of whom had voted for John. Then a warmly phrased official message was sent to the pope: "The Soviet government and its prime minister, Nikita Khrushchev, value to the highest degree the pontiff's endeavors to foster the cause of peace among all peoples." The climate was such and the direction of the pope's thinking was so clear that the audience could not be refused. The protocol division, however, let it be known that Adzhubei's presence in the Vatican could be possible only because of his status as a journalist—editor in chief and special correspondent of *Izvestia*—and as such he would take part in a collective audience granted to forty-eight Italian and foreign newspapermen.

Mr. and Mrs. Adzhubei did in fact take part in the group audience, sitting in the third of the four rows of chairs. The pope spoke to the group about the complete supranational neturality of the Church, and, before withdrawing, he paid some compliment to each person present. He was talking with an Australian and voicing his regret that distance would probably always prevent him from visiting that country, when it was observed that the Adzhubeis had been separated from the group and had vanished. At

195

the same time the antechambers and the threshold of the pope's private library were cleared, and all spectators who might have lined the short passage from room to room had been removed.

These were specific precautions intended to maintain secrecy concerning the reception of the Adzhubeis, but their only effect, of course, was to establish it as a certainty whereas until a short time earlier it had still been regarded as uncertain. The audience was actually held, it lasted eighteen minutes, and it was learned that the pope had seated Khrushchev's relatives in two armchairs in a corner of the library. Mrs. Adzhubei, according to custom, had covered her head in a black scarf trimmed with gold sequins along the edges, and she said later that she had constantly smiled and nodded as John spoke, though without being able to say very much in reply: "When the pope rose from his chair, I looked at his hands as he greeted us and blessed us, and I wanted to tell him that his hands were peasant hands, like my father's. Of course I did not have the courage to tell him so, but it is really true. I looked closely at his hands again when he was giving us symbolic gifts—for me, for Alexis, and for my father. Then he said to me: 'This is for your papa.' "

The symbolic gift to Mrs. Adzhubei, the atheist daughter of atheists, was a blessed rosary, and John said to her: "My associates have explained to me that I am supposed to give a non-Catholic princess either two medals or two gold coins. Instead I give you this rosary so that it may be known that, in addition to the great prayers of the psalms, the pope also says this family prayer, which he learned at the fireside while his mother was cooking dinner, which was always very poor and frugal. It is the prayer that the pope says every day for all the children who are born into the world so that each of them, Catholic or not, may find a blessing and salvation." Then, more directly, he added: "You tell me, *signora,* that you are an atheist; but it will not offend you, will it? to have an old man's blessing for your children. What are their names?" Shyly Mrs. Adzhubei murmured: "Nikita, Alexis, and Ivan." "What fine names!" the pope commented. "Ivan, that's fine, he is my namesake. When you return home, kiss your children for me, and particularly Ivan, without making the others jealous."

Adzhubei too was tongue-tied, and he kept glancing at his interpreter, Alexis Makov, the Rome correspondent of *Izvestia* and the Soviet Embassy's cultural attaché. But Makov too was silent, and the translations had to be made by Father Kulik of the Russian Institute of Rome. John, meanwhile, had gone over to his relaxed, even if not impeccable, French, and in that language he recited the verses from Genesis on the creation of the world, concluding fittingly: "So the first age was the age of light: the light of my eyes met the light of yours. May the Lord bless the road of good will, if such be his pleasure." Then John gave Adzhubei a personal message for Khrushchev, already written in Russian and signed by him in Cyrillic characters: "Johannes PP. XXIII"; the whole was adorned with the keys of paradise, crossed, tied, and surmounted by the tiara that symbolizes the triple pontifical power of the father of kings and princes, the chancellor of the world, and the vicar of Christ. Showing it to his Soviet press colleagues and discussing it with them, Adzhubei seemed to be attempting to make some joke on the subject, as if to maintain his integrity as a Communist atheist, but in the end he was constrained to say: "As for my father-in-law, I can tell you only that the pope asked me to thank him for the attentive attitude that he has always had toward him. Then he gave me an envelope covered with a number of seals. As for the pope, I must say that he is a man of great and genuine simplicity. You open your eyes, you take a long look at him, and suddenly you are filled with profound respect for him and at the same time with unexpected trust."

Even if he jested somewhat, then, Adzhubei made no secret of his pleasure in the success that he had had. The message and the signature were the crown of the policy of conciliation followed by the Soviet Union and the Catholic Church, and indeed the pope was unreservedly reproved by the so-called right-thinking and God-fearing people who found him guilty of the most culpable naïveté in his readiness to see the most unlikely signs of Providence where there were only the propaganda and speculation of an enemy with whom there must be no dealings: "*Adzhubei, qui tollis peccata mundi* (Adzhubei, who taketh away the sins of the world)," the irreverent chanted, but Pope John was untroubled by them. "Perhaps I delude myself," he said one evening to Monsignor Capovilla, "but it could also be a direct thread of Providence, and I do not have the right to break it."

He was encouraged, too, by the reception that the Soviet press had given to his encyclical, *Pacem in terris.* Tass had quoted long excerpts from it, commenting:

The new encyclical that Pope John XXIII has addressed to the clergy, to Christians, and to all men of good will has aroused a tremendous echo in the entire world because it is dedicated to problems that preoccupy mankind, and above all the preservation of peace on our planet. Hence it is understandable that the section devoted to relations among states has stimulated particularly keen interest among all international observers, including atheists and non-Catholics.

On April 22 Khrushchev granted an interview to Italo Pietra, editor in chief of *Il Giorno*, saying, among other things:

> We cannot refuse to take account of the position of Pope John XXIII. Many are aware today that the pope, in contrast to certain of his predecessors, has a realistic position on a number of the most crucial problems of our epoch, and in particular on that of peace and disarmament. . . . We Communists do not accept any religious concept: but at the same time we believe that in the interests of the preservation of peace all forces must be united.

The Soviet radio and press served as the chorus for the interview, and subsequently it lent credence to the insistently circulating rumor that Khrushchev was going to visit the pope in August.

The Deutsche Presseagentur, a West German news agency, distributed a story dealing with work and preparations under way in the papal palace of Castel Gandolfo for Khrushchev's welcome, but a Vatican spokesman expressed astonishment, saying that there was no need "to renovate the palace," as the DPA had reported, because all needed restoration had been carried out in earlier years. The delicacy of the phraseology by which both confirmation and denial were avoided was in the best tradition of the Curia, and it was clever too in its ironic digression from the major subject to a minor detail; so the story of the meeting was thus made the more believable. There was talk of a form of tactical coexistence that would be initiated by the Church and the Soviet Union, and the Vatican replied that coexistence is neither tactical nor strategic but arises from the reciprocal recognition of respective existences. If a new chapter was destined to be initiated in the history of Vatican relations, the aim of the Church was nothing more or less than the attainment of that "honorable coexistence in truth" that Pope Pius XII of sainted memory had already expressed as an aspiration in his radio message to the world on December 23, 1950: "How the Church desires to cooperate in smoothing the way to this contact among peoples! To her East and West do not represent opposing principles but share in a common heritage to which both have contributed mightily and are called again to contribute in the future!"

The invocation of the late pope whose inflexible crusader intransigence was recalled with regret by all those who feared possible surrenders by the reigning pope was a felicitous stroke of political acumen. No less welcome was a second quotation employed at the same period, not of papal rhetoric this time but of American opinion as expressed in the Jesuit publication of the United States, *America*, which seemed to encourage the new course: "The pope and his collaborators well know what perils exist in negotiations with the Soviets, but the Church can never slight any possibility of regularizing or improving communications between the Holy See and the Catholics of any country."

This was not enough to prove that the meeting would be held, but it was certain that preparations for it were under way before John's health broke. Furthermore, his diary entry of December 26, 1962, confirms that he himself had been preparing for it for some time; he was even planning to learn some Russian words and sentences in order to be able to welcome his guest properly. "Tonight," he wrote in his diary, "after much meditation and a reading of the introduction to Ettore Lo Gatto's Russian grammar (which Monsignor Capovilla gave me yesterday as a Christmas gift), I got out of bed and, kneeling before the Crucified, I consecrated my life in ultimate sacrifice of my entire being for whatever He desired of me for this great undertaking of the conversion of Russia to the Catholic Church." His confessor, Monsignor Cavagna, too, had some knowledge of this: "Just in these last months," he recalled on the day of John's death, "he showed me a Russian grammar, telling me that, since he already knew a little Slavic, it would be easy for him to learn at least a few words in Russian and by this means too to show how much he loved that great people, for his reaffirmation of the divine redeemer's words was unremitting: *Non veni vocare justos sed peccatores* (I came to call not the just but the sinner)."

IX

The Separated Brethren

John the good Catholic.
The Anglican archbishop of Canterbury at the Vatican.
The situation of non-Catholics in Italy.
"Holiness, we are making history."
The Secretiat for Christian unity.
Protestants and Orthodox at the Council.
"In my heart you will find much more
than in my words."
Excess of pomp in Saint Peter's.

THE return of all Christians to a single fold in which they would be united under a single shepherd was one of John's great dreams. *"Et alias oves habeo quae non sunt ex hoc ovili* [And other sheep I have, which are not of this fold]," he would say in the words of the Gospel (John X:16). In the exaltation of his faith he strove passionately for the achievement of unity among the churches, but in practical fact, because of the healthy realism that was his unfailing talent, he cherished few illusions. First of all he was aware, even in the circle of his closest collaborators, of a certain spirit of distrust and resistance toward any possible "pro-unification openings" in the direction of non-Catholics, and he fully recognized that the very term, "pro-unification opening," represented opposition. In the second place, although he himself was not inclined to ascribe importance to the historical-theological reasons for the division, which to him must have seemed little more than opportunist in the eyes of God, he nevertheless knew that they had left incrustations on Christianity that it would be difficult to remove nothing but the ardor of evangelical *caritas.*

What was more, he was not at all disposed to abdicate the primacy that the Catholic Church has always claimed for itself. In even the most "ecumenical" of his utterances, there was never a shadow of so-called theological concordism or of the equally deprecated practical pan-Christianism. In all his enthusiasm, in all his zeal of charity to hasten the era of union, John never omitted to point out that it was the Catholic Church that had been willed by Christ: "We therefore believe that the church for which Our Lord prayed and sacrificed himself on the cross, and to which He has pledged His eternal presence, has always been and remains *one, holy, Catholic,* and *apostolic,* as it was established." In other words, and specifically by way of reply to the charges that were always being lodged against him by the reactionaries, Pope John had to be acknowledged as a good Catholic; and such a statement should not seem foolish or contradictory.

The Anglicans were the first to give him credit for this, and one day Doctor Geoffrey Francis Fisher, archbishop of Canterbury, said that John "was careful always to reassure the Catholic Church: the dogmas would not be touched, they would remain as intact and strong as the columns of Saint Peter's. But there is considerable space between one column and the next," Fisher pointed out, correctly interpreting the pope's thinking, "and it is possible to move about in it without having to touch them." In the closed circle of the Vatican, however, the suspicion persisted, as a typical episode shows. When John heard that Sir Marcus Cheke, the British minister to the Holy See and an Anglican by religion, was nearing death, the pope had the spontaneous wish to pay him a visit and try to comfort him. When Sir Marcus saw him at the bedside, he thanked the pope "for the honor that he was thus paying to Her Majesty, the Queen of England" (later, returning to the Vatican in his car, the pope had smiled in affectionate appreciation of this modesty), and added that "anyway" he was proud to offer his life for Christian unity. "But do not concern yourself with that," John replied. "Just tell me one thing: may I bless you?" "Yes, thank you." "Good; and now the Lord will take care of the rest. Let us say the *Pater Noster* together." When John was back in the Vatican, several persons asked Monsignor Capovilla: "Did the Englishman convert, at least?" "But that was not the purpose of the visit," Monsignor Capovilla objected, only to be told, in one form or another: "Perhaps not, but this pope with those devilish Anglicans . . ."

If non-Catholic Christians were still the targets of such angry or contemptuous epithets in the apostolic palace, it was because for centuries the Vatican had omitted to carry through to the end a survey of the historical position of Catholicism. It still behaved as if the Church had not suffered the major amputations of the Reformation and the schisms, or as if these had been mere random occurrences of which no account need be taken and the Church of Rome could continue to be regarded as not only the majority but also the unchallengeable, above all criticism. This was a presumption, an arrogance based on nonexistent or arbitrarily stated facts, backed by a simple artifice similar to the assumptions as to the Catholic loyalty of the masses simply because of the statistics on baptisms.

John was more concerned with truth and therefore more demanding. Even many years before his election to the papacy, when he was still the apostolic delegate in Turkey, he had had occasion to remark at Epiphany in 1938:

> Look at this country of Turkey. For so many generations it was the scene of the highly dramatic life of the Church: here the ancient dioceses were as numerous as the stars in the sky. Now everything has vanished and it is difficult merely to be certain of names.

Hence, in the Lord's plans, what is purely material and mutable in its nature is of no importance. . . . When the tempest blows, it shakes the most solid structures, it lays waste, it changes everything. Nothing matters. In the Lord's designs everything serves for his glory, everything corresponds to his doctrine, which purifies and renews the generations of man.

Not everyone could understand this, for understanding would have required far more faith than generally inspires the souls of Christians. This was demonstrated when John received Doctor Fisher, the archbishop of Canterbury, on the morning of December 2, 1960. It was the first time in more than four hundred years that an archbishop of Canterbury had come to talk with a Roman pontiff. The last previous such occasion had occurred in 1414, when the Englishman was the Earl of Arundel, the savage persecutor and burner of Lollard heretics, but, on the other hand, the pope by whom he was received was in truth only an anti-pope, one of the four who at the time were contesting for Peter's throne: in fact, he was that same Baldassare Coscia who had assumed the same name later chosen by Pope Roncalli: John XXIII.

The arcana of Providence are indeed mysterious. In any case, a new visit to Saint Peter's by an Anglican seemed almost a scandal to many Catholics, including collaborators of the pope. *Noi uomini (We Men)*, a Catholic Action magazine, printed an article composed entirely of suspicions and seeded with disobliging allusions both to Doctor Fisher personally and to the Anglican Church in general. Even *Civiltà cattolica,* the Jesuits' fortnightly, adopted a position of distrustful aloofness. Left to itself, the publication would have preferred to ignore the matter completely, and it was only as a result of pressures brought to bear by

208

the secretary of state that the Jesuits honored the special
vow of obedience to the pope that they solemnly pronounce
in addition to their other priestly vows. Consequently
Father Roberto Tucci wrote an extremely cautious article
in which he acknowledged that the Anglican reform is one
of the least distant from Catholic positions because it has
preserved

> . . . a rather striking appreciation of the visible Church, an
> ecclesiastical structure founded on the bishops, a quite rich liturgi-
> cal piety, a theology that in general does not neglect the most
> ancient tradition and that is therefore alien to the unlimited exer-
> cise of the principle of unhindered exploration of Scripture: but
> this, of course, is not enough to heal the deep differences.

Caution was manifested on the Anglican side too. The
initiative for the meeting had been taken by the archbishop
of Canterbury in the spring of 1960, when he had written
to a personal friend, Jan Bernard Alfrink, archbishop of
Utrecht and one of the most progressive of the cardinals,
to say that he was planning to visit the Orthodox Church
in Constantinople as the guest of Patriarch Athenagoras.
On his way home from the East, he added, he would be
delighted to seize the opportunity for a meeting with Pope
John if this would be agreeable to Rome. With the pope's
authorization, Alfrink replied at once with enthusiastic
approval, and during July Monsignor Johann Willebrands
met secretly with the Anglican Canon J. B. Satterthwaite,
who was in charge of interdenominational relations for the
Church of England, with a view to establishing the details
of the "courtesy visit." In August the central committee of
the World Council of Churches met in St. Andrew's, Scot-
land, and Doctor Fisher published a statement in his
episcopal bulletin in which he noted with satisfaction the

"rapid change of attitude in Rome in connection with our efforts for spiritual unity and mutual understanding with the Baptists, the Congregationalists, the Methodists, the Presbyterians, and also the Roman Catholics."

This statement created a stir among the non-Catholic Christians of Italy, the closest of the separated brethren, who in fact had had little cause for satisfaction in Italian Church policy throughout the reign of Pius XII. Stupid harassments, some of them even unconstitutional in their nature, had been initiated by the police, always prompt in their zeal to restrict Protestants' freedom of worship. The Protestant churches had not been allowed even to place identifying plaques on the doors of their establishments, and the most childish pretexts were invoked for a policy of outright persecution of their clergy.

One of these clerics, Anthony Caliandro, had been expelled from Italian territory because he had established an institute in Portici named after Girolamo Savonarola, in which he offered hospitality to Catholic priests who had abandoned their priesthood and needed special help, particularly in the initial period when they were seeking to build new lives. On another occasion the Milanese police commissioner forbade Jehovah's Witnesses to hold a convention for the expansion of biblical studies, on the pretext that the premises that they had rented, known as the Odéon Winter Garden, was restricted by its "regular restaurant license, and therefore the manager should have requested and obtained a special permit from police headquarters for its use as a meetingplace of a different character." Protests and even American diplomatic intervention had never been able to accomplish anything, and even in December of 1959, after John's accession to the papacy,

the deputy police commissioner of Vicenza ordered prosecution "for calumniation of the state religion" begun
against an American pastor, Howard Bybee, who had
written a short essay on the worship of images and relics.
The essay contained statistics on the "multiplicity" of
relics and showed precisely how many arms, ribs, big toes,
shoulder blades, and jawbones of a single saint were still
venerated on the altars as they had been for centuries in
Catholic churches in Italy and other countries.

These and other precedents had led Italian Protestants
to fear that the meeting at the summit of the Vatican between
the archbishop of Canterbury and the pope might mean
surrender to the Catholic Church or recognition of Italian
ecclesiastical policy. Therefore the highest dignitaries—
Mario Sbaffi, chairman of the Federal Council of Evangelical Churches; Ermanno Rostan, moderator of the Walden-
sian Church; and Roberto Ronchi, president of the Union
of Baptist Churches—had transmitted a joint resolution to
Doctor Fisher, calling on him to exert every effort to make
his visit result favorably for greater understanding among
the churches "that serve all peoples and beyond all theological conflict," without in any way compromising Italian
Protestants' independence of Peter's throne.

On his arrival at Ciampino Airport on December 1,
Doctor Fisher made a point of reassuring them at once: "I
will discuss everything and anything with His Holiness.
We will talk about Christian friendship. Mine is a happy
visit but not an official one." Then he repaired to Rome's
Anglican church, All Saints' Church of England in Via del
Babuino, and there he was much more explicit and precise
in the sermon that he preached on a text from the Gospel
of John (VIII:32) in which it is said: "The truth shall

make you free." He strongly emphasized this theme of freedom, basing his discourse also on a verse from Luke (IX:50): "He that is not against us, is for us." Then he explained:

Doctrinal diffrences are never purely theological; they are determined by differences of race, of temperament, of personality, and all these have certainly influenced relations between the Church of England and the Church of Rome. By vocation and by the grace of God, England and the English church are passionate lovers of freedom, even when they do not know or do not care how to make the best use of it. This passion for freedom was one of the major factors that led to the separation from the Church of Rome, because at the root of all the separations and all the schisms there is always a question of authority and jurisdiction.

Having thus restated the firm Anglican intention of yielding in no way on the question of independence, Doctor Fisher added:

Rival jurisdictions can coexist peacefully, cooperate, and create. This is the truth by virtue of which all churches are free in Christ, all gloriously free together for Christ and for the true unity of the Church. I say *unity* and not *union* advisedly, because union is a jurisdictional problem while unity is a thing of the spirit and of reciprocal love among the churches.

Then he turned to the subject of his visit.

For the first time in four hundred years an archbishop of Canterbury has come to Rome in his official capacity not to protest or complain but solely to greet His Holiness the pope in the courteous spirit of Christian brotherhood. This could happen, and I could suggest this visit, only because the pope had made it known that he would receive me in the same courteous spirit of Christian brotherhood. So here we are on a Lord's day much like many other Lord's days —normal, not spectacular, almost unnoticeable, like a whisper of a still barely audible voice of the Holy Spirit.

The next morning the archbishop arrived at the Vatican a half-hour before the time of his appointment. He was attired in all his robes of office: a purple cloak over a violet cassock, the violet episcopal sash girding his waist, on his head the four-pointed black velvet cap—the Canterbury cap—and at his breast a cross of gold and mother-of-pearl.

"He should not be kept waiting," John said when, in spite of protocol, the archbishop's presence was announced to him ahead of schedule. Doctor Fisher proceeded through a series of eleven rooms, and midway, in what is called the throne room, he saw the canopy and above it the strip of black velvet bearing the legend: *Ubi Petrus ibi Ecclesia* (Where Peter is, the Church is). What this is intended to convey is that, removed from Peter's successor, there is no true church. This was a new inscription that had not been on the canopy the day before, but John, in his punctilious conscientiousness as a Roman Catholic, had had it installed that evening. He had had an armchair so placed in his private study that his guest would be able to contemplate a tapestry depicting Christ surrounded by his apostles and entrusting Peter with the mandate of ruling His Church, saying to him: *"Tu es Petrus et super hanc petram aedificabo ecclesiam meam* (Thou art Peter and on this rock I will build My Church)." If, John had pointed out, the archbishop of Canterbury "should look at it, he will be able to see what is the basis of our point of view." In the same spirit the pope had also prepared, as a gift to the archbishop, a large medallion bearing his own image surrounded by his papal motto: *"Oboedientia et pax* (Obedience and peace)"; and this idea of peace founded on obedience was also a reminder of the principle of discipline, which, in contrast to the Anglican claims of free-

213

dom, is the essential foundation of the Catholic hierarchical conception.

Fisher too had had a purpose in choosing his formal gifts for the pope: among other things, a book of pictures of the various stages in the ritual of Queen Elizabeth's coronation, presided over by himself, as if to demonstrate to John the singular privilege granted to the first arch-bishop—even if *primus inter pares*—of the Church of England.

Very English in his appearance, energetic but open, deeply committed yet tolerant, Doctor Fisher began his talk with the pope on a felicitous note: "Your Holiness," he said in English, as he extended his hand, "we are making history." Subsequently, in an English television program, he recounted that there had been not the slightest constraint when the two men met:

> In a few minutes we were already talking with the ease and the cordiality of old friends about our respective spiritual experiences as Christians, and the conversation, in which there was not a moment's pause or boredom, lasted an hour. I had been warned that he would do all the talking. He is old, and old people, you know, often have a tendency to be loquacious. But that was not the case this time. The tone of the conversation was friendly and relaxed from the start. The Vatican people had given me to understand that protocol would be punctiliously observed and rather burden-some. And I was received with all the honors of an official guest; ceremony, however, ended right there.

John, for his part, describing his impressions the next day to a group of eighteen cardinals, archbishops, bishops, prelates, and priests of the Roman Curia in the Matilde Chapel, observed: "We did not go beyond the threshold of the great problems." This was his way of saying that there had been no discussion of doctrinal questions on the merits, but at the same time of expressing his confidence that, with time, through personal contacts and exchanges of ideas, as a result of fraternal discussions, the day of understanding in charity and truth would ultimately arrive. His faith was strengthened, he said, by the very fact of the friendly warmth displayed toward him by Fisher, which he did not hesitate to describe as "the not inconsiderable fruit of a courageous meeting that marks a date in the relations between the Catholic Church and the Anglican Church."

In order to receive Fisher, John had broken off the spiritual exercises held in the Matilde Chapel in preparation for Christmas. "It would be our wish," he told the cardinals, "to spend the days of the exercise in prayer, in meditation, in pious devotional practices. But the necessity arises of submitting to one or another departure from the prepared program." It seemed to him that it would be well to give "the fullest courtesy to the reception of a request properly transmitted and well received." The request was that for the audience, which had been prepared by Cardinal Alfrink of Utrecht and to the successful progress of which in Rome much work had been devoted by Augustin Cardinal Bea. The archbishop acknowledged Bea's help when he went to call on the cardinal that afternoon in the offices of the Secretariat for Unity, which had been established by John with a view to the Council. The conversation was cordial, "and the greater part of it," Bea said later, "dealt with matters of a general nature touching on the relations among the various Christian churches."

Mere mention of relations "among the various Christian churches" from a Catholic source was in itself a major innovation. It was an indication that representatives of the "other churches" might be able to attend an Ecumenical Council of the Roman Church—a thing that had never happened under the reign of any of John's predecessors. In 1919 some Episcopalian bishops from the United States had been received by Benedict XV, who had welcomed them warmly, but, before they left the Vatican, he had a note delivered to them in which he said that, if outside the Catholic Church there were Christians who were concerned with the unity of the churches, they knew quite well what they ought to do: become converts to Catholicism. Then, in 1928, there had been an encyclical of Pius XI, *Mortalium animos,* the inspiration and tone of which were extremely hostile to non-Catholics, at least in the sense that he continued to impose on them the pure and simple duty of conversion to Catholicism. This encyclical began by stating that never before had there been so strong a desire among men "to reinforce and broaden those relations of brotherhood that bind and join us all by the very fact of our common origin and nature," but then the text reemphasized "the unique rights of the single truth" represented by the papal throne. The possibility of any approach to other Christian churches was not even envisaged; indeed, the encyclical apparently made its greatest concession in the sentence in which it blessed and encouraged studies and activities the intention of which was to foster "a more rational knowledge of Catholicism."

So Pius XI followed Benedict XV, and Pius XII, as far as he was concerned, had accepted and ratified *Mortalium animos.* In 1947, in fact, it was harshly recalled to mind in an admonition from the Holy Office that it was strictly in force. John, however, was of a different view and a dif-

ferent inspiration. When he had celebrated Christmas Mass
in 1934 in Bulgaria in his capacity as apostolic visitor, he
had said in a fine access of pastoral charity:

My dear brothers! Who knows the roads the future will take?
In whatever part of the world I may come to live, if anyone from
Bulgaria has occasion to pass by my house in the middle of the
night, amid all the problems of life, he will always find a lighted
lamp in my window. Let him knock, knock at the door. I will not
ask him whether he is Catholic or Orthodox: Bulgarian brother,
knock and enter; two fraternal arms will embrace you, a friend's
warm heart will offer you a feast.

In his first radio broadcast after his election as pope, on
October 29, 1958, he said again:

We open our heart and our arms to all those who are separated
from this Apostolic Church in which Peter himself lives in his successors. We ardently desire their return to the house of our common father. . . . Let them all come, we exhort them, in unreserved,
loving good will. They will not be entering a strange house but
coming into the house that is their own.

Thus the old Catholic theory of the mandatory "return"
of the separated brethren to the bosom of the Church began
to lose the polemic connotation that it had had since the era
of the Council of Trent. It was no longer a return in the
sense of a repudiation of the reasons for the separation. As
Lamberto Furno observed in *Testimonianze per papa Giovanni (Bearing Witness for Pope John)*, John's Church
held itself forth in a new manner, more hospitable, more
in the sense of a "meeting farther on" as a result of the
progress that everyone had been able to make after the
centuries since the Reformation and the schisms. John said,
indeed: "This is the road that leads to meeting, to return.

Come and take or resume your places, which for many of you are those of your ancient sires."

He himself had already made a great step forward by establishing a special Secretariat for Christian Unity under the leadership of Cardinal Bea. As far as its dignity and its prerogatives were concerned, it was in every respect assimilated to the commissions of Vatican Council II and, moreover, vested with a very broad jurisdiction of its own. The Holy Office was losing its old function of supervision over relations with the non-Catholic churches, which, as is obvious, it had always exercised in an exclusively negative fashion. Cardinal Bea said:

... the origins and the foundation of the Secretariat for Unity were remarkably like the grain of mustard seed in the Gospel, by reason of their extreme simplicity and virtual insignificance. I do not know whether such an agency of the Holy See had been requested also from other sources, but I myself do know that I received an official petition from Germany in the early months of 1960 for transmittal to the Holy Father. After thorough study and meticulous detailed description of the project, I conveyed the request to Pope John on March 11. Only two days later, on the thirteenth, the pope informed me of his complete agreement and his desire to discuss further details of the matter, and he gave me an audience on that same day.

In itself the swiftness of the decision was a favorable sign: John wanted to give the Council a practically ecumenical meaning, and, in fact, it was on Pentecost that he issued his *motu proprio* * *Superno Dei nutu (By the Lofty Will of God)*, which instituted the Secretariat.

* Literally, "on his own motion." The term was applied originally to a new Church law that came directly and exclusively from the pope; it has since come to mean any ecclesiastical decree, whatever its source, in which the pope is especially interested.—TRANSLATOR.

There was an immediate change in the language employed by the Vatican in its still cautious but already frank contacts with the various churches. Arrogance was put aside in favor of courtesy and delicacy of approach. Bea sent his trusted agents to ask the leaders of the various denominations "whether they would welcome invitations to the Council," and then the invitations were dispatched to those (all except the Baptists and the Greek Orthodox) whose replies had been affirmative, thus averting the risk of formal rejections. At the same time, during August of that year, the Ecumenical Council of the Reformed Churches invited Catholic observers to its youth assembly in Lausanne, and in the next year to its Congress in New Delhi. For the first time the invitations were accepted, notwithstanding the fact that many persons in the Vatican had second thoughts on these "unionist" enthusiasms that might prove to be mere illusions and that in any case created the risk of major perils "to the purity of the faith," doomed the missionary era, to the profit of that of coexistence, opened the gate to apathy, and offered the temptations of syncretism.

Dangers there unquestionably are [Cardinal Bea told Lamberto Furno]. What is more, not everyone can do everything. A Catholic without theological training cannot take the risk of entering into a discussion or a dialogue with a learned non-Catholic professor of theology. Therefore caution is necessary and one must not overestimate one's own strength, but this is the kind of prudence that is required in all undertakings, even in secular life. Possible perils, however, are not and cannot be a reason for dereliction in the especially sacred duty of concerning ourselves in prudent and deliberate fashion with all who are baptized in Christ and who are our brothers.

What was above all to be surmounted was a question of principle. According to the Orthodox and the Protestants, a council is not ecumenical unless it brings together the representatives of all churches on a footing of absolute parity. The Catholic Church, therefore, could not call the council of its bishops ecumenical. Kristen E. Skydsgaard, professor of systematic theology at the University of Copenhagen, described his astonishment on the day when he read in the newspapers that John XXIII had convoked an "ecumenical" Council:

Interpreting this word as it has been construed in the ecumenical movement of the past fifty years, I had to reflect, marveling, that the pope wanted to bring together representatives of all the Christian churches. This, of course, was a misinterpretation of the word *ecumenical*, which in the Catholic Church has a different meaning.

The difficulties with the Russians were even greater and also more varied in nature. The patriarchate of Moscow had complained because the first invitation to attend the Roman Council had been sent to Patriarch Athenagoras of Constantinople as the representative of all the Orthodox. But the patriarchate of Moscow recognized no valid primacy in that of Constantinople, and indeed in its own official publication it printed a refusal in an article given a Latin title for comic effect: *Non possumus* ("We Cannot"). Monsignor Nicodemos, archbishop of Yaroslav and Rostov, who was responsible for foreign relations on behalf of the patriarchate of Moscow, was in Paris in the summer of 1962, when he made further public statements that were almost disparaging. It was guessed or known, however, that the stand taken by the Russians was determined not only by theological motives; politics played the major part; and so, properly, political approaches were attempted.

Cardinal Tisserant discussed a first opening with Nicodemos when he had the Russian as a guest in his country house near Metz. Tisserant asked frankly what conditions the Russian Church would lay down and what guaranties it would demand for the dispatch of a representative to the Council in Rome. It was agreed that Monsignor Johann Willebrands, Cardinal Bea's closest collaborator in the Secretariat for Christian Unity, should at once set out on an exploratory journey to Moscow. Time was pressing: it was already the end of September, and only little more than a week remained before the opening of the Council. Willebrands flew to Moscow, where he arrived on the twenty-seventh. He was welcomed as the representative of the "patriarchate of Rome" and given quarters in the Zagorsk monastery, the seat of the Moscow patriarchate, about forty-two miles outside the Soviet capital.

Patriarch Alexis was not there; he was resting in Odessa. But the rectors of the ecclesiastical academies of Moscow and Leningrad joined Nicodemos in the negotiations with Willebrands. In only five days an agreement was reached and embodied in the terms of a formal compromise. The delegates of the patriarchate of Moscow would have to report to Nicodemos at least once a week on the progress of the Council's labors, supplying him at the same time with all available informational material both official and unofficial. Furthermore, "and within the limits of the Council status established for observers, they would not omit to state the precise position of the patriarchate of Moscow in the appropriate quarters of the Roman Catholic Church." For his part, Monsignor Willebrands gave formal assurance that the Council would be devoted exclusively to religious matters. It was the pope's command that religious affairs that might in some degree extend into the political domain (atheism, Communism, the Church of silence, and similar questions) would be handled with great circumspection.

Agreement having been reached on these bases, Willebrands returned to Rome on October 2; two days later Cardinal Bea sent the official invitation to Nicodemos, and on October 12 Archpriest Vitaly Borovoy, a professor at the theological academy in Leningrad, and Archimandrite Vladimir Kotlyarov, vice chairman of the Russian Orthodox mission in Jerusalem, arrived at Fiumicino Airport. As they were driving into Rome, they asked Willebrands, who had gone to welcome them, whether they could stop at the Basilica of Saint Paul Outside the Walls in order to pay tribute to the saint. Then, when they had arrived at Saint Peter's, they went straight to the altar of confession. The next morning they were present at the opening of the Council, and in the afternoon they took part in the audience granted by John to non-Catholic observers. Greeting him as the "patriarch of Rome," they prostrated themselves devoutly before him.

There were thirty-two Catholic observers at the ceremonies that inaugurated the Council on October 12; in addition there were representatives of the Anglican commission, the World Lutheran Federation, the Evangelical Church of Germany, the World Convention of the Churches of Christ, the worldwide consultative committee of the Society of Friends, the International Congregationalist Council, the World Methodist Council, the World Council of Churches, the Old Catholic Church, the Coptic Church of Egypt, the Syriac-Jacobite Church, the Church of Ethiopia, the Armenian Church, the Orthodox Church Outside Russia, the Patriarchate of Moscow, and the International Association for Free Christianity and Religious Freedom.

These were all separated brethren who were oppressed by the problem of their division, who perhaps cherished the hope of unity, but who certainly felt a kind of united-front complex face to face with the Catholic Church. Doctor John Moorman, the Anglican bishop of Rippon, reported: "We were accompanied to Saint Peter's and we expected to be placed in one of the balconies above the seats of the Council fathers, but, to our astonishment, we found that places had been reserved for us in front of the diplomatic section. In other words, we were in the very front row, so that between us and the pope there was no one."

Pope John had also anticipated that not all the observers would be familiar with Latin, and therefore he had ordered that interpreters be available for them—the only interpreters permitted in the basilica. Copies of all working documents were then distributed to the thirty-two Catholic observers with the request that they divulge nothing but with authorization to inform their respective communities of the contents as conscience dictated. The Secretariat for Unity held weekly press conferences in order to provide explanations and to listen to comments: "Pope John seemed very happy to have us at the Council. He saw to it that we had every assistance and accommodation, like special guests; he wanted us to understand and appreciate everything that was taking place." The bishop of Rippon was enthusiastic, and he was overcome by emotion on October 13 when the secretary general of the Council, Monsignor Pericle Felici, gave the signal for deliberations to begin by pronouncing the *exeant omnes*—the order that all non-

223

working delegates depart; but at once he added: *"Possunt remanere patres, periti, observatores, et officiales*—Fathers, technicians, observers, and officials may remain." Even non-Catholics, then, could be present at the discussions and listen to the debates: *"Horresco* [I am horrified]!" Ottaviani said quite audibly. But, to quote Doctor Moorman again, "Later John XXIII received us in the Hall of the Consistory. When he entered he did not wish to take his seat on the throne but ordered a chair placed on the floor. We remained standing in a large circle, and then he came and shook hands with each of us."

The Hall of the Consistory is where the pope announces the names of new cardinals. After the greetings and introductions, John sat down in a red velvet armchair, not really a throne, placed on a low platform only slightly raised above the floor. Without the perspective of the steps, his chair, even if higher, would have had to be considered to be on the same level as those of his guests, and, while observations of this character may not be pleasant in their lack of religious and pastoral meaning, it must nevertheless be pointed out that the protocol officers of the Curia placed compelling importance on such details.

John was moved and he eyed the non-Catholic observers with a kind of trembling love. He indulged in a real confession as he recalled the ceremony in Saint Peter's that had inaugurated the Council:

In that providential hour I was concerned above all to wholly perform my duty of the moment, which was to meditate, to pray, to thank the Lord. But from time to time my eyes wandered among so many sons and brothers, and, when they came to your group, to each one of you, I found in your presence a source of comfort.

He conducted himself like a model host. Hospitable and warm, he allowed himself the pleasure of reminiscences of his past life among non-Catholics:

How, my dear friends, could I forget the ten years I spent in Sofia? And the ten others in Athens and Istanbul? They were twenty happy, hard-working, well-spent years, in the course of which I came to know many venerable leaders and young men filled with generosity. I looked on them with friendship even though my mission as the Holy Father's representative in the Near East did not concern them directly.

Moving easily from friendship to edifying quotation, John proceeded:

Ubi caritas et amor, ibi Deus est; congregavit nos in unum Christi amor [Where charity and love are, God is; Christ's love has united us in one]. In Paris too, which is one of the world's meeting-places and which was particularly such immediately after the Second World War, I had many contacts with Christians belonging to various denominations. Never that I can recall was there any conflict among us over principles or any dissension in the field of the charity of the work that circumstances imposed on us. We never argued; we talked. We did not discuss; we made friendships.

Since he was not given to rhetoric, he remarked:

The Christian virtue of patience should not impair the virtue of prudence, for this too is fundamental. So enough for today. The Catholic Church is at work, a serene and generous work, and you are performing your duties as observers with ever refreshed and benevolent attentiveness.

This was the historic meeting, the most important in centuries, among the Christian denominations, but John did not want to go to excesses or exploit the opportunity. Like a wise man, he avoided triumphal declarations, and, conscious of the limitations to which even he was subjected by the orientation of the Curia and therefore not wishing to claim credit, he confined himself to urging: "Gentlemen, please read what is in my heart. You will find much more there than in my words. But understand in any event that your presence here fills my priest's and bishop's soul with emotion." The fact that he did not say "my pope's soul" was a difference far more important than a mere shading.

When the audience was over, Cardinal Bea said with emotion: "It is a miracle, it is a miracle!" The miracle was the new attitude of the Catholic Church toward the other Christians, and in fact one of the observers, Oscar Cullmann, the Protestant theologian, attested explicitly to the fact:

When we go every morning to take our places, which are almost places of honor, in front of the cardinals, when every morning after Mass the secretary of the Council pronounces the *Exeant omnes*, while we can remain in our seats, I am always newly stunned by the way in which we are received in this Council and really made part of it. Outwardly we are passive observers, but inwardly we live these actions with our Catholic brothers. And, appropriating Cardinal Bea's remark about the miracle, I too am thinking of what past Councils meant for Christians who were not Catholics. I am not sure whether everyone fully appreciates what our presence here signifies.

In a large hotel in Rome (the Columbus, in Via della Conciliazione), Cardinal Bea gave a reception for non-Catholic observers. "I beg you," he said, in the tone of one assigned to public relations, "to tell us frankly whatever you do not like; to let us have your criticisms, your suggestions, your requests." The most pertinent and pointed reply came from a Lutheran: "One thing bothers me: if at a press conference I demonstrate my approval on any subject whatever, I am suddenly the object of emphasis, repetition, flattery, constant emulation. If, on the other hand, I express any reservations, they are always glossed over." Very subtly Bea replied: "Courtesy can indeed lead to unpleasant confusions." The thrust at the Curia was much appreciated.

John was convinced that, if Protestants could have the opportunity to see the Catholic Church as it really was, they would change their views of it: "Eliminating everything that from a human point of view could be an obstacle and taking a smoother road, we will show the church in all its splendor, *sine macula et ruga* [without stain or scar], and we will say to all the others who are separated from us— Orthodox, Protestant, etc.: 'See, brothers, here is the Church of Christ; we have striven to remain faithful to it.' " Perhaps the notion of splendor was wrongly interpreted, and indeed little was lacking from precisely the point of view of outward appearance in the ceremonies inaugurating the Ecumenical Council to make Protestants find the Catholic Church anything but acceptable. In order to be *sine macula et ruga,* as Cardinal Alfrink constantly argued, it would have had to appear less Roman and more Christian, denuded of the pagan pomp of its ritual manifestations. The splendors of the inaugural ceremonial, however, outstripped every known precedent and exceeded every possibility of the imagination.

John himself professed to be overwhelmed by it. "Going into St. Peter's," he had to admit on the evening of October 11, 1962, "I lost my breath." Even he had not expected such a spectacle, but the best—or the worst—was yet to come in the course of the ceremonies because of a staging that brought back to mind the thundering denunciation by Luther in his scornful phrase, *"Regnum papae* (The pope's kingdom)." Yet a contrast was to be found between the outward pomp and the meditative face of John, who sought to fulfill his functions with modesty and humility. "If I did not suffer too much during all that ceremony," a French Huguenot said, "it was precisely because of the bearing of the pope, who of course had to obey the system but who, from all the evidence, did so without the slightest enthusiasm."

As an impression it was quite accurate. It is easier, however, to understand John's state of mind if one recalls also a reply that he gave to a Calvinist monk, a sincere advocate of Christian unity, who had respectfully asked him when at last he would have made up his mind to strip his court and the Catholic Church of the last vestiges of princely ritual. Wisely John replied: "It is not for me to do everything."

X

Ecumenical Council
Vatican II

The announcement in the Basilica
of Saint Paul Outside the Walls.
Pius XII had given thought to a Council.
It would have been rigidly controlled by the Curia.
Why the preparations for it were broken off.
How many condemnations were
in prospect and what they were.

THE idea of convoking an Ecumenical Council, as John said, came to him without warning by divine inspiration. In his *Giornale dell'anima* he said that he first mentioned it to his secretary of state, Cardinal Tardini, during a regular Tuesday audience on January 20, 1959. He was discussing his concern over the state of general upheaval and the need for peace in the world, as well as the paucity of faith that made matters more difficult for the Church; and he was wondering what he could do, when—he wrote—there came spontaneously to his lips: "A Council . . ." Tardini, equally overwhelmed by the inspiration, said: "Yes, yes, a Council. It is a magnificent idea. I like beautiful new things. This is what our time needs."

Supposedly this was the start of the whole project, and John numbered it among the blessings that he had received from Providence: "Without ever having thought of it before, bringing out in a discussion with my secretary of state on January 20, 1959, the term *Ecumenical Council*, contrary to all my suppositions or imagination on the subject." It was certainly a blessing, and indeed John said again: "The first to be amazed by this proposal of mine was I myself, without anyone's ever having given me a hint of it. And to think that after that everything seemed so natural to me in its immediate and continuing development."

In actuality—divine blessing to one side—he had men-

231

tioned his plan to others before that January 20: in November of 1958 to Cardinals Ruffini and Urbani and Monsignor Girolamo Bartolomeo Bortignon, bishop of Padua; on January 9, 1959, to Don Giovanni Rossi of Pro Civitate Christiana of Assisi; and then, of course, to Monsignor Capovilla too: "With trepidation imploring support and consent in prayer." It has also been ascertained that, before he received Cardinal Tardini that Tuesday morning, John had already written the speech that he was to deliver the following Sunday, January 25, as his official public announcement. That Sunday, the observance of the conversion of Saul the Jew and the last day of the solemn octave, John went to the Basilica of Saint Paul Outside the Walls, attended a solemn ceremony, and during the Mass delivered a sermon calling for prayers for the Chinese brethren. Then he went into an apartment that had been made ready for him by the Benedictine monks of the Abbey of Monte Cassino, who were in charge of the basilica, and who were supposed to pay homage to him there. Unexpectedly, however, he said that before he received the monks he wished to be alone with the seventeen cardinals who had attended the ceremony.

He began speaking to them in a friendly tone, with that honest sense of realism that was new to the Vatican after the days of Pius XII: "We are aware that the pontiff's work is observed in many quarters with great friendship and devotion and in others with hostility and uncertainty . . ." He said that his responsibilities as bishop of Rome seemed serious to him, but not even remotely comparable to those of the pastor of the universal Church: "If we broaden our gaze to the entire world, oh, what a spectacle it is!" He explained that it was a spectacle that was blissful and sorrowful at the same time, and with broad strokes he painted a picture of the world's problems, the Church's needs, the perils that menaced the spiritual life of the Christian people, the necessity for its edification, the call to be addressed to the separated communities in the quest for unity.

Finally he came to his announcement:

Venerable brothers and beloved sons, we pronounce in your presence, certainly trembling somewhat with emotion but at the same time with humble resoluteness of purpose, the name and the proposal of the double celebration of a diocesan synod for the city and of an Ecumenical Council for the universal Church. We beseech you all for a good beginning, continuation, and happy outcome for these proposals of great labor for the enlightenment, the edification, and the joy of the whole Christian people, for a renewed invitation to the faithful of the separated communities that they too may follow us with love in this quest for unity and grace after which so many souls yearn from every part of the earth.

His conclusion was a great affectionate compliment to his fellow cardinals, to whom he gave the greeting of Saint Paul in the terms in which it is reported by San Leone Magno: "You are my crown and my joy if your faith, which from the beginning of the Gospel was preached in the whole world, subsists in love and sanctity. Oh, what a tribute that is!" he said with genuine emotion.

It was a splendid speech, but the reception that it was given by the cardinals was, as John said later, "strange." During a relaxed conversation one day with a group of pilgrims from Venice, he disclosed in fact that those seventeen cardinals, almost all members of the Curia, had received the news of the Council in silence and remained cold, even when he quoted Saint Paul according to San

Leone Magno. "Ordinarily," John said, "it might have been expected that, after they had heard the announcement, the cardinals would have pressed round us to give their approval and good wishes. Instead there was a dramatic, devout silence," which was probably a sign of irritation or fear or uneasiness. "In the days that followed, however," John continued to the Venetian pilgrims, "received in audience individually, the cardinals explained that they had been overcome by sudden, over-intense emotion: 'We could not find words to express our jubilation and unlimited obedience.' " John said that they had come and told him this, and his smile was almost mocking at the same time that it was indulgent and ironic, showing plainly that he had seen through their excuses.

That coldness, however (even if it were mixed with uneasiness, fear, or irritation), was natural enough. An Ecumenical Council is an irrevocable undertaking that can have disturbing effects on the Church, as the cardinals were easily able to imagine when John told them of his project. For this very reason, which intuitively he grasped completely, Pius XII in his own time had abandoned the idea of convoking an Ecumenical Council in spite of the fact that secret preparatory work had been under way for three years, from March of 1948 until early January of 1951. Pope Pius XII had then decided to abandon the notion, saying that he was quite convinced of the value of a Council to the Church but at the same time felt that he was too old to be able to hope to see it through to its conclusion.

If he had really wanted it, he would have had enough time, and too because the project as it was then conceived was for a Council *sui generis,* centralized and domesticated, that would have started, moved, and stopped at the pleasure of the pope and the Curia. Precise details on the matter were furnished by Father Giovanni Caprile in *Civiltà cattolica* (August 6 and 20, 1966, Nos. 2787–2788); he had been permitted to consult the relevant documents in the archives of the Congregation for the Doctrine of the Faith (formerly the Holy Office). In fact, Father Caprile said that he had been given assurances that "Pius XII himself had incidentally alluded in a speech to his desire to convoke a Council if he had not been deterred by his advanced age. We have not succeeded, however, in finding this remark in the vast ocean of his utterances."

A cardinal who had known Pius XII well, however, told Father Caprile that Pope Pacelli "would never have convoked a Council, not so much because of his age as because his character could not have adjusted to the immediate presence of such a body with the powers and the influence of a Council." It was this that made him afraid, and on this score it must be acknowledged that he was perspicacious and far-sighted. In spite of the fact that he was offered the possibility of a Council tailored to his specifications, Pius XII actually allowed himself no illusions, knowing that, once the much feared "dynamic thrust of the ecclesiastical periphery" had been unleashed, it would be impossible to restrain and effectively combat the sempiternal demands of the bishops and obtain recognition of the apostolic sovereignty.

Of all the reactionaries in the Curia, Pius XII, while he could not be called the most enlightened, was beyond doubt the most intelligent, or at the very least the shrewdest. The first suggestion of a Council had come to him from Ernesto Cardinal Ruffini, archbishop of Palermo, who had gone to talk to him on behalf of Monsignor Alfredo Ottaviani, the assessor of the Holy Office and not yet a cardinal. Ruffini himself described the discussion in a speech that he gave at the Lateran University on October 28, 1959, the first anniversary of John's election. Having selected that day for his endeavor to ascribe to Pope Pacelli the credit for having initiated Pope Roncalli's undertaking, Ruffini said righteously:

> Ten years ago, at the feet of Pius XII, I dared—I, the least of the priests—to suggest an Ecumenical Council. It seemed to me to be urgently required by circumstances and that it would have as many matters on its agenda as did the Council of Trent. The venerated pontiff did not reject the suggestion but indeed made notes on it, as it was his custom to do in important matters; I know that subsequently he spoke of it to some prelates, but divine providence has reserved to his successor its difficult and arduous execution.

We know that on the day in question—February 24, 1948—Ruffini told the pope that he had mentioned the matter also to Ottaviani, who was in complete agreement. A few days later, on March 4, the pope received Ottaviani. It was Pius himself who brought Ruffini's proposal into the conversation, and Ottaviani promptly supported it: in the light of the mass of philosophical and theological, social and moral errors that were abroad, the necessity of clarifying and defining a number of doctrinal points was obvious. Then too there were the problems posed by the war and by Communism, as well as the prospect of new wars. The code of canon law needed modernization, and a quick survey was enough to show how many other actions would be necessary in the various domains of ecclesiastical discipline, Catholic Action, culture, etc. And, too, in Ottaviani's view, an Ecumenical Council would have been highly appropriate for the then planned proclamation of the dogma of the physical assumption of the Virgin Mary, the immaculate mother of God, into heaven.

Pius XII agreed in part. He pointed out at once, however, that to bring several thousand bishops to Rome and maintain them there for a considerable time, far from their dioceses, was no small undertaking. He mentioned the existence of other "unfavorable circumstances," which he omitted to identify, but in the end he gave his consent to the initiation of preliminary work, such as consideration of matters to be placed on the agenda and the selection of the persons to be asked to become members of the preparatory commissions. And further, for "reasons of prudence," he ordered that all work be carried out under the cloak of the Holy Office, wrapped in canonical secrecy.

Ottaviani moved so quickly in his execution of the pope's directive as to give rise to the suspicion that in combination with Ruffini he had already worked out at least the bases of a council organization some time before. On March 15—only eleven days after his audience—he was in fact already in a position to bring together a commission consisting of a half dozen consultants in whom he had confidence, most of them Germans (*Monsignori* Luigi Hudal and Virgilio Dalpiaz; three Jesuits, Franz Hurth, Josef Creusen, and Sebastian Tromp; and Fathers Ulrich Beste, O.S.B., and Josef Grendel of the Society of the Holy Name); they immediately established the number and titles of the commissions to be appointed: two theological, one canonical, one missionary, and one cultural. At the top there was to be an executive committee composed of members "drawn from the Roman Curia and equipped with

237

good organizational talents and adequate knowledge of languages."

Work continued at a rapid pace and on March 22 it was decided that the Council's commissions should all be headed by members of the Curia and that the commissioners should be the advisers of the Roman congregations. In a later phase others were to be brought in from outside and even from abroad, appointed on the basis of the judgments of the papal nuncios in their respective countries or of the bishops of major dioceses.

Informed of this by Ottaviani, Pius XII remarked that it was unnecessary to have recourse to foreign bishops or papal representatives, since the speed and frequency of modern means of communication enabled Rome to have first-class knowledge of men, their positions, and their abilities. Some twenty experts living in various parts of the world and permanently established outside Italy were therefore officially inscribed on a list put together by Ottaviani. None of them, however, was ever summoned to Rome. On July 9, however, there was a meeting of the cardinals who were advisers to the Holy Office: Francesco Marchetti-Selvaggiani, Pietro Fumasoni-Biondi, Domenico Jorio, Giuseppe Pizzardo, and Nicola Canali. In his capacity as assessor, Ottaviani made a report on the work that had been accomplished in the preceding four months; then, following procedure, he asked what were the views of Their Eminences. Their Eminences replied: *"Ad Assessorem cum Sanctissimo,"* which meant: "Let the assessor take the matter directly to the Holy Father."

Ahead of everything else Pius XII looked to the hierarchical structure of the Council. His choice for the presidency of the central commission was the apostolic nuncio in Italy, Monsignor Francesco Borgognini Duca; for the secretariat general, Father Pierre Charles, a Jesuit and professor of dogmatic theology in a college in Louvain— he was the only member of the commission who did not live in Rome. This in itself was not enough to give the commission a supranational quality or the semblance of independence of the Curia, but Charles was preferred above the other candidates—apostolic nuncios and visitors and delegates—precisely because he preserved appearances, or at least some appearances, outside the circle of the central pontifical bureaucracy.

Again because of the desire to have an international aspect, which would be all the more appropriate for an Ecumenical Council, it was decided to ask a small number of bishops secretly for their views. There was long debate over the criteria to be employed in the selection of the prelates who would be questioned, and exceedingly secret information was requested from the secretary of state and the Congregation for the Propagation of the Faith on the greater or lesser importance and the kind of position enjoyed by this or that bishop in South America or the mission territories. There were also proposals to question some superiors general, at least of those religious orders—the most important—that are normally invited to a Council. Then there were suggestions that all the cardinals without exception be consulted, but in the end, however, a shorter list was compiled, limited to some sixty persons representing about thirty countries on all six continents: twenty-seven Europeans, eight Asians, three Africans, nine North Americans, seven Central and South Americans, and one Australian, as well as two cardinals, a patriarch, two titular bishops of the Eastern Rite, and two titular superior archbishops and one bishop of the missionary institutes.

In short, a very restricted group was being organized, unsuited to the purposes of a Council that was supposed to be ecumenical. Be that as it might, the sixty chosen ones were to receive a letter in Latin, which, after much introductory circumlocution, requested the recipient to inform the pope in all frankness *("candide Domino aperies")* and in clear, succinct terms *("paucis quidem clarisque sententiis")* of his views on all matters of doctrine, morals, law, social affairs, missions, or discipline of the clergy and the Christian people that a possible Council might be able to discuss. It was understood, the letter pointed out by way of conclusion, that questions and replies would be wrapped in the secrecy of the Holy Office *("arctissimi tamen S. Officii secreto servato")*, the most severe of all canonical secrecy, according to the constitution of Benedict XIV, *Sollicita ac Provida,* of July 9, 1753, reiterated in the *Normae peculiares* of Pius X of September 29, 1908.

Before dispatching these sixty confidential personal letters, however, the central prepatory commission presented a question to the cardinals who were advisers to the Holy Office—Marchetti-Selvaggiani, Fumasoni-Biondi, Jorio, Pizzardo, and Canali. They were asked whether it would be proper to confer also with prelates who did not belong to the Holy Office (". . . whether it was appropriate to consult the other members of the Sacred College and some members of the episcopacy; *quatenus affirmative* [if the reply is affirmative], which bishops should be selected . . ."). The most eminent replied: "Let the commission begin by drafting projects on the most important matters. As for communications *ad extra, dilata"*—in other words, let it proceed with its doctrinal labors without for the moment initiating contacts abroad.

This was perhaps a wise precaution, because no one as yet had a clear idea what type of Council might be held, whether long or short, plenary or limited, free or precast. After the speed and ease of the initial preparations, obstacles now sprang up everywhere. Father Caprile related that many wanted a short Council because they were concerned primarily by the harm and inconvenience that would be attendant on prolonged absences of bishops from their dioceses. Moreover, housing three thousand prelates —that was the estimated count of Council fathers—in Rome created serious logistical problems. Hence a maximum term of three or four weeks was envisaged, inasmuch as the bishops "have also to think of the affairs of their dioceses. There is the further fact that not all bishops are equally concerned by all questions or equally prepared to deal with them."

The solutions suggested were varied, but all were inspired by the well-known desire of Pius XII "to reduce the term of the Council sessions to the unavoidable minimum." One proposal amounted in essence to holding the Council by mail. Each of three commissions—for dogma, for morals, and for discipline—would send its own preliminary drafts from Rome to all the bishops, asking each one to present his written comments. When all the replies had been received, the commission would prepare a new draft and send it too by mail to all the bishops with the request for further criticisms, which would be taken into account in the definitive version. Then the plenary Council would be convoked in order to ratify the prepared texts.

According to another suggestion, the Council could be held in a series of sessions—for example, one every year if not every two years. Properly organized, each session could be concluded in not more than a month, with limited meetings, because bishops would be asked to participate on the basis of only one for each ecclesiastical province: "This would substantially reduce the number of fathers without depriving the Council of anything of its ecumenical character," according to one of the documents in the Holy Office. The restricted meetings would have been pure working sessions, without any special pomp or occasion for doctrinal pronouncements. Only at the end would there have been a plenary session, to which all the bishops would be invited for the proclamation of the theories of dogma prepared by the working groups. A possible variant (according to details published several years later, on November 7, 1962, by *La Croix*) provided for a Council composed of five or six hundred fathers elected by the episcopates of the various countries and entitled, as in the congresses of political parties, to votes in proportion to the size of their constituencies.

Moreover the Council could also be reduced to a mere formality after the central commission had drafted "a short, complete document in which the major truths of faith professed by the Church and considered of major importance by the contemporary world would be set forth with clarity and in positive form." It would be necessary for this document to avoid all possible controversial issues, because it was believed to be absolutely necessary to give the world a solemn testimonial of unity and unanimity "in order not to provide the enemy with a means by which to exploit and emphasize possible divergences of views and opinions."

The only way of attaining this end was obviously that of restriction to generalities what could be accepted by the Council, "possibly even by acclamation." Such a system would have been of no value to the Church, but it was thought that it could be incorporated with a list of errors to be condemned and reforms to be effected that would be separately presented to the bishops, each of whom would be free to offer amendments, additions, or deletions. Thus, when the Council had concluded amid acclamations, the bishops' proposals—collected, catalogued, classified, and distributed among the various ministries of the Curia into whose jurisdictions they fell—would be examined subsequently by special commissions that would prepare the final texts of the condemnations and reforms *ad mentem Concilii*—that is, on the basis of the indications and intentions left behind by the dismissed Council fathers.

This would have been hardly more than a joke, and indeed there was no lack of criticisms of the idea and of the membership of the central commission. It was remarked that either a Council is conducted according to the traditional rules or, better, it is not held at all: "A Council must be taken seriously, and therefore it must be given as much time as it requires," to quote one of the documents consulted by Father Caprile. For the same reasons the Council fathers should be allowed complete freedom, with meticulous care to avoid the creation of any outside impression that they are being manipulated or that they are responding to cues. The fathers themselves, furthermore, should be relieved at all costs from the idea "that everything had been arranged in advance by the Roman Curia."

It was at this point in the decisive phase of the preparations that Pius XII recognized danger. Displaying more sagacity than his collaborators in the Curia, he understood that it was impossible to achieve two contradictory results: that is, that the Council accomplish any serious work without causing changes or compromises in his system of personal government of the Church. Early in January of 1951, therefore, he issued orders that nothing further be done on the project for the Council and that all the preparations be enveloped in canonical secrecy.

Apart from the disagreements on the standards to be adopted, the mass of work completed was impressive. A report by the secretary general, Father Pierre Charles, stated that the proposals for condemnation of errors, for reinforcements of discipline, for moral precepts to be inculcated, etc., *"mole et numero excedunt mensuram earum quae ab uno Concilio expediri possunt*—in their mass and their number were more than could be dealt with by a single Council." Even the chairman of the central commission, Monsignor Borgognini Duca, spoke of *"immensa materia a nobis praeparata* [immense material prepared by us]," expressing the fear that it was *"inepta ad formam conciliarem recipiendam* [unsuited to the form of the Council receiving it]."

If this was true of the quantity, one may say of the quality that the general inspiration, the tone, and the sense of the documents that should have been or, as the case might be, actually were prepared were dominated by concentration on condemning the mounting tide of errors *("ingruentium errorum colluvies")* and emphasizing the differences between the Church and the secular world *("Ecclesiae civilisque consortii discrimina")*. After the Council of 1870 errors and differences had not diminished; rather, they had been aggravated *("quinimmo graviora facta esse videntur")* and the new Council would have had to act therefore on a long series of errors, both traditional and specifically modern.

Thus we should have had a kind of new Syllabus brought up to date in the middle of the twentieth century and flashing with anathemas against:

1. those who deny the capacity of the human intellect to know God *"per rationem* [through reason]";
2. those who hold Saint Thomas and scholastic philosophy in contempt;
3. the various forms of existentialism, materialism, protopagan humanism, and naturalism;
4. all errors concerning the primary purpose of marriage—in other words, against birth control and artificial insemination;
5. the so-called paramount right of the state in the field of education;
6. those who deny the existence of a social problem or who seek to resolve it by violence;
7. men in public life who stoop to agreements with non-Catholics that lack regard for the rights of the Church;
8. those who are guided by Communist doctrines and regard the social doctrine of the Church as obsolete;
9. those who seek to resolve international disputes by war;
10. those who wage total war;
11. those who contend that any "honest" man, even if unbaptized and without any visible dependence on the head of the Church, is rightly and properly *(vere et proprie)* a member of the Church;
12. those who assert that dissenters differ from the faithful only in name (ecumenism);
13. the right of secular sponsorship, particularly on the part of governments elected by popular vote, in the selection of bishops.

After so much "against," so much anathema, there were very few proposals favorable to anything or anyone in the Council as projected by the Holy Office. There was one noteworthy one, however, that envisaged "the propriety of gathering into the patrimony of the Church everything that is not tainted by sin," thus claiming the right to usurp or annex whatever, for example in the domain of culture, suited the Church. A similar desire for conquest or abuse was to be found in the view on ecumenism, which under No. 12 of the anathemas, was condemned as a relaxation of vigilance or prudence in matters of faith. The whole problem of unity and of relations among Christians, according to the Holy Office, came down to the manner *"de alliis ovibus ad unicum ovile unumque pastorem adducendis* [in which they must be brought from other folds to the one fold and the one shepherd]," and in this sense the chairman of the central commission, Monsignor Borgognini Duca, proposed in his final report that the basic goal of the Council be recognized to be that of "calling" into Peter's fold the dissenters and the unbelievers of the entire world. There exists, in fact, a *Concilii Oecumenici Declaratio authentica (Authorized Statement of the Ecumenical Council),* put forward by the secretary general, Pierre Charles, which was a solemn profession of Catholic doctrine, closing with the outspoken summons to all other Christians to "return to the common table, even if at one time their fathers ate the sour grapes of controversy." A similar invitation was extended to the Jews: after having endured so many undeserved disasters, let them too acknowledge in Jesus Christ their Messiah and Redeemer.

These model solutions by the Holy Office to the problems of ecumenism, furthermore, reflected the attitude of

246

Pius XII as it was depicted by Cardinal Bea, who was Pope Pacelli's confessor:

Many fine things could be said that are perhaps widely un-suspected. In his encyclical on the Church as the mystical body of Christ, for example, Pius XII employs expressions of so tender a love for the separated brethren that I would call them surprising in a jurist such as Pius. It is also known how many times he ex-pressed hope for a closer collaboration among all Christians in fields that do not directly concern faith—for example, in social and welfare work, peace, and so on. Let it be remembered too with what fatherly charity he welcomed all non-Catholics of good will who came to him in search of a word of exhortation or encour-agement.

Ostensibly paying tribute to breadth of views, Cardinal Bea in *L'unione dei cristiani (Christian Union)* has por-trayed the narrowness of Pope Pacelli's limitations, his rejection of ecumenical conceptions: a lawyer of religion, he was therefore the more easily led to recognize what divides rather than to value what unites.

XI

John's Holy Madness

Widespread opposition to the Council.
"We need to emerge from our ghetto."
The moods of the conservative Curia
and of the restive "ecclesiastical periphery."
The arrival of the Council fathers in Rome.
The inaugural address, "written wholly by
the pope from the first word to the last."

JOHN did not know the extent of the studies that the Holy Office had already made for a Council during Pope Pius' reign. Bound by canonical secrecy, neither the original promoters of the venture, Cardinals Ruffini and Ottaviani, nor anyone else among the experts or the members of the congregation had told him anything of what had happened. Thus Father Caprile was able to ascertain that "John's initiative was completely individual and independent: only later did he learn of the preparations that had been carried out under his predecessor."

It was in April of 1959, at the first meeting of the pre-preparatory commission appointed by John to plan for the Council, that someone mentioned the existence of documents that were being kept in the archives of the Holy Office. Cardinal Tardini reported this to John, asked him to dissolve the interdict of canonical secrecy, and thus was enabled to make the work achieved by the collaborators of Pius XII available to the new incumbents, who were then in a position to make use of it if it lent itself to their endeavors. Unfortunately this led to a subsequent confusion as to the facts, partly too because attitudes on the matter within the Roman Curia were uncertain and contradictory.

Many churchmen believed that the Ecumenical Council Vatican I of 1870 had forever concluded the epoch of councils by its dogmatic proclamation of papal primacy and infallibility. The ageless maxim, *Roma locuta causa finita* (Rome has spoken, the case is closed), was still highly favored because one of the consequences of the dogma, and the effect most pleasing to the men of the Curia, had been the concentration of all power in the Curia. Now that John threw everything open to question again in a single stroke, unleashing the inordinately dreaded "dynamic thrust" of the ecclesiastical periphery, "the placid bureaucratism of certain Curia cardinals and prelates naturally looked on the Council as a threat, a problem, a ground for anxiety," as Mario Gozzini wrote in *Concilio aperto (The Council Opens).*

Opposition to John was widespread. Irreverent witticisms ran through the Curia: "We are paying for fifteen minutes' insanity in the pope," even those assigned to the preparatory work used to say. "The Council? It's a sickness of the Church." They studied the state of John's health, and, whenever there was a sign of illness, it was interpreted as evidence of the anger of God, who wanted the whole Council to go up in smoke. "I do not believe that the pope wanted to convoke a Council," the late Francis Cardinal Spellman of New York said, "but he was pushed into it by people who had misconstrued what he had said."

Different in character, the frightened reaction of Archbishop Lercaro of Bologna was no less intense: "How could he have dared to convoke a new Council after a hundred years, and within less than three months after his election? Who else in his position, however convinced he might be of the rightness of it, would not rather have conceived it to be his duty to give it further thought, at least until he was in a position to make a better evaluation of

252

the real state of the Church and of the possible consequences of so vital and extraordinary a decision?" According to Lercaro, there was a genuine dilemma: "Either Pope John has been rash and impulsive, with a lack of breeding and experience that borders on the paradoxical, in which case it would no longer be possible to talk seriously of any holiness in him because a fact of such proportions would negatively envelop all his sanctity and his spiritual and religious personality and knock down the whole castle of his supposed moral and theological virtues; or else in actuality Pope John has done this with calculated audacity, though obviously not being capable of foreseeing all the details or even the material content of certain future developments, and in that case it must be conceded that he was aware of the solid foundations of some of his doctrinal theses . . ."

However *nuancé* his conclusions, the alternatives posed by Lercaro were not flattering for John. The pope, however, was not shocked by them; still less was he upset by them. Regarding the Council as a grace bestowed by God, he said that "without a little holy madness the Church does not broaden its dominion." He was convinced that what was needed was "a gust of fresh air in the Church, because we need to emerge from our ghetto without wasting time throwing stones at the Communists." Furthermore, he knew very well what was really exciting certain persons round him in the Vatican: "not the division in Christianity, not the worldwide menace of theoretical and practical materialism, not the growing loss of souls, but proposals for reform, innovations that might threaten Curia careers." The statement, with all its bitterness, was reported by Otto Roegele, a German Catholic writer.

The Curia cardinals disapproved of the Council, seeing it as a threat to their power as well as a menace to faith: "They are certainly zealous men," John said of them, "but it is not they who are ruling the Church. That post is mine, and I do not wish anyone to hobble progress toward a Council." In addition he recognized the risks that were present during the preparatory period, when the commissions might so conduct their labors as to produce a conflicting, counter-productive result that would distort the very foundations of the Council in perhaps irreparable fashion.

In fealty to his own principles, he had allowed full freedom to the commissions even as he trembled at the thought of the use to which they might turn it, and he followed their work attentively. He confined himself, however, to encouragement and even praise, endeavoring always to avoid the mere appearance of interference, if only in order to prevent the growth of resentment, and in his diary he wrote: "Preparations for the Ecumenical Council Vatican II occupy a large part of my daily activities." He prayed a great deal and he exhorted others to pray, trusting in God: "I shall be awaiting some happy inspiration."

A champion of freedom, he allowed the theologians and the Curia to work as they wished, himself prepared to intervene only in the event of any surrender by them to their hoary passion for anathemas. Father Robert Rouquette related that one day a prominent prelate visited John in his study, where the pope brandished a ruler at him and said: "Look here, Monsignor, just look: in this document there are twelve inches of anathema!" He warned the preachers of Lenten sermons that "God has

254

called us to enlighten consciences, not to bewilder and coerce them . . . he has called us to heal our brothers, not to terrorize them." The very concept of anathema was repugnant to him. He had always rejected it, ever since he was only a young teaching priest in the seminary in Bergamo: "If the truth and the whole truth must be told, I do not understand why it has to be accompanied by the thunder and lightning of Sinai, rather than with the calm and the serenity of Jesus on the Sea of Galilee and the Mount."

So he had been scandalized by the vehemence of one Father M., a preacher who had gone to Bergamo to give battle to modernist error. Now that he was pope, he was in the same situation. He reacted with a certain impatience if he had to deal with the oversubtle pettifogging casuists of theology: "Knowledge swells us," he admonished them, paraphrasing his beloved Saint Paul's first Epistle to the Corinthians; "it is charity that builds." When he was asked for summary decisions that would dogmatically resolve some question, he knitted his brows and clenched his fists almost as if he were repressing some fierce impulse; then, with a tolerant sigh, he himself would ask a question, very often an embarrassing one: "What is the real problem? What can be done?"

It was a professional theologian, John Courtney Murray, an American Jesuit, who said that in this attitude he saw John's real modernity, or at least the change made by him in the Catholic Church. It was also his need for direct communication in the broadest sense that made for conflict between him and the Curia. When the council fathers were arriving in Rome, Monsignor Capovilla was charged by John with making a long series of telephone calls because John wished them to be discreetly apprised of a certain separation of responsibilities between the pope and the Curia as to the manner in which the preparations for the Council had been made.

In some instances it was John himself who made the explanation. "My hands are tied here," he said one day, for example, to Richard Cardinal Cushing, archbishop of Boston, when he was feeling especially discouraged. He knew the moods of the so-called ecclesiastical periphery because demanding cries were reaching Rome from all the most remote provinces of the Church. A collective statement by the United States bishops declared that it was not the business of the bishops "to give rash answers to questions drafted by the preparatory commissions or to approve their recommendations by a mere vote of ratification: but rather to deliberate with all serenity, to express mature judgments, and to render conscientious votes after sufficient time."

Franziskus Cardinal Koenig, archbishop of Vienna, had told his flock that it was his intention to propose that the Council decentralize the powers held by the Curia. "And let it be clearly understood," he concluded amid applause, "that we are not going to Rome to be a yes-man." Julius Cardinal Doepfner, archbishop of Munich, had spoken to his people of "Peter led by Paul." The pope, he said, as Peter's successor, should have been more systematically assisted by the bishops, Paul's and hence the apostles' successors. Wider freedoms for the bishops, he argued, would have a favorable influence on the thinking of the separated brethren by giving the Church of Rome a more hospitable aspect.

Jan Bernard Cardinal Alfrink of Utrecht had said in

256

The Netherlands that the Council would be useful only if it succeeded in "bringing more of the government of the Church into the hands of the bishops and making it less dependent on the central body." He reserved the right to demand the internationalization of the Curia and of the entire Vatican Foreign Service, saying that, if the Church really wished to become *sine macula et ruga,* it must be made more Catholic and less Roman. Accused of being intransigently anti-Roman, he replied honestly that, if anti-Roman meant anti-papal, the charge was unfounded, but, if what was meant was rather a protest "against certain methods of the Roman governing apparatus and against the way in which certain persons in Rome employ certain methods, then I neither can nor wish to deny the existence of an anti-Roman spirit in The Netherlands. *Non timeo Petrum, sed secretarium Petri* (I fear not Peter but Peter's secretary)."

By way of clarification and amplification, he concluded: "It would be a grave error, however, to think that this anti-Roman sentiment exists only in The Netherlands. It is to be found everywhere in varying degrees: even in Rome." Be that as it might, the arrival of The Netherlands' delegates in Rome was preceded by their notoriety as anti-Roman activists (this was the term used by *Il Corriere della sera* for Alfrink himself when it accused him of the sin of crossing his legs during the solemn ceremonies in Saint Peter's). Distrust of them was aggravated by the fact that the Church of The Netherlands had expressed its opposition to the decision to make Latin the official language of the Council without simultaneous translations during its sittings. In addition, some time earlier the apostolic charter, *Veterum sapientia (The Wisdom of the*

Ages), which stipulated that Catholic universities everywhere in the world must conduct their courses in theology, philosophy, and Holy Scripture in Latin, had evoked a collective protest from the Church of The Netherlands.

The most serious of all the so-called impertinences of the Netherlanders, however, was the letter in which their bishops' conference defined "the sense of the Council." Among other things it said:

> The sudden interruption of the Ecumenical Council Vatican I created the impression that the separate definition of papal infallibility was an isolated dogma. In actuality this personal infallibility is part of the official infallibility of the worldwide episcopate, which in turn is the fruit of the infallible faith of the whole community.

Made public in Rome, translated into Italian, and placed on sale in religious bookshops, this document seemed to exude the reek of heresy on the eve of the opening of the Council. The problem was placed before John; he was told that it was essential to take the thing out of circulation and in any event to confute it. *Divinitas*, the publication of the Pontifical University of the Lateran, had already prepared an article condemning it, and this was shown in proof to the pope. Inasmuch as he had no choice, John handed down a judgment of Solomon: he allowed an order to be issued to the religious bookshops to withdraw the Netherlanders' letter from sale, but he did not permit *Divinitas* to publish its condemnation.

It was just at this time that thousands of bishops, bishops' secretaries, and bishops' theological advisers were pouring into Rome. For the first time in its history the city really seemed, even physically, to be the center of Catholicism. The Termini railway station and the Fiumicino airport were converted into vestibules of the Council, full of ecclesiastics in clerical collars, prelates *in longis* (that is, cassocks), cardinals in embroidered caps and lavish trappings. Most of the visitors were arriving at this time. By noon of October 10, 1962, twenty-two hundred Council fathers had already recorded their presence, and more were still alighting from every train and every plane—one by one, in groups, in shoals.

They included the archbishop of Rubaga, Monsignor Joseph Kiwanuka; the archbishop of New York, the late Francis Cardinal Spellman; the bishop of Al-Kosh, Ablahad Sana; the archbishop of Kirkuk, Rafael Rabban; the bishop of Accra, Andraus Sana; the patriarch of Babylon, Paul II Sheikcho; the archbishop of Bassara, Joseph Gogue; the bishop of Abançay, Alcides Mendoza Castro. Not all of them, as they arrived, presented normal passports; many offered the most improbable of documents, or papers written in languages that even the most accomplished of the interpreters could not decipher. One Japanese had nothing in his wallet or his briefcase that could attest not merely to his rank or his position but even to his own personal identity; and he smiled a seraphic smile as he blessed the Italian border guards who took his word for everything and unanimously regarded him as a guest of honor, following a special protocol that was intended to be at the same time speedy and deferential, thorough and respectful, for all the prelates of the world.

By way of Paris, Monsignor Paul Etoga, the residential bishop of Mbalmayo in the Cameroons, arrived exhausted and famished. Having with the utmost difficulty succeeded in canvassing his diocese for pitiful contributions that together amounted to the price of a tourist-class plane

259

ticket from Africa to Paris, he had arrived in France with barely enough money left for a second-class railway ticket to Rome. But, when he had paid for this, he had no money at all for food, and for two days he ate nothing. In Rome he was turned over to the pious institution of the *Peregrinatio romana ad Petri sedem (Roman Pilgrimage to Peter's Chair)*, which fed him at once and then harbored him for the duration of the Council. He had long since decided to rely on Providence to manage his return to the Cameroons. The *Peregrinatio romana* also found accommodations in monasteries, religious hospices, and modest boarding-houses for others like him—Council fathers arriving in general from the mission territories of Asia or Africa or from the remote and desolate dioceses of South America. Little hotels, rented from cellar to roof for the purpose, took on an entirely new appearance, and in every one of them at least one altar was set up so that every morning and afternoon the episcopal customers could celebrate Holy Mass at home.

As if in response to orders issued in revenge against the Netherlanders, Rome seemed after centuries to be reverting to the daily use of the Latin language, and this enriched the cultural content of the Council climate. An automobile-rental firm advertised in the newspapers that it had reserved for the Council fathers *"novae automobiles quacumque amplitudine omnibusque numeris absolutae etiam sine raedario"*—in other words, new cars of all sizes and even without drivers—and *"sine munere minimi itineris circumvehendi"*—without any minimum mileage charge. A bank announced that it had established *"peculiarum mensam argentariam apud additionem procurationis sedem quae eorum necessitatibus inserviat"*—a special

260

foreign-exchange department at which they could obtain as well whatever extra money they might need. Another branch of the same bank pointed out that it could be useful *"quae cum ad Petrianae basilicae forum adiaceat"*— because of its convenient proximity to St. Peter's Square.

While these were typical of the profane or touristological preparations for the sacred ceremonies that would inaugurate the Council, the liturgical preparations were described in a solemn document issued by the prefect of apostolic ceremonial:

> *Ordo ex caeremoniali praesertim S.R.E. excerptus Concilii oecumenici celebrandi in sacrosanta basilica vaticana jussu Domini nostri* (Order of Ceremonies Prescribed by the Holy Roman Church for the Use of the Ecumenical Council to Be Celebrated in the Most Holy Vatican Basilica at the Command of our Lord)

On the morning of October 11, pursuant to this document, 2498 Council fathers—cardinals and patriarchs, archbishops and bishops— marched through St. Peter's Square in a procession that was one and a quarter miles long and that took a full hour to make its way past a crowd of two hundred thousand spectators, cheering and shouting and more excited by the parade than plunged in prayer. Monsignor Arnaldo Fattinnanzi, master of papal ceremonies, stood before the bronze gate at eight thirty in the morning and shouted like a colonel: *"Procedamus!"* The march was led off by a color guard of the noble guards, followed by two sergeants of the Swiss Guards, a train of "lay nobility," secret chaplains in red cassocks, consistory lawyers in great black robes, referendaries * and *votandi di segnatura* in violet robes and ermine mantles and hoods,

* Bearers of the gestatorial chair.—TRANSLATOR.

261

judges of the Rota in surplices and stoles, honorary chamberlains in white rochets, secret chamberlains in Spanish cloaks, a chaplain with the pope's tiara, a subdeacon with the pope's cross, and then the Council fathers, the "bearers of God."

In their van were the snowy caps of the generals of the Dominican, Trinitarian, Premonstratensian, and Carthusian orders; the tobacco-colored habits of the generals of the mendicant orders; the chasubles, dalmatics, and copes of abbots occupying episcopal functions, abbots general, prelates and abbots *nullius;* then came twenty-five hundred miters on the heads of as many Council fathers marching two by two in a slow solemnity—miters gently bobbing, matched in the subtle variety of their styles— pure white miters, miters veined with gold, laminated miters, sparkling miters, long miters peaking toward the sky, lower and broader miters of the African bishops, jewel-studded closed-crown miters of the bishops of the Eastern Catholic Rite, shining damask miters of cardinals: the Roman patrician dress of the two guardians of the Council, Prince Don Aspreno Colonna and Prince Don Alessandro Torlonia; the hooded mantle of the chamberlain of the Holy Roman Church, Monsignor José Nunes da Costa, the first of the four "tasseled prelates"; the purple of the cardinal-first deacon who would intone the Gospel, Francesco Roberti; the purple of Alberto Cardinal Di Jorio, deacon of Santa Prudenziana; the purple of Alfredo Cardinal Ottaviani, deacon of Santa Maria in Dominica; and then, at the end, in his gestatorial chair, Pope John.

He moved forward under the protection of the canopy and between two bearers of the flabella, the fans of ostrich plumes; he was followed by the dean of the tribunal of the Rota, the court physician to the papacy, the mace bearers with their silver weapons, the six cantors, the auditor and the treasurer of the apostolic chamber, the participating prothonotaries, the undersecretaries and officials of the Council, and, to close the whole procession, the forty-two young priests trained in Latin shorthand, the most sober of all the marchers in their ankle-length robes with their short black cloaks. John was constantly repeating blessings, the bands were playing the pontifical anthem, the soldiers of an Italian regiment arrayed in parade formation on the frontier between Church and State stood presenting arms, and the throng clapped and shouted amid the pealing of all the church bells in Rome.

Inside Saint Peter's, meanwhile, the Council fathers, whose procession had brought them back to the basilica, went in pairs to their seats, where they sat smoothing out their white cloaks as they waited for the pope, who, when at last he arrived, dismounted from his gestatorial chair at the foot of the statue of Saint Peter at the beginning of the apse. He knelt on the faldstool, rose, and began to chant the hymn of Pentecost, *"Veni, creator spiritus, mentes tuorum visita* (Come, creating spirit, and enter the spirits of thy people) . . ."* The cantors responded and the bishops joined in the chorus: *"Qui diceris Paraclitus/altissimi donum Dei* (Thou Holy Spirit who exaltest/the gift of Most High God) . . ."* through all seven stanzas to the final exaltation: *"Deo Patri sit gloria/et Filio qui a mortuis/resurrexit, ac Paraclito* (Glory to God the Father/and to the Son who from the dead/arose again, and to the Holy Spirit) . . ."* And then, three times, *Oremus* (let us pray), again sung

263

in chorus to the Holy Spirit, to God the Father, and to the Son.

The Mass was celebrated by the senior cardinal, Eugène Tisserant, who sang it in a fine voice trained in the French pronunciation of Latin, with stresses falling on the final closed *u* in *Dominùs* and *Oremùs* and on the broad *e* of *Patèr nostèr*. When it was concluded, after more than an hour, the pope embraced the cardinal and the fathers in their pews embraced one another, first the neighbor to the right and then the neighbor to the left, hands resting lightly on shoulders, in series along the entire length of the endless rows. John, meanwhile, was putting on his gala pointifical robes, from stockings and shoes to maniple and pallium; then he took his place on the throne and received the pledges of obedience from the Council fathers.

All the cardinals took part, but only two from each category of archbishops and bishops, abbots and fathers general performed the rite, in order to conserve time. According to their rank (in descending order), they bowed and kissed the pope's hand, his knee, or his foot; but John was cordial and kind with all of them, clasped hands warmly with each, chatted, laughed, made little jokes, and, in the spontaneity of his conversation, transformed the ritual of pledging obedience into a reunion of brothers met in joyful love. He greeted Thomas Cardinal Tien ken-sin of China in Latin, and the prelate blushed with embarrassment but made an elegant Latin response. Twice the pope warmly clapped Laurean Cardinal Rugambwa of Tanzania on the shoulder: in the cardinal's native tongue his surname means "future fame" and John reminded him that the prophecy had been truly fulfilled. He joked with Pietro Cardinal Ciriaci, a typical Roman, and orally and by gesture he repeatedly signified his agreement with his beloved primate of Poland, Stepan Wyszysnki, opening and closing his hands, and spreading his arms affectionately.

He became solemn again when it was time for him to pronounce the profession of faith, the episcopal creed: *"Ego Johannes, Sacrae Romanae Ecclesiae Episcopus* (I, John, Bishop of the Holy Roman Church) . . ." He affirmed his belief in the revelation, the teaching, and the doctrine of the Church, in the seven sacraments, in the doctrine of original sin, in the interpretation of the Holy Scriptures (*"amplector et recipio*—I embrace and accept") in the supremacy and infallibility of the Roman pontiff, in the presence of Jesus Christ in the Eucharist, in purgatory *("constanter teneo purgatorium esse*—I have always held that purgatory exists"), in prayer for the souls of the dead, in the Madonna, in the saints, in the relics (*"teneo reliquias esse venerandas*—I believe that relics should be venerated"). All these things he promised, making vows and oaths to respect them (*"spondeo, voveo, et juro*—I promise, I vow, and I swear") and to repudiate and condemn (*"reicio et anatematizo*—I reject and anathematize") evil wherever it might lie hidden. His voice was sonorous, with a few traces of northern Italian accent audible in his Latin, which he pronounced in an assured manner, like a teacher who expounds in order to persuade gently, with full regard for punctuation and the meaning of ordinary words, and taking care to enunciate the more difficult ones with clarity —such as *anatematizata* (anathematized)—so that there could be no misunderstanding; and, when he felt that it was necessary, he resorted to gesture to stimulate attention and to the motion of the finger to underline an idea: "And so," he concluded, "may God help me, with these his Holy Apostles."

At the command of the secretary general of the Council, Monsignor Pericle Felici, the fathers rose and in chorus they repeated the oath; then the prayer *Adsumus* (We are here) was sung and the litany of the saints was recited, invoking Saint Michael, Saint Gabriel, Saint Raphael, all the sainted angels and archangels, all the sainted patriarchs and prophets, Saint Andrew, Saint John, Saint Thomas, and Saint Philip, *orate pro nobis, libera nos Domine, Te rogamus, audi nos ut Ecclesiam sanctam regere et conservare digneris* (pray for us, set us free, o Lord, we beseech thee, hear us that thou mayest see fit to let Holy Church reign and endure). Francesco Cardinal Roberti, first deacon, began to sing the Gospel for the great day. It was the sequence in Matthew (XXVIII:18–20), which tells how, after the Crucifixion, Jesus appeared to his disciples on a mountain in Galilee and said to them: *"Data est mihi omnis potestas in coelo et in terra* (All power is given unto me in heaven and in earth). Go ye therefore, and teach all nations, baptizing them in the name of the Father, and of the Son, and of the Holy Spirit: teaching them to observe all things whatsoever I have commanded you: *et ecce ego vobiscum sum omnibus diebus usque ad consummationem saeculi*—and, lo, I am with you always, even unto the end of the world."

The mission of the apostles, from whom the bishops are in direct descent, having thus been stated in Latin, the supremacy of Peter, on the other hand, was proclaimed in Greek. From another section of Matthew (XVI:13–20), prelates of the Eastern Rite chanted the arrival of Jesus "into the coasts of Caesarea Philippi," where, when He asked who in the opinion of the people was the Son of Man, the disciples replied: "Some say that thou art John the Baptist; some, Elias; and others, Jeremiah, or one of the prophets. He saith unto them, But whom say ye that I am? And Simon Peter answered and said, Thou art the Christ, the Son of the living God. And Jesus answered and said unto him, Blessed art thou, Simon Bar-jona: for flesh and blood hath not revealed it unto thee, but My Father which is in heaven. And I say also unto thee, That thou are Peter; and upon this rock I will build My church; and the gates of hell shall not prevail against it."

Here the Greeks proceeded with a supplication from their own rite, an invocation to the Paraclete, the Holy Spirit. They sang in loud voices, repeating an exalting *Kyrie eleison* three times as if it were a battle hymn. Shrill at the beginning, the Greek voices went from the long-drawn-out tones of eastern music to sharp, stressed rhythms, scanned and measured by the accents: *"Tòn Paraclitòn, Tòn Paraclitòn, Tòn Paraclitòn"* roared and reechoed beneath the dome of Saint Peter's. Once more there was singing in Latin: the *Pater noster*, Psalm LXVI, the great litany, the plea to Mary, the lesser litany, the final litany. The pope sang, the cardinals sang, the Council fathers and the cantors of the papal musical college sang: "O Good Shepherd who hast promised to bring together the strayed lambs in a single flock . . . we pray thee, O Lord, fulfill our hope and have mercy on us."

Finally the singing was ended and the pope once more sat on his throne. He put on his eyeglasses, took from Monsignor Capovilla the speech that he had prepared for the Council, and began to read it quietly, holding the text firmly and taking care to keep the pages in proper order.

He raised his hand to mark the passages that he regarded as important, calling the fathers' attention to them, and frequently he looked round in order to make sure that they were giving it. Judged on the basis of his gestures and looks, the passages that seemed most important to him were those that dealt with understanding the modern world and the primacy of pastoral over theological doctrine: in other words, of persuasion over condemnation. In fact he said:

In the daily exercise of our ministry our ear is sometimes offended by suggestions from persons who, though ardent in their devotion, are not overabundantly endowed with discretion or a sense of proportion. Modern times to them mean only falsehood and ruin; they are always saying that our age, in comparison with those of the past, is steadily deteriorating; and they behave as if they had learned nothing from history, which is nonetheless the teacher of life, and as if in the days of the earlier Ecumenical Councils everything proceeded in the fullness of the triumphs of the Christian idea and practice and of proper religious freedom. To us it seems [here, placing his manuscript in one hand, he threw wide the other arm] that it is our duty to disagree with these prophets of doom who constantly foretell disastrous events as if the end of the world were at hand.

Drawing a deep breath, he looked round to make certain that everyone had understood. More tranquilly, patiently didactic, he proceeded to explain the reasons behind the Council and the tasks before it as he viewed them:

The *punctum saliens* [salient point] of this Council is not debate over this or that thesis of the fundamental doctrine of the Church in prodigal repetition of the teaching of ancient and modern fathers and theologians, which is presumed always to be vividly present and familiar to the spirit. For this there was no need for a Council.

Again he gestured generously with his arm, his hand flat like a blade scything the weeds that mar the beauty of a field, and then he explained how errors should be identified and dealt with.

We always see, as one age is followed by another, that men's opinions also change, one set canceling another, and errors are no sooner born than they vanish like fog before the sun. The Church has always opposed these errors: often, indeed, she has condemned them with the utmost harshness. Now, however, the Bride of Christ prefers to apply the medication of mercy rather than that of severity. She believes in meeting the needs of our day by showing the validity of her doctrine rather than by renewing her condemnations.

With this everything that was necessary was said, and at the conclusion John removed his eyeglasses, put them away, returned the perfectly arranged sheets of his manuscript to Monsignor Capovilla, and rose to deliver his benediction in the names of Saint Peter and Saint Paul, from whom, he said, he derived his own authority. Six voices were raised then in Pier Luigi da Palestrina's *Tu es Petrus* (*Thou Art Peter*), which translates into music the Gospel according to Saint Matthew; two verses of it were sung and then the antiphon was repeated, while John mounted the gestatorial chair, the referendaries raised it, and his little procession set off toward the doors of the basilica at a slow pace amid applause and singing.

This speech had been written completely by John himself, in Italian: "It is all flour out of my own sack, and no one has thrust his beak into it," he told a foreign cardinal. Then it was translated by the Vatican's Latinists, but John ordered that *l'Osservatore romano* also "print the first draft in the Italian language in order that everyone know, not

269

because I seek personal satisfaction but because I have discharged the responsibility that I have assumed, that it was all written by the pope from the first word to the last . . ." He took pains too to make his own check of the Latin text of *Pacem in terris* so that it suffer no damage, but even in the period of the Council he felt the need to act directly, to step in, to oversee, to keep his finger on everything: "I am incapable," he wrote in his diary, "of giving up my personal determination to write everything myself. There is a little vanity in this: *Dominus mihi parcat,* may the Lord forgive me; and vanity makes for a certain amount of suffering."

The next day, in the Sistine Chapel, John received the members of the eighty-six special missions that had come from every part of the world for the Ecumenical Council: twenty-two from Africa, twenty from America, eighteen from Europe, sixteen from Asia, and one from Australia; the others represented such international entities as the Order of Malta, Euratom, the European Economic Community, and the United Nations' Educational, Scientific, and Cultural Organization. So mixed a group had never before been brought together in the Sistine Chapel in all the years of its history, and John, standing beneath the Pentecostal tapestry, looked round on his guests with great satisfaction. As usual, he greeted them by throwing out his arms and gesturing with his hands, while the chapel's singers intoned the *Surge illuminare,* a work for six voices by Pier Luigi da Palestrina.

The pope at once made very effort to put everyone at ease, good-humoredly repeating: "Your Excellencies . . . my dear sirs . . . " He explained that he had wanted to show special respect to so select a group by receiving it there in the Sistine Chapel, "customarily restricted to liturgical

270

ceremonies and also, as you know, to meetings of the cardinals when a new pope is to be elected." Then he spoke of the purposes of the Council:

Beyond its religious significance, the Council has a social aspect that concerns the lives of nations, and this has been given special prominence by your presence in this place. It is well known and obvious that a Council involves above all the Catholic Church. It is intended to demonstrate its vitality and emphasize its spiritual mission. It seeks further to modify its methods and instruments to the end that the dictrine of the Gospels be realized and more easily accepted by the peoples. It is intended too to smooth the way that will lead to the meeting of so many brothers, because it is a renewed call to the faithful of the separated communities that they too may follow us in friendship on this quest for unity and grace.

Next he spoke of the Church's goal of peace:

. . . a true peace destined to foster respect for the human individual among the peoples and to achieve true freedom of worship and religion, a peace that fosters harmony among states even if this requires them to make certain sacrifices. The logical results will be mutual love, brotherhood, and the end of the conflicts among men of diverse origins and different mentalities. This will expedite the aid so badly needed by the developing nations, and it will further the campaign for their well-being by eliminating all thoughts of domination.

This was a repetition of a passage in *Mater et Magistra* in which John had denounced neocolonialism, a phenomenon that, "however cleverly disguised, is no less enslaving on that account than what many peoples have recently thrown off and that would exert a negative influence on international relations because it would constitute a menace and a danger to world peace." Having thus reiterated that one of the bases of world peace was the harmonious and

271

orderly development of the newly independent countries, John once more addressed to rulers a call to peace negotiations:

Let them continue to meet, to discuss, and let them arrive at honorable, generous, and just agreements. Let them be ready, too, to make the sacrifices necessary for the preservation of the peace of the world. Then the peoples will be able to labor in a climate of serenity, and all the discoveries of science will serve the cause of progress and contribute to the continuing amelioration of man's sojourn on this earth.

By way of conclusion John recited a psalm, the sixty-seventh, rhythmically accenting the third and fourth verses: * "Let the people praise thee, O God; let all the people praise thee. O let the nations be glad, and sing for joy; for thou shalt judge the people righteously, and govern the nations upon earth." He came down from the throne, chatted with his visitors, then went back to the throne to give them his blessing. After that, he said again: "Last night, in a good talk with the Romans who had come into St. Peter's Square to greet me, I told them to kiss their children when they went home and tell the children that that was the pope's kiss. Well, let the benediction that I am giving you also be like a caress to all the peoples whom you represent."

* In the King James Version.—TRANSLATOR.

XII

Freedom in the Church

The fathers refuse to vote.
John accepts and approves their explanations.
Cardinal Montini acknowledges the
inadequacy of the preparations.
John cuts short the debate on the liturgy.
Ottaviani is called a liar.
John withdraws the draft
on the sources of divine revelation.
The second session should be quicker.

THE Council opened under the auspices of freedom, for which Cardinal Ottaviani himself had volunteered to stand surety. In his capacity as secretary of the Congregation of the Holy Office, he was functioning as the judicial guardian of the faith. Indeed, he had promised in a speech that the broadest liberty of discussion would be allowed; and probably he was not enthusiastic at the prospect. It appeared rather that he had said this only in order to evade making a prediction: "Who knows anything about it? there will be complete freedom."

This freedom was actually mere pretense from the very first general session on October 13, 1962, which, moreover, lasted only fifteen working minutes after the opening Mass. This was supposed to have been the occasion for the election of the 160 members of the 10 Council commissions, and the secretary general, Monsignor Pericle Felici, presented the Council fathers with a list of names of those who were already members of or consultants to the preparatory commissions—all appointees of the Vatican and probably creatures of the Curia and the Roman congregations. Such lists could have a considerable power of suggestion, particularly on those Council fathers described as "deprived," the heads of dioceses scattered over distant continents, who were strangers to Vatican procedures and thus easily manipulated by Monsignor Felici.

In explicit Latin the bishop of Lille, Achille Cardinal Liénart, refused to vote: "Under the existing conditions we are in no position to appraise and choose. Not all of us know one another well; we feel the need for preliminary consultation among the various ecclesiastical provinces and the diverse episcopal conferences." At that moment there were at least fifty such conferences in Rome, both national and continental; this was a new state of affairs for the capital of Catholicism and it created problems unknown to the men of the Curia.

Joseph Cardinal Frings, archbishop of Cologne, rose to introduce a motion to postpone the vote; it was seconded by the archbishops of Utrecht, Vienna, and Munich, Cardinals Alfrink, Koenig, and Doepfner. Thus the vanguard of the fifty national conferences, the episcopates of France, Germany, The Netherlands, and Austria, launched their battle against the Curia on a matter of procedure, which, however, had a certain substantive character. The vigorous applause that arose from the benches of the "deprived" fathers, who formed the majority, raised the specter of even larger forces in the future. The chairman of the session, Cardinal Tisserant, taking cognizance of the prevailing mood, decided in favor of the postponement and announced that the vote would be held three days later, on Tuesday, October 16. It was not even ten o'clock in the morning when the Council fathers began pouring down the grand staircase and through the bronze gates to fill the colonnade and adorn St. Peter's Square with the white, red, and violet of thousands of rochets, mantlets, and *mozzette.*

The episode, which was a real blow to the opening of the Council, was not kept secret. Just as there had been freedom of discussion, so, too, though unanticipated, there

276

was freedom of information. Within a half-hour the details of the matter were publicly announced through the sober description of them in an official bulletin.

The lack of reticence on the deliberations of the opening day of the Council was probably also the result of the admission of Italian television cameramen to that morning's session by special exception in order to record the proceedings, which Monsignor Felici had expected to be purely formal. Hence the unanticipated discussion had taken place for the eyes and ears of outsiders ("Vatican II, born under the intrusive glare of a few spotlights, has made the existence of these and other problems matters of public knowledge: not only is this the case, but there was no time allowed to review them in such a way that their disclosure could be accomplished without shocks and misunderstandings": thus the lament of the conservative *Giornale d'Italia*), and, notwithstanding the fact that all the speeches had been made in Latin and that the television people had quite honestly insisted that they had not understood a word, Monsignor Felici deemed it wiser to assume that theirs was a feigned ingenuousness. He preferred to grasp the initiative by himself providing information that at least would not shockingly aggravate the truth.

John sent for the ten cardinals of the so-called "presidium": Tisserant and Liénart of France, Tappouni of Syria, Gilroy of Australia, Frings of Germany, Pla y Deniel of Spain, Spellman of the United States, Ruffini of Italy, Caggiano of Argentina, and Alfrink of The Netherlands. They had been the chairmen of the ten preparatory commissions, which were now to be replaced or made permanent according to the Council's vote. Liénart spoke for all of them, explaining to the pope the situation that had given rise to the ill humor of the fathers. Each commission was composed of twenty-four members: eight appointed by the pope and sixteen elected by the Council. The choice of the 160 names by the Council fathers was a very complex procedure: in theory, each of the 2500 voting fathers should have had access to a list of 2500 names among which he could make a free—but, in practice, random— choice. Therefore the list distributed by Monsignor Felici, the secretary general, could become an instrument, if not of limitation, at least of hidden persuasion. What was worse, simultaneous voting on 160 names distributed among the 10 lists of the 10 commissions would have brought about inevitable duplications, unmerited defeats, infinite dilutions. Having taken all this into account, Liénart told the pope, he had on his own initiative summoned the majority of the French fathers the day before to the church of Saint Louis in Via della Scrofa.

This Cardinal Liénart, the dean of his country's bishops, the inspiration of the Mission de France in Pontigny—one of the most vigorous and modern institutions in the Catholic Church—was among the most aggressive of the prelates. He had gained notoriety and prestige for the campaigns that he had waged on behalf of the worker priests and trade-union unity and against the use of torture in Algeria. In comparison with such things, the electoral battle that he was now preparing to mount against the Curia was a minor affair.

In the session in Saint Louis des Français he had in fact successfully championed the necessity to modernize the weapon of the ballot and indeed to make it practically efficacious, insisting that in every case it be free in a Council that intended to be an innovative force in the life of the

Church. The French fathers had expressed their approbation, and, on their initiative, so had all the Basque bishops and a large number of the Catalans, who politically gravitated more toward the French bishops than toward the other Spanish prelates. In addition to the French, the Basques, and the Catalans, the Belgian bishops had held a meeting under the chairmanship of the archbishop of Malines, Léo-Joseph Cardinal Suenens, in the premises of their country's seminary, and forged a unity of their own; subsequently Cardinal Bea had gone there to advise them that the German bishops too, holding their session in the church of Santa Maria dell'Anima, had aligned themselves against the Curia. On behalf of the Netherlanders Alfrink had made a similar announcement.

Thus, through these exchanges of information among the national episcopates, they had reached agreement on the motion for the postponement of the vote and laid the foundations for accords on future lists of candidates. Each episcopal conference was to be able to present its own restricted list of names to be inserted by prior agreement into the ten different lists: three or four names for each of the larger national conferences and proportionate representation, appropriately arrived at, for each of the others in every list. In substance, the purpose was to have the lists of candidates prepared not by the Roman Curia but by the national or continental conferences.

John acknowledged that there could have been no better solution; for that matter, he showed no unhappiness over the business. He pointed out that in the history of the Ecumenical Councils there had often been instances of even quite bitter conflict. So Vatican II was falling into the right tradition, and, with a certain malice, John added that there was no compelling reason for haste in the voting: "Do not be dismayed if things go slowly. He travels far who travels slowly." He told the fathers that he himself had given close study to the precedents. As early as June of 1959 he had borrowed from the Jesuits in Villa Malta the bound volumes of *Civiltà cattolica* that contained the accounts of the preparations for and the progress of the Ecumenical Council Vatican I. Other books too, also borrowed from the same library, had served him as sources on the subject, and from them he had learned that the voting in Vatican I for its commissions, which were called deputations, had proceeded much more deliberately:

> In order to choose four of them, elections were held during four general meetings on December 14, 21, and 28, 1869, and January 14, 1870. So why improvise this time? It would be imprudent, and it could also give rise to the suspicion that the central preparatory commission wanted to consolidate those principles of bureaucratic centralization in the government of the church that, in contrast, are quite far from the spirit of our Council.

He had *l'Osservatore romano* say that

> . . . all validity would be stripped from a Council insofar as it permitted the suppression of projects, proposals, and statements that clarify the truth. . . . Nothing is more dangerous and prejudicial than to imagine the Council fathers as passive, mechanical duplicating machines, lifeless dummies in an assembly.

The election battle having been won, the more energetic of the Council fathers found cause for criticism in the doctrinal theses that had been drafted—there were 70 of them—and then brought together, glossed, explained, and annotated in 119 pamphlets dispatched in July of 1962 to all the bishops in the world. In return, they had sent a total of 8792 votes of approval or disapproval, comments, and analyses to the central committee in the Vatican, but in the end all this material put together to provide a doctrinal fabric for the Council proved to be of deteriorating quality, as John himself had very much feared.

Many fathers found these theses too scholastic, too canonical, too legalistic, and therefore far from adequately pastoral, in addition to being very scantily evangelical. The work of evaluation had been immeasurable, but the result could have been called the birth of the mouse after the labor of the mountain. Many of the fathers who had come from remote areas found that they all agreed that the best thing that could be done with these theses was to give them decent burial: *"Sepelire reverenter* [Bury them with respect]," they suggested. Cardinal Montini himself, the archbishop of Milan, handed down a most harsh judgment:

> The material is tremendous [he wrote in *Italia*, the daily newspaper of his archbishopric]; it is excellent but heterogeneous and unequal; it would have called for courageous editing and condensation if some authority that was not merely external and disciplinary had dominated its logical and organic preparation and if a central architectonic idea had polarized and perfected this work.

It might seem that Montini was criticizing John for inadequate participation. While John had posed the problem of freedom within the Catholic Church, both for the present and for the future, Montini viewed it only in terms of the difficulties that it entailed. In any case, employing the conventional terminology of deference, Montini continued:

In conformity with that ideal of freedom and spontaneity that gave birth to this Council, there is still lacking a focal point for its program, which, however, has fortunately been given solemn and wise delineation by the Holy Father's words in those years that preceded the Council.

The French bishops were consistent in their request that all the theses be reviewed "in the light of the speeches of John XXIII," and they quoted the pope's exhortations that the Council not run aground on abstract considerations or devote itself to condemnation of the errors of our age. For that, John had said, "it would not have been necessary to have a Council." Now, therefore, the way must be found for a pastoral, evangelical Council, "because any pastoral method that does not come down to evangelical simplicity is doomed to failure." It was essential to fight free of doctrinal and disciplinary schematism and to resolve rather on a Council "that strives for the very essence of Christian life, corroded and ambushed in these times from all sides."

Cardinal Siri, on the other hand, descended to direct controversy with John in explicit terms that were harsher than those used by Montini. In *Orizzonti*, a Catholic weekly with a large circulation, he said that the Ecumenical Council ought properly to concern itself with "doctrinal matters of extreme importance" because it was precisely these that constituted "the major duty of the Council," while the pastoral task should have been appropriately reduced:

It is absolutely false that the pastoral mission can characterize a Council. . . . The primary pastoral obligation is to tell the whole revealed truth. . . . Pastoral care does not consist in distributing caresses, smiles, and acts of grace at any price. . . . None of us can dilute the Gospel: on the contrary, the most important requests that Christ has made of his followers can arise as cogent imperatives.

He then put forth as certain the condemnation of a number of modern errors, though he took pains not to identify any of them, and finally he allowed himself a certain irony on the so-called separation of the Church from Western politics. "The West," he declared, in contrast to John's position of complete supranational neutrality, "is absolutely not to be repudiated."

Aside from any polemic theme, the problem of the orientation of the Council and a necessary programmatic schedule for it undoubtedly existed, and indeed even the temperate Cardinal Montini wondered: "What will be the comprehensive, logical plan for this vast and overwhelming discussion? It would not appear that any plan has been prepared. Will it be possible to establish one now? Will it be made public?"

There was a certain tentative groping in the early days. Alfrink's Netherlanders contended that first of all the bishops' power must be reexamined because only after satisfaction on this point had been achieved would the fathers have the full authority and stature required for the resolution of other questions. This would also be a means of establishing a direct connection between Vatican II and Vatican I if the thesis of the Netherlands bishops' conference were to be accepted: that the dogma of papal infallibility was not isolated and self-supporting but must be extended and reinforced by the proclamation of the collective infallibility of the bishops, which in turn was the fruit of the infallible faith of the entire community.

To work through dogmas, however, did not seem useful. If the Netherlanders had insisted on their own point of view, they would have had to endure the counterattack of the advocates of the new Marian dogmas, or even of the references to Saint Joseph, which some Italian theologians were holding in reserve. So, instead, work began in an area that seemed best suited for accomplishing the first steps and also for gaining some idea of the efforts and obligations that the Council would require. Thus it was liturgy that was quietly selected as the subject. Even this, however, was the occasion for clashes or at least skirmishes between two tendencies, one called "numinous" and the other called "luminous." The numinous group, from *numen*, the divine will or the sense of grace, was a conservative minority that was concerned with preserving the sacral and mysterious aspect of worship and therefore favored the retention of Latin, which is musical, poetic, and concise, even if incomprehensible to the masses. The "luminous" group, on the other hand, championed the necessity of assuring enlightenment, *lumen*—in other words, the help that liturgy should give to teaching. In view of the fact that often the liturgy is in practice the only means of teaching the people (in the case of the missionary churches and also that of the churches of silence), it would be better, this group argued, to eliminate Latin in part or wholly, since it is an unknown language to most and no one can be enlightened by obscurity, even if the obscurity is holy.

John, even though he had praised Latin in his constitution, *Veterum Sapientia,* as an irreplaceable tool of culture in the seminaries and the theological schools, declared that this constitution did not apply to the liturgy. "It is quite natural," he explained, speaking in Italian at the Mass celebrated in Saint Peter's in honor of the fourth anniversary of his election, "it is quite natural that changes in times and circumstances should suggest different forms and methods for the external transmittal of doctrine itself and endow it with a new appearance." Members of the Curia protested to him that one must proceed with caution because venerable problems of tradition were at issue: and the reply that he made then is still a model: "Tradition? But do you know what that is? It is the progress that was made yesterday, as the progress that we ought to make today will constitute the tradition of tomorrow."

The debate between the numinous and the luminous continued in the meantime, and, in order to overcome the opposition between *numen* and *lumen*, recourse was suggested to a third word, *culmen*, the summit, by which was meant the liturgy as the highest point in the mystery of the Church. So it appeared as if madness lay ahead, as in the Byzantine theologians' controversies over the sex of the angels. It was in fact from the Orient that the shock came this time when Patriarch Maxim IV Seigh of the Syrian Melchites rose to speak. Although he was more than a master of Latin, he spoke this time in French for polemical reasons. He said that actually there was nothing sacred about Latin, that in any event neither his own Melchite Church nor any other Catholic Church of the Eastern Rite used Latin, and that not even Jesus Christ and the apostles had spoken Latin: "Almost like our colleague, Cardinal Spellman, who when he speaks Latin has an incomprehensible accent."

There was much laughter, but there was also a cry of protest from Monsignor Enrico Dante, secretary of the Sacred Congregation of Rites and prefect of the sacred ceremonies: "Everything has been settled by tradition, and you want to change it all." Maxim IV retorted that there was a definite date at which the tradition had begun, because it was only in the second century of the Church that

285

Latin had been introduced into the liturgy: and even earlier, anyway, Saint Paul had resolved the question once and for all, so that one could say that the tradition had begun with Saint Paul. He quoted Paul's First Epistle to the Corinthians, from the tenth through the nineteenth verses of the fourteenth chapter: "There are, it may be, so many kinds of voices in the world, and none of them is without signification. . . . Wherefore let him that speaketh in an unknown tongue, pray that he may interpret. . . . Else, when thou shalt bless with the spirit, how shall he that occupieth the room of the unlearned, say Amen at thy giving of thanks, seeing he understandeth not what thou sayest? For thou verily givest thanks well, but the other is not edified. . . . Yet in the Church I had rather speak five words with my understanding, that by my voice I might teach others also, than ten thousand words in an unknown tongue."

It was then that Cardinal Ottaviani rose to defend tradition in a most polished Latin. It might indeed have been a pleasure to listen to him, because his Latin was beautifully harmonic, and, unlike Cardinal Spellman's, pronounced with a good accent. When, however, the ten minutes allowed to each speaker had passed and Ottaviani showed no sign of stopping, Cardinal Alfrink, whose turn it was that day to occupy the chair, asked him to finish. Having a great deal more to say, perhaps of importance, Ottaviani pretended not to have understood. When five minutes more had elapsed, Alfrink did not repeat his request but simply disconnected the wire that ran to the speaker's microphone. Initially Ottaviani did not notice, and he went on speaking; the audience could see his lips moving but there was no sound in the vastness of the basilica. What alerted him to the situation was the handclapping of the laughing Council fathers applauding Alfrink's firm action. Piqued, Ottaviani departed not only from the speaker's platform but also from the meeting hall, and for thirteen days he took no part in the Council's labors.

This gave John pain. He might not have shared Ottaviani's views and his defense of so-called tradition à l'outrance, but the pope was offended by the discourtesy of the treatment that had been needlessly inflicted on the cardinal. He let his regret be known; and then he suggested that the general discussion on the problem of the liturgy could be concluded; he proposed to the governing commission that it declare the debate closed and suggest that any further comments be submitted to the Secretariat in writing. Then he did something still better. As if to point out that the pope's power was still intact even when the Council was sitting, on his own initiative, while the controversies over the liturgy were still flourishing, he issued a decree that modified the Canon of the Mass. He ordered that, after the words *Communicantes et memoriam venerantes*, Mary's name be followed by that of Saint Joseph.

Since the year A.D. 610—in other words, since the time of Saint Gregory the Great—the Canon of the Mass had remained unaltered throughout the world. John's change, therefore, was a real event, even if, or even because, the Council had had no part in it. "The pope has acted counter to the wishes of many fathers," it was officially announced. This was little less than an estimate, because there had been only a modest petition signed by some three hundred Canadian, Italian, and Yugoslav bishops. Hence the announcement of the change that was made in the basilica by Monsignor Felici, the secretary general, was received with the briefest and chilliest applause, purely for the sake of form. But the moral was not missed, and at least in the matter of liturgy a final vote was ultimately arrived at; the majority approved a preamble that explained simply how the option was left with the national bishops' conferences to decide whether certain parts of the Mass might be celebrated in the ordinary language of their respective peoples. The later paragraphs of the preamble were submitted to a commission that was charged with amending them in accordance with the new spirit: and this was now the spirit of Paul's First Epistle to the Corinthians.

If it proceeded in this manner, however, it was clear that the Council would never accomplish anything concrete, or in any event that it would go on endlessly. John had assumed that everything could be completed in a single session, and in fact the logistical organization had been worked out on the presumption of a short Council. The metal supports that held up the speakers' platform of the Council fathers in the nave of Saint Peter's had been leased from a firm in Milan for only three months, and it was in November that the decision was made to buy them after a rebate of £IT100 million on what had already been sunk into the rental.

From a practical point of view, the almost exclusive function of the entire first session of the Council was to make the best rectifications possible in the mistakes and defects of the work carried out by the preparatory commissions. The seventy theses that had been elaborated and that in their number and extent exceeded in their mass and volume all the decrees approved by all twenty Ecumenical Councils held during the history of the Church were reduced to some twenty. This was a commonsense move, and it was also decided to evolve better positions on some of the matters that the preparatory commissions had neglected, such as the problems of hunger, justice, peace, population expansion, and the evangelization of the poor. The fact that the Council had recognized these as basic problems of the modern world and that it had reduced the number of areas of work, interweaving them differently, was already an initial victory for the so-called progressive tendencies among the bishops, as firm as they were vigorous in their demand for episcopal privileges against Roman centralization, yet on the other hand open to world problems.

Their spokesman became Léo-Joseph Cardinal Suenens, the archbishop of Malines. He pointed out the main road to be followed, which was that of reviewing all the theses in terms of two dominating ideas: the opening of the Church *ad intra* and the opening of the Church *ad extra*. Through the opening *ad intra* the Church would reexamine its own nature and constitution, its central power, its members—bishops, priests, the laity—its educational and redemptory mission. *Ad extra* it would confront the problems of the world from war to justice, from peace to poverty, social justice, etc. Thus the Council would find the guideline that it had lacked from the outset.

The result had been not only that unfortunate loss of time that had pained John but also a disorderly battle between two sides; and to John this was more serious, especially because the major clash occurred over a matter of ecumenical Christian importance: divine revelation. Were two discrete sources of this revelation— the Holy Scripture and tradition—to be recognized, or only one with two different expressions? According to the Catholic traditional-

289

ists there were two sources: Holy Scripture, and tradition handed down orally since the time of the apostles. According to the reformed believers and Protestants in general, only Scripture was acceptable.

Those Council fathers who were not rigid traditionalists and who were better disposed toward an approach to the other Christian churches would have liked to profit by Vatican II to reduce the gap, but unfortunately the thesis on the sources of revelation had been prepared by a theological commission presided over by Cardinal Ottaviani and made up for the greater part of theologians in his confidence. It had produced a text that could not have been more rigidly traditionalist. It asserted that the sources of revelation were separate; it reiterated the law laid down by the Council of Trent to the effect that the Bible might be interpreted only with the spiritual guidance of a theologian; and it rejected the theory that modern scientific methods might be applied to the interpretation of Scripture.

If this thesis had been approved, the problem of the union of the churches would have been set back at least a century. A Protestant observer remarked: "I feel as if I were at Vatican I. But what am I saying? At Nicea! No, I mean at Ephesus!" Siri, Ruffini, and Ottaviani, Italian cardinals of the conservative guard, supported by the archbishop of Los Angeles, James Francis A. Cardinal McIntyre, a man of the strict Irish tradition, gave battle for the confirmation of the age-old integrity of Catholic doctrine. Against them Cardinals Frings, Liénart, Koenig, and Ritter began to contend that the thesis was too doctrinal and scholastic, excessively rigid, not sufficiently explored in depth, but above all incomprehensible not only for the separated brothers but to Catholics themselves.

Conscious of the responsibilities that were incumbent on him as secretary for Christian unity, Cardinal Bea attempted to mediate. A man of great spontaneous courtesy, he was lavish in his praises of those who had drafted the thesis, paying full tribute to the labor, as accurate as it was exhaustive, to which they had subjected themselves. The result of so much effort, however, seemed unsatisfactory to him, if not completely negative, because so rigid a thesis would have inflicted incalculable harm on the cause of the union of Christians: not only that, but "it would also have shut the gates against intellectual Europe and refused the outstretched hands of the separated brothers of the Old and the New Worlds."

Aware that he had lost ground, Ottaviani rose. He said that the thesis had been meticulously prepared by bishops and theologians, approved by the central commission, ratified by the pope. Therefore it could not be repudiated. "*Ista propositio est falsa* (This statement is false)!" an enraged but still anonymous father shouted. Branded a liar, Ottaviani went white. There was a moment of shocked silence—no one would have ever imagined that a cardinal could be called a liar in Saint Peter's, to say nothing of a cardinal who was secretary of the Holy Office—and then Julius Cardinal Doepfner, archbishop of Munich, spoke. He did not stress the direct accusation of Ottaviani, but he destroyed all the latter's arguments, taking them apart piece by piece. As for the ratification by the pope, he said, that should impress no one. The pope had ratified all the theses, obviously, in order that they be submitted to the Council. The commission, however, far indeed from being unanimous, had evidenced many reservations, which Chairman Ottaviani had assumed that he could dismiss from consideration. This was a most grave charge.

John himself was not on the side of the rigorists of tradition. With his belief that tradition was the progress of yesterday and that the progress of today was the tradition of tomorrow, he was not frightened of any possible evolution. Above all he was resolved not to deepen the gulf between Catholics and separated brethren, and too, as far as Bible reading was concerned, his ideas were of the broadest. In his opening address to the Council he had said that doctrine would be examined and expounded "through the forms of analysis and literary expression of modern thought," and it was beyond doubt that he had not had in mind the necessity of any guidance by a theologian for students of the Bible.

While discussions were going on in the Council with so much heat, John spoke in the manner of a commandment to a group of the faithful who were attending a general audience one day during the latter half of November: "Each of you, when you return home, look and see whether there is a Bible there. If you have one, open it often to those pages that are best for the nourishment of the spirit. If you do not have a Bible, lose no time in buying one and giving the place of honor in your home to the book of books." He was convinced that, as far as Catholics were concerned, the separation among Christians was very largely the result of insufficient familiarity with the Holy Scriptures. And so he alluded to the discussions that were under way: "In olden days," he said, as if in response to the rigorists, "there was a certain reluctance to familiarize oneself with the Bible because, some of our Christian brothers having left the Church on the ground that they were standing on the Bible and that faith did not require the pope, the Church, or the priesthood, it was feared that there was almost the same danger of thinking and acting like them."

But John did not believe in this danger. Having thwarted Ottaviani's attempt to bring the pope into the ranks of the integralists, in fact, he procured the transmittal to the steering committee of the Council of a motion to suspend the discussion of the thesis on the sources of revelation. Thirteen hundred seventy-eight fathers voted for the motion and 822 voted against it. To be effective a two-thirds majority was required, but the affirmative vote fell short by fifty-three. Hence the battle would have to continue, paragraph by paragraph, in a state of tension and mutual incomprehension such as to raise the threat of new scandals. Already Monsignor Biagio Musto, bishop of Aquino, had expressed in his loudest tones and his most accusing manner his grief that voices could have been raised beneath the dome of Saint Peter's against the fundamental principles of the institutional and hierarchical Church. Shrewdly quoting Saint Paul, he denounced as false doctors certain bishops who because of their love of innovation were capable of throwing themselves into a cause that would earn them the vengeful punishment of God. Protests went up at once, accompanied by the hammering of pastoral rings against desks, until the prelate from Aquino was silenced as, on a similar though less dramatic occasion, his master, Ottaviani, had been.

Now it was for the pope to make a decision. Anything but satisfied with course taken by the discussions, John followed them from his study on the monitor of a closed-circuit television relay. Perhaps he was grieved not so much by the actual events as by the hair-splitting and rancorous states of mind that lay behind them: "It is good, it is necessary that the Council debate," he told the French bishops when he received them in audience. "It must do so with a feeling of brotherhood, and everything will go well. As for myself, I am an optimist." Perhaps he was not completely an optimist, but he concluded by applying to himself the sentence that was used by Jacob in Genesis (XXXVII:11) in testimony of the dispute between the sons: *"Pater vero rem tacitus considerabat* [The father, however, contemplated the matter in silence]."

John too considered "the matter"—that is, the dispute among his sons—and reached the conclusion that it must be cut short. It was clear that the majority was opposed to Ottaviani's thesis, even if fifty-three votes were still needed to reach the quorum of the two-thirds required by the rules. That was too bad for the rules and the quorum; good faith required that the moral majority rather than the merely arithmetically correct figure be respected. Therefore, on November 21, the day after the vote, John sent word to the Council that the thesis on the sources of revelation was being withdrawn at the request of the Holy Father and transferred for revision to a special mixed commission composed of all the members of the Council's theological commission and all the bishops belonging to the Secretariat for Christian Union, under the joint chairmanship of the standard-bearer of each of the conflicting camps, Cardinals Ottaviani and Bea.

The applause that day, when the announcement was made, exceeded in volume and duration any and all that had occurred previously during the Council's sittings. "Today will go into history as the date of the end of the Counter-Reformation," Father Gregory Baum, the Canadian theologian, asserted. And John, sitting at the monitor in his study, said: "Now our real Council is beginning." There was a universal feeling that the atmosphere had been cleared and the fathers had regained confidence that they could debate not only freely, as before, but in addition with some benefit. Almost gaily Monsignor Thomas Roberts (for many years bishop of Bombay, which he had left in order to make the position available to the first Indian in the Sacred College, Valeriano Cardinal Gracias) declared: "The Council is a football game with the pope as referee."

In his capacity as referee John succeeded in preserving a judicial calm, but it cost him some effort. Actually he did not trust the theologians, and one day, when an Anglican observer was visiting him, the pope asked suddenly: "Are you a theologian?" The Anglican was not, and John added: "Good, *Deo gratias!* I am not either, although I cannot say so. But you too know how many disasters the professional theologians have brought down on the Church with their subtleties, their vanity, their mental narrowness, their stubbornness. And now it is up to ordinary Christians like you and me to get out of this mess."

Ottaviani, however, was preparing another stroke. Toward the end of the Council—in its final days, in fact—he proposed the study of a thesis on the Virgin Mary instead of that *De Ecclesia (Concerning the Church)*. He had evolved a tactic that was not devoid of guile, because the thesis on the Madonna was short, only five pages in all, while *De Ecclesia,* which was much more complicated, required eighty pages. Hence the Council might be tempted to take up a matter that could be disposed of easily and to make a satisfactory finish with the definitive settlement of one more thesis.

Another Marian proclamation, however, would have been an error at the end of the first session of a Council that had as its announced purpose the paving of the way for the unity of the churches. Any new statement having to do with the cult of Mary could in fact only create new obstacles to the return of the separated brethren, but an endeavor of this kind on Ottaviani's part could shock no one. A cardinal such as he, who in practice had never had a pastoral ministry, whose training was exclusively juridical and theological, bureaucratic and authoritarian, who knew the whole range of religious problems only through the texts of the scholastics and who had a horror of unpetrified ideas, would have found it extremely difficult to grasp the mentality of the fathers who had been in contact with men of all confessions, who knew the world and secular culture, who enjoyed dealing with unbelievers. In fact, first the executive committee and then the assembly as a whole rejected Ottaviani's proposal, which was therefore the real great defeat in the first session of the Council.

On December 8, the date set for adjournment, John said that the labors of the first session had been only "a slow and solemn introduction to the great work of the Council. These heaven-sent discussion have caused truth to spring forth, displaying to the eyes of the world the holy freedom of the sons of God as it exists in the Church." Having thus once more confirmed freedom as the salient point of his conception of Christianity, he went on to deal with another of his deepest concerns, the expeditiousness that he wished for the Council.

"The new session that will begin next September," he said, "will have an assured, uninterrupted, and swifter pace, which will have been made possible by the experience gained in these two months of 1962, so that we hope to be able to see its conclusion, on which the eyes of all the faithful are focused." Then and only then, he said, would it be possible to extend the Council's indications and directives to all the domains of the Church: "At that point all the pastors will be united in a gigantic effort of preaching sound doctrine and applying laws that they themselves wished. It will be the new Pentecost, a new leap forward by the Kingdom of Christ on earth, a new proclamation of the good tidings of redemption."

He made his farewell and his benediction, and it seemed that the fulfillment of his office was costing him pain or exceptional fatigue; with a certain sadness he left the basilica amid applause, walking irregularly, now and again hurrying, then slowing again as if to assure himself of safer progress. His health was already very bad, he was aware of its deterioration day by day, and, frankly, he was much displeased by this.

XIII

" . . . Stupid Pope Who Takes It Straight"

"I love life!"
The first attacks of disease.
John's concern with the fate of the Council.
Long and painful suffering.
The meaning of freedom for Christians.

JOHN would have liked to live much longer, and not only in order to officiate himself at the concluding ceremonies of the Ecumenical Council but also because as a man with a good mind he appreciated the gift of life. "Pray for your pope," he said one day at the termination of a general audience, "because to tell the truth, if you will allow me to say so, I hope to live a long time. I love life!" On another occasion—it was January 28, 1959, only a few days after he had first informed the world that there would be a Council—he allowed himself to indulge in some bargaining with God. It was the feast of Saints Agatone and Vitaliano, both seventh-century popes: the first had reigned two and a half years, the second fourteen.

John said that he could not demand the treatment accorded to Vitaliano but that he hoped for as much as Agatone: "I, who attained to the papacy at so late an age, do not despair of being granted by the Lord at least as much time as he gave to Saint Agatone: there are so many things to be done!" He was joking, and he cited still another precedent that puzzled him: "Leo XI, who was Alessandro de' Medici, a Florentine, occupied the papal throne for only twenty-five days, in 1605, and one might comment that it was not worth the trouble of disturbing oneself for so little. But that is how it is," he concluded, smiling and consigning himself to the will of God. In his *Giornale*

301

dell'anima, however, when he was beginning the fourth year of his pontificate and thus had somewhat exceeded Agatone's tenure, he wrote with some satisfaction:

When on October 28, 1958, I was appointed to the supreme responsibility for the universal flock of Jesus Christ at the age of seventy-seven, the conviction was general that I would be merely a temporary, transitional pope. Instead, here I am in the fourth year of my papacy and with the prospect of a vigorous program to be carried out before the eyes of the whole world, which is watching and waiting.

But it was during this same fourth year of his reign, in July and August of 1962, that the symptoms of an ailment that might be an ulcer or a tumor appeared. In September, when he was living in seclusion in Saint John's tower, where an apartment that overlooked the Vatican gardens had been fitted out for him, John was afflicted by recurrent attacks. They did not cause him to give up his preparatory work for the Council; but in addition he subjected himself to the strain of a journey to Loreto and Assisi on October 4. He had to remain standing for long periods, suffering constant discomfort, but he refused to allow himself more than the briefest rest during the hour when the cardinals were taking luncheon together in one of the halls of the basilica of Loreto.

At the inauguration of the Council on October 11 those who were close to him and familiar with his expressions remarked that "his inmost delight was certainly accompanied by the bite of physical suffering." More than once, when he covered his face with his hands and bowed his head, it was in order not only to concentrate on meditation but also to attempt to endure and conceal his pain. On October 28, the fourth anniversary of his election, he was much paler than usual during the Solemn Pontifical Mass in Saint Peter's; he did not complain, however. "If I did not have some suffering and vexation," he said almost gaily, "what kind of pope should I be?"

The experience of physical pain was almost a novelty for him at the age of eighty: he had always enjoyed robust health. He had had some gastric trouble in 1954, and from time to time it had recurred, but he always dismissed it cavalierly as some "mere annoyance." Out of a habit of obedience he followed the regimen that his doctors prescribed for him and he took certain precautions though he regarded them as exaggerated: "But I should like to repay the physicians' affection properly." His condition deteriorated, however, and in the meantime his personal physician, Doctor Filippo Rocchi, had died. John was asked to select a successor, and he chose Professor Antonio Gasbarrini, who lived in Bologna, because he was an old acquaintance of whom John was fond. Gasbarrini, in turn, appointed Professor Pietro Mazzoni as his assistant and went to Rome for a visit. In the best of circumstances, he believed, the problem was an ulcer, or else it was a tumor, and he was much impressed by John's serenity. "Even if it is a tumor," the pope said, "well, let God's will be done. But do not concern yourself for me, because my bags are packed and I am ready to leave. *Nec mori timeo nec vivere recuso* [I neither fear to die nor refuse to live]," he said, quoting Saint Martin the bishop.

It was November 20, a serious day for John because the tension in the Council over the thesis on the sources of divine revelation had risen to its peak. So circumstances contributed to the intensification of his affliction, and indeed the following Sunday, which was his eighty-first birth-

303

day, John felt completely weak. From the window of his apartments looking out on St. Peter's Square he replied to the good wishes of the crowd with an effort that was visible. The next day, Monday, he seemed to be exhausted, and Gasbarrini insisted that he remain in bed. John obeyed because he wanted to regain his strength for the next public audience, but during the night of November 26–27 he had a hemorrhage.

The usual Wednesday audience had to be canceled, and the Vatican announced that the pope was confined to his bed by "a severe influenza." The next day there was a vaguely phrased bulletin that the pope was still ill. Twice in twenty-four hours Gasbarrini called on him; Mazzoni did not leave the Vatican throughout the day. On Thursday the twenty-ninth *l'Osservatore romano* said that all audiences had been suspended "because of the heightened symptoms of a gastric disorder for which the Holy Father has for some time been receiving appropriate medical and dietetic care and that has brought on a rather severe anemic condition."

On that same day, however, John rallied. He left his bed and was able to sit up at the television set in his study for a performance of Beethoven's Ninth Symphony that was being broadcast from the Basilica of Saint Paul's Beyond the Walls on the occasion of a large reception given there for the Council fathers, which he was supposed to have attended. Forbidden to leave the Vatican, he decided, however, to resume his normal activity to the full extent, and the news was conveyed to the Council by its secretary general, Monsignor Felici. Sitting before his television set in the study, John listened to the prolonged applause of the fathers. On Sunday, December 2, he appeared again

304

at his window to recite the *Angelus* with the throng below, and he said: "Good health, which was threatening to flee, has returned: more than ever!"

On Wednesday, the general-audience day, he made a longer speech: "My children, as you see, Providence is helping us. Every day brings us farther along not toward the end but toward recovery. Little by little we are moving from illness to convalescence; and we are convalescent, and your presence gives us joy and strength and vigor." The Council fathers too were standing in the square, the morning's session having been completed, and they were mingling with the crowd. John watched and was pleased: "Here is a new sight today. The Church is gathered in its full representation. Here are the bishops! Here are the priests! Here is the Christian people! The whole family is present here, the family of Christ!"

In spite of the interdict of his physicians, John unexpectedly appeared before the fathers gathered in Saint Peter's on Friday morning, December 7, the day before the Council was to end. He was taken by car to the side entrance of the basilica, made a surprise entrance, and seated himself on the little throne to declare: "Although we have not taken part in your general meetings, we have been closer to them than ever all the same through prayer and our single-minded observation of your labors on television." The next day, which was that of the solemn concluding ceremonies, he could not be present at the Mass for the Immaculate Virgin, which was celebrated by Paolo Cardinal Marella, and he did not appear in Saint Peter's until eleven o'clock in the morning. As he was walking toward Bernini's canopy (the gestatorial chair would have been too painful for him), everyone remarked how pale

305

and thin he had grown: the facial features were drawn and he was walking more slowly than usual down the endless aisle. And as he mounted the steps to the throne it was clear that he was making a great effort; only his voice, which held up unfailingly for a fifteen-minute address in Latin, was still as strong as when he was well.

Because of the healthy optimism that he had always nurtured, he still had a wisp of hope and he rejoiced at every indication of improvement. On December 25, after the three Christmas Masses had been celebrated, he began to joke about the state of his own health: "By all means trust the doctors when they say that the pope has suffered some minor disorder, but now you can see for yourselves that nothing is wrong with him: the eyes, the ears, the tongue, and especially the heart are fine, and the heart situation is the best and most precious of all." He was hanging to life by his teeth, however, and three days later he said resignedly to the cardinals who had come to present their New Year's greetings: "Our humble life, like everyone's, is in the hands of God."

This was perhaps an indication that inwardly he was consumed with mounting anxiety over the fate of the Council, which had been adjourned until the following year. To John the interval seemed long, perhaps insuperable. This was another reason why he had wanted the Council to begin in 1962, in opposition to those who would have preferred to postpone it until 1963. He had nursed the illusion that it could conclude its business in a single session, he had disapproved of the extent of the preparatory work, and finally he had been dismayed to see that the Church, in its involved theological-bureaucratic complexity, was much more difficult to reorganize than he had thought.

One day he remarked rather sadly to Father Roberto Tucci, the editor in chief of *Civiltà cattolica:* "My speech at the opening of the Council was not understood until the end of the session." Again on February 6, 1963, addressing a group at a general audience, he felt it necessary to explain how unjust it was to cry out in shock—as had been so much the case—because conflicting opinions had been freely voiced in the Council: "Some hotheads, acquiring unreliable information on one or another difference in language, sought at once to utter rash judgments: see, they said, they can't agree. On the contrary: harmony held full sway and could not have been greater."

He added that the question came down to a very simple fact. Everyone shared absolutely in the same truth, but, as free men, all could disagree only on the choice of the methods by which it was to be propagated:

What is wrong with that? Of course it is an arduous undertaking, but it has the blessing of God. Conflicts are prominent and deep in the world; one has only to think of what happens in any human gathering. But in the Council those who have expressed themselves have put forward their individual views but always with the most profound respect in their hearts for the integrity of doctrine and the persons of their brothers. Truth is always accompanied by peace and by meekness.

This was substantially true, and this capacity in John of seeing through things to their essence, never allowing himself to stop with appearances, especially when these tended to be less than auspicious, was among the major sources of his strength. It was indeed for this reason that, in spite of disappointments and unpleasant experiences,

307

he was able to go on recognizing in the Council the continuing observance of all its venerable structures of every kind and level. When he felt that he had reached a point that was beyond his own mental qualities or physical strength, he committed himself to God.

In his final addresses to the faithful, when the tortures of his illness were at their height, he alternated between resignation and optimism, not without a certain grief or foreboding, in an elegiac tone. One morning at the end of January he told a gathering of the faithful in St. Peter's Square: "What befalls all men will perhaps happen very soon to the pope who is speaking to you today." On the other hand, visiting the patients in the children's hospital of the Infant Jesus on February 2, he asserted in high spirits: "I have come here, as you see, in an excellent state of health. I am not exactly in condition to run a race or take part in a contest, but, thank God, I still have the fullest use of all my senses and of my whole organism, so that I am able fully to appreciate this impressive spectacle of charity and innocence and hope."

He believed, furthermore, that it was part of his duty to assume certain risks. When the ceremonies for the presentation of the Balzan Prize were arranged for April, his physicians did not wish him to subject himself to the burden of a massive audience in the grand hall of the Vatican. "Holy Father," Mazzoni said, "Suppose something happens to you during the audience?" John's reply was quick: "What could be finer for a father than to die in the bosom of his assembled children?" It was even less advisable for him to go to the Quirinal: "Holy Father, you cannot go out on the street like that," Monsignor Capovilla warned him; and John replied: "Why not, Don Loris? So many people die in the street: why can't the pope die there too?"

On April 30 he suffered a new hemorrhage, more violent than that of the night of November 26. More detailed information began to seep out of the Vatican: the pope had a "gastric growth," a tumor, perhaps a cancer; only exploratory surgery could make certain. He was given intravenous feeding and for twenty-four hours Professor Mazzoni administered transfusions, coagulants, and injections of morphine, preliminary measures to enable the surgeons to decide whether to resort to the knife or to radiation therapy. He seemed to make some gains, but on May 21 it was announced that the pope was going to have to have nine days of complete rest during which he would prepare himself in prayer for the forthcoming feast of Pentecost. On the morning of Wednesday the twenty-second, normally a day of audience and the eve of the Ascension, he fainted. He was extremely weak; in a few months he had lost almost fifty pounds. When he regained consciousness, he managed to appear at his window at ten thirty and address the crowd below, although his voice was trembling. He himself made the announcement that the Wednesday audience had been canceled:

I was expecting you at noon, but instead we are advancing our appointment somewhat. So here I am. I remember that our meeting was to have taken place inside Saint Peter's. But what's the difference? inside or outside, as long as it is at Saint Peter's, it is still all right. And besides we are anticipating the noon appointment. Happy Ascension Day, greetings, greetings, greetings.

The next day, the actual celebration of the Ascension, was marked on his *calendarium* for a visit to the Abbey of Monte Cassino, and he would have preferred to adhere to

309

his program. He was told that this would mean the danger of another hemorrhage, and he replied tranquilly: "One more hemorrhage would not be the end. It would mean, if it came, that the monks would put me to bed in one of the cells of the monastery. To die in Montecassino: what a fine death!" He was dissuaded, however, by the argument that any such event would also have caused great embarrassment for the Italian government. Hence he confined himself to making another appearance at his window, from which he could offer a few remarks, pronounce a blessing, and join the faithful in the recitation of the Marian antiphon, *Regina coeli*. After that day no one ever again saw him from outside.

On Saturday, May 25, however, he was still able to record a radio broadcast intended for the Catholic workers of Poland, who, in conformity with their tradition, were preparing for their annual pligrimage to the shrine of Piekary on the last Sunday of the month. He told them:

You know how important it is to us and to the Church to defend your rights, to improve your living conditions, and to proclaim in accordance with the precepts of the Gospels what is proper for the well-being of you and your families while at the same time preserving that priority by which eternal and spiritual good is paramount while earthly prosperity is made to accord with it. This is what we have sought to accomplish, especially by means of the encyclical letters, *Mater et magistra* and, more recently, *Pacem in terris*. We will not spare ourselves, as long as we live, in constant solicitude and effort for you. Have faith in the love of the Church and entrust yourselves to it unafraid, with the certainty that its thoughts are thoughts of peace and not of suffering.

He was photographed, too, on that day, for the last time in his life. He would have liked to go up to his lofty suite

in the tower of Saint John, but the doctors argued against
this because it would have been difficult to equip the tower
with the various devices required for his treatment. He
had fresh hemorrhages on May 26 and 27. Mazzoni gave
him more transfusions and conferred with Gasbarrini, who
had been summoned from Bologna, and with a Roman
surgeon, Professor Pietro Valdoni. The announcement issued on May 28 by the three professors, however, was
quite reassuring, because John was holding out: "The effects of the gastric growth have now diminished, and the
organic consequences are limited and countered by the
therapeutic measures that have been adopted."

Early that morning Cardinal Cicognani, the secretary of
state, had arrived to inform John: "Most Blessed Father,
the whole world is praying for your health." He had returned at about noon for a discussion of business, and
John, who had apparently been thinking about the comforting announcement of the morning, greeted him with a dis-
ciplined argumentation: "By reason of the fact that the
whole world is praying for the ailing pope, it is quite
natural that there be an intention given to this supplication.
If God wishes the sacrifice of the pope's life, let that
sacrifice mean the beseeching of innumerable blessings on
the Ecumenical Council. If on the other hand it be God's
will to continue this pontifical service of ours, let that be
for the sanctification of the pope's soul." He knew that
Rome and the Vatican too were full of predictions that,
when he was dead, everything would be over, everything
would have gone up in smoke: both the Council and the
modernization of the Church. He was convinced, however,
that Providence was on his side, and in fact he said to
Monsignor van Lierde, the sacristan of Saint Peter's: "May

311

it be God's will that the Council fathers be able still to crown the great work that they have begun. I offer all my suffering *ut unum sint* [that they may be one], that all may be a sole entity in Christ."

John's nephew, Monsignor Giovanni Battista Roncalli, arrived from Bergamo and was immediately admitted to his uncle's room. "When he saw me come in," the nephew related later, "he gave me a smile filled with affection. Even before I could ask him about his health, he asked me how our relatives were, and about our house in Sotto il Monte; what the spring was like in our part of the country, what I was doing, and whether I liked it. He also asked for news of various persons in Bergamo of whom he was fond. Then, slowly, he said: 'Look, you come here and find me in bed. The doctors say that I have something wrong with my stomach. But let us hope that everything will turn out for the best and that soon I can once more devote myself to the Council and the Church.' "

For that matter, there was a further remarkable improvement on May 29. Mazzoni left the Vatican for the first time in a week, and the next morning, Thursday, the thirtieth, Gasbarrini went back to Bologna, telling the newspapermen that his august patient had "an iron constitution to match his iron will." Actually John had got out of bed, conducted Church business, and even laughed at newspaper reports that he was preparing to visit America and to be host to Khrushchev, but he said too that he hoped to live to see the end of the Council.

At about midnight, however, Professor Mazzoni, sleeping in a room next to the pope's, heard John complaining softly and calling for help. He had just had another hemorrhage, complicated by an attack of peritonitis. Gasbarrini hurriedly came back from Bologna and Valdoni also returned to the Vatican. The three physicians agreed that they must convey to John that his condition was hopeless. The information was given to him by his secretary, Monsignor Capovilla: "Holy Father, I have talked to the doctors."

"Yes? What did they say?"

"Holy Father, I will be honest with you, as you wish me to be. I have to tell you that today you are summoned to paradise."

"Thank you, Don Loris, for having treated me with so much kindness and let me know in time. Now, from this moment on, I can put aside all earthly thoughts and concern myself only with my soul."

John sent for Professor Mazzoni, smiled at him, and said: "I should like to express my thanks to you too, but I have nothing here to give you, except this fountain pen. Take it, it is almost new, you know: I have never used it." Then came Monsignor Cavagna, who heard the pope's confession and gave him communion, and Monsignor van Lierde, who administered extreme unction. John was still fully conscious. According to *l'Osservatore romano*, he even expressed to Monsignor Cavagna "in a firm, clear voice his great love for the Church and for all the souls that were entrusted to it. Once more he offered his life for the successful conclusion of the Council, and again and again he repeated to those present, who were deeply moved: *'Ut unum sint.'* " He sent for Cardinal Cicognani and quoted the Book of Psalms (CXXII:1) to him: "See, *laetatus sum in his quae dicta sunt mihi: in domum Domini ibimus* [I was glad when they said unto me, Let us go into the house of the Lord]." He confided to Monsignor

313

Capovilla, however, that he was still looking forward to two or three more weeks of life; and, when Cardinals Tisserant and Ottaviani called on him, he first blessed them and thanked them for their collaboration (indeed, for their help, as he humbly corrected himself), and then admitted: "But how I dislike going!" Ottaviani's reply was almost admonitory: "You must regard it as the work of God."

At seven thirty in the evening Cardinal Montini arrived with the pope's relatives: his sister, Assunta, and his three brothers, Zaverio, Alfredo, and Giuseppe, all of whom had come by plane from Bergamo. John was in a coma and recognized no one. His nephew, the monsignor, described how the four old people were led into the pope's bedroom and urgently requested "not to weep. They were to leave if indeed they could not hold back their tears. Those poor old things were trembling, and still all upset from their plane trip, which was the first for any of them. There was a very dim light in the room. We were all standing back because the pope was having great difficulty breathing. He needed air, and it was as if we would deprive him of it if we stood close to him." Later that night, about three in the morning, John emerged from his coma, saw his brothers and sister and greeted them festively with the words that Christ used to Martha, the sister of Lazarus: *"Ego sum resurrectio et vita* [I am the resurrection and the life]" (John XI:25). More personally, as if recalling old family memories, he went on: "Do you remember how I never thought of anything else or imagined doing anything else in life but being a priest? Now I embrace you and bless you. Do you remember our father? do you remember our mother? I have always thought of them, and I am glad because in a little while I shall see them again in heaven.

314

Now pray, let us pray together for our father and mother."

Some hours had already elapsed since the Vatican announcement that the pope had "begun his final agony" and was dying; "He is no longer suffering," the announcement assured the world. But John's heart—a heart of exceptional strength, "the heart of an ox," as the intimates of his illness said, not out of irreverence but out of amazement—still would not give in. John was repeatedly in and out of coma, and every time he regained consciousness he blessed those round him and dedicated his suffering "to the Council and to peace." The chaplain of the noble guards, Monsignor Oddone Tacoli, told him that he looked as if he had been reborn, and John replied: "I have watched my death minute by minute. Now I am quietly departing into the final stage." He apologized to Monsignor Capovilla: "I am sorry to have made you neglect your mother, Don Loris. But, when I am dead, think of her, do not forget her, go and see her."

At four o'clock in the morning of June 1, the Saturday before Pentecost, Cardinal Cicognani arrived to celebrate Mass. John was able to follow it, and he recited the responses that he had learned in the Roman seminary—*Mater mea, fiducia mea* (My mother, my hope)—and then, again, *Ego sum resurrectio et vita, Jesus, Jesus, Jesus.* His temperature was rising because of the peritoneal inflammation, which was spreading, and he alternated between periods of stupor and flashes of rationality. In the afternoon he recognized and greeted Baron Prosper Poswick, ambassador of Belgium to the Holy See and dean of the diplomatic corps accredited to the Vatican, and toward evening his pulse became normal again. On Sunday, June 2, which was Pentecost, Cardinal Cicognani cele-

315

brated Mass at dawn and John repeated the Gospel for the day: "Peace I leave with you, my peace I give unto you. Let not your heart be troubled, neither let it be afraid. You have heard how I said unto you: I go away, and come again unto you" (John 14: 27–28).

In the afternoon his temperature rose to almost 104 degrees F. He talked very little now because his voice was quite weak. But he motioned to Professor Mazzoni to bend down and then said to him: "Death is the beginning of a new life: the glorification of Christ." Death was unmercifully slow in coming. "I am suffering with love," John murmured, "but with pain, so much pain." The night dragged on, and he continued to whisper: *"Cupio dissolvi et esse cum Cristo* [I want to vanish and be with Christ]." Again he recalled Christ's words in the garden of Gethsemane (John:XVII:11): "Father, keep through thine own name those whom thou hast given me, that they may be one, *ut unum sint . . . ut unum sint . . . ut unum sint . . ."*

The final coma was close at hand, but John had time still to voice another thought: "In September, in September. It will be I or some other pope, but in September everything will be completed in a month." Then there was an uncompleted sentence, which was his last and which is still a mystery: "At least as far as the bronze gates." It was seven fifty in the evening of June 3, 1963. In the courtyard of the Basilica of Saint Peter's the Mass was being celebrated by Cardinal Traglia, the pope's vicar for Rome, and it would appear that John died just at the moment when, reading the final Gospel text of the mass, the cardinal was intoning: *"Fuit homo missus a Deo, cui nomen erat Johannes* [There was a man sent from God, whose name was John]" (John I:6).

316

Even if the coincidence in time is not established, and it may well have been invented by the hagiographers, it would still have been a better tribute than that other reaction, quite different in character, that John's death apparently aroused in the mind of Cardinal Siri. In the days immediately after the event he was believed to be the author of the irreverent observation: "It will take forty years to repair the damage that this pope inflicted in four years."

Fact or fiction, the statement epitomized the quite widely held opinion that in a moment of insanity John had exposed the Church without preparation to one of the most serious crises in its history. This was the view expressed, for example, by *Il Giornale d'Italia* in an article that was believed to have been inspired by the same "eminent layman" who had earlier been a topic of conversation when Italy was facing the question of deciding whether to have a Center-Left government. "The real difficulty of the Council," the still mysterious eminence pontificated, "consisted in the fact that it had been conceived by John XXIII as a manifestation of testimony of religious piety and pastoral zeal on the part of all the highest officers of the Christian apostolate rather than as a supreme theological tribunal." Having thus deplored the doctrinal deficiency, the eminent layman asserted that theology and the pastorate were in the full course of development and therefore could not have provided the fathers with certain, definite data on which to base "effective decrees." John, therefore, would have done better not to convoke the Council, since there was absolutely no hope of confronting "still undeveloped problems without upheaval and equivocation." The equivocation, it appeared, was caused "by a vast effort on the part

317

of the Marxists to make a tool out of the image of the *good* pope. According to this sectarian view, a Council opened by the *parish priest of Rome* could not help being the Council of political and social doctrinal tolerance, divorce, contraceptives, and *yé-yé* masses."

It is better to stop here rather than fall into vulgarity, but it is certain that John was and still is very much an object of reproach for his decision to convoke an Ecumenical Council that would have revealed to the world the internal problems of the Church, its difficulties, and the conflicts in its day-to-day life. It is argued that he intensified all of these through his ingenuous attempt to heal them by means of impracticable expedients. The crisis of Catholicism had actually been made evident by the ferments that were seething among the clergy, the conflicts of views expressed in the Council, the sharpness of the discussions on subjects that traditional conformism regarded as forbidden to all Catholics.

The truth is that the crisis of the Catholic world antedated John's pontificate and was not its consequence. Having not only inherited but above all understood it, John had sought the remedy for it in the Gospels, which are tidings of freedom. Regardless whether one believes in the institutional dogmas of the Catholic Church, the Christian God is conceived as the Creator of the freedom of man, who by reason of his own dignity cannot be deprived of it. The return of men to the Church, which was the great problem that John faced, could be accomplished only through the course of freedom. "Outside freedom, salvation is impossible," he had written in his diary.

Today the Church is still at grips with exceptional difficulties, even more severe than those that it suffered during the centuries through the recurrent persecutions to which it was subjected. Today's problems are different in nature and more difficult because courage is not enough for their solution, any more than the heroic level of sanctity that sustained the martyrs in the early centuries of Christianity. Today the Church is not called on to defend itself against its enemies; in general it may be said that the Church is no longer assailed but rather abandoned by the world, which is becoming progressively less Christian. Therefore John went out to meet the world, almost in pursuit of men who no longer recognize the Church. He declared the necessity of starting again from the beginning with new tidings for men whom the Catholic Church has itself shown that it no longer understands, men with new needs, burdened by problems different from those to which the Church has become accustomed in its history.

The tidings were to remain those of the Gospels, but purged of adulterations and incrustations that had grown up in and among them to such a point as to make them unrecognizable or unacceptable. Outmoded traditions too, only ostensibly respectable, were to be challenged afresh or repudiated because all institutions, even the noblest, are susceptible to decay, because they are all human and hence fallible. If the remedy indicated by John (who firmly believed in its validity, so that he did not hesitate to allow the Church to be swept by the fierce wind of revolutionary evangelical freedom), if even this remedy had failed, the failure would have entailed a negative appraisal of the tendency of modern men to religious sentiment.

John indeed was purely religious, as he had resolved to be from the start of his pontificate. If he had had to take a position on Cardinal Suenens' thesis of the opening of

319

the Church *ad extra* and *ad intra*, John would have said that, in order to thrust the Church in the direction of the world through an opening *ad extra,* an opening first of all *ad intra* was required in the sense of a return to the supernatural sources, and this would have been demonstrated by the youthfulness of a church capable of throwing off historic superstructures—in other words, of being modern and more profoundly true to itself.

These are difficult theses for the majority of Catholics because it is given only to the genuine believer to understand them, and in addition the problem of John's life and pontificate—his so-called "mystery"—comes down to no more and no less than the simple fact that he really believed, in contrast to the majority. And Siri's condemnation of Roncalli's work was a denunciation of the shock, indeed the scandal occasioned by the occupation of Peter's throne by a pope who taught the Gospels, the whole Gospels, and nothing but the Gospels. There is no irreverence in the thought that it was as if Giuseppe Giusti's fantasy had come to life, his dream that Father Pero, a happy, simple, practicing Christian, had been elected pope: *

> . . . questo papa spiritato
> che vuol far l'apostolo,
> ripescare in pro' del Cielo
> colle reti del Vangelo
> pesci che ci scappino.
> Questo è un Papa in buona fede,
> è un papaccio che ci crede,
> diamogli l'arsenico!

* Giuseppe Giusti (1809–1850) was a satiric poet whose early works had to be printed outside Italy and circulated there surreptitiously.—TRANSLATOR.

". . . Stupid Pope Who Takes It Straight"

(. . . this our pope possessed by devils,
who aims at apsotolate,
casting, on behalf of heaven,
nets of purest Gospel weaving
for the fish that get away.
Here's a pope who has real faith,
stupid pope who takes it straight:
poison him this very day!)

That the whole difference lies between believing and
not believing is evidenced by the fact that the things that
John said on the subject of peace and war, or of the sacred
and the profane, or love for one's neighbor, were anything
but new. The freedom of Catholics to make their own decisions in politics was established as early as 1885 by
Leo XIII in his encyclical *Immortale Dei* ("wherever there
is debate on purely political matters, such as the best form
of government, or whether a state should be organized according to this or that system, it is beyond all doubt that
on such points there can be honest diversities of views"),
but there is no doubt that it was never given a thought until
it was restated by John. And the same was equally true
of everything that had to do with international matters of
war and peace and collaboration among peoples. Even
among the speeches and messages of Pius XII there are
very splendid, very noble utterances of the kind, and
Mario Massiroli was quite right when he wrote that the
very exhortations of John XXIII "had been uttered and
stressed by all his predecessors, who, in spite of everything, never attained to such a peak of consensus"—or dissension.

The fact is that every pope has always spoken well of
peace and ill of war; always well of good and ill of evil.

Notwithstanding the words, it has so happened that some popes have managed to be convincing and some have not, because some, like John, really believed and others believed less.

Index

Index

Index

Index

Index

Index

Index

329

Index